# The South African Communist Party

# The South African Communist Party
### Exile and After Apartheid

## Eddy Maloka

First published by Jacana Media (Pty) Ltd in 2013

10 Orange Street
Sunnyside
Auckland Park 2092
South Africa
+2711 628 3200
www.jacana.co.za

© Eddy Maloka, 2013

All rights reserved.

ISBN 978-1-4314-0766-8

Cover design by Maggie Davey and Shawn Paikin
Set in Sabon 10.5/15pt
Job No. 002040
Printed and bound by Ultra Litho (Pty) Ltd Johannesburg

See a complete list of Jacana titles at www.jacana.co.za

# Contents

Introduction ................................................. 7
1: The Reconstruction Period ............................... 14
2: The Morogoro Aftermath ................................. 25
3: The Soldiers of Luthuli ................................. 35
4: People's War ............................................ 42
5: Ideological Hegemony ................................... 68
6: Internationalism ........................................ 83
7: Towards Home ........................................... 95
8: The Alliance ........................................... 107
9: Building a 'Mass' Party ................................ 116
10: Negotiations .......................................... 132
11: Elections and Freedom ................................. 155
Conclusion ................................................ 173
Acknowledgements .......................................... 183
Notes ..................................................... 184
Index ..................................................... 197

# Introduction

THE HISTORY OF THE SOUTH AFRICAN Communist Party (SACP), formed in 1921 as the Communist Party of South Africa (CPSA) and subsequently banned in 1950, has generated a rich and fascinating literature. During the first phase of its existence, between 1921 and the early 1930s, the CPSA battled with being a largely white organisation having to adapt its Marxism-Leninism to conditions in which the African majority, irrespective of class affiliation, was living under one of the most oppressive systems of settler colonial rule. Thus the CPSA supported the 1922 white miners' strike whose main objective was the protection of the job reservation regime for white workers. The Communist International, the Comintern, intervened in the form of the famous 1928 'Native Republic' resolution which called upon the CPSA to work with the nationalist movement for "an independent native South African republic as a stage towards a workers' and peasants' republic with full, equal rights for all races".[1]

During the second phase, from the late 1930s to the outbreak of World War II, the CPSA underwent a strategic reorientation and was fully Africanised. The period 1931–35 was, however, one of the most difficult, as the CPSA had to survive purges and expulsions, which saw the organisation's membership drop from about 3 000 in 1929 to below 300 in the mid-1930s. The first generation of African CPSA leaders emerged during this phase, beginning with Albert Nzula who became the first African general secretary of the organisation. Other notable African figures who emerged during this phase were Moses Kotane (who became general secretary in 1938), Edwin Mofutsanyana, and JB Marks.

The third phase, 1940s to 1950, witnessed the massive growth of the CPSA, thanks to Kotane's efforts which not only rescued the organisation from the decline of 1931–35, but also rooted the CPSA in the struggles that were taking place in black townships, mines and factories. It was during this phase that relations between the CPSA and the nationalist movement, the African National Congress (ANC), improved, and some of its leading figures were elected to senior positions in the latter.

The fourth phase, 1950 to 1963, began with the banning of the CPSA. It, however, resurfaced underground in 1953 as the SACP, thanks to the efforts of, notably, Kotane, Lionel 'Rusty' Bernstein, Michael Harmel and a number of young communists, such as Joe Slovo, Ruth First and Harold Wolpe. During the first few years of its underground existence, between 1953 and 1960, the SACP did not publically acknowledge its existence. Nonetheless, the new Party continued to play its part in the liberation struggle, participating in the mass struggles of the 1950s, which included the Defiance Campaign of 1952 and the Congress of the People that adopted the Freedom Charter in 1955. This period resulted in the consolidation of the liberation movement in two important areas. Firstly, the notion of non-racialism was integrated into liberation politics. This resulted in the break-away of the Pan-Africanist Congress (PAC) from the main nationalist movement, the ANC. Secondly, and thanks to the cooperation among organisations representing the oppressed, the Congress alliance made up of mainly the ANC, the South African Indian Congress (SAIC), the Coloured People's Congress, the Congress of Democrats (COD), and the South African Congress of Trade Unions (SACTU) was consolidated. The Congress alliance was also important in that it enabled the ANC as an organisation, then open only to Africans, to cooperate intimately, both organisationally and politically, with Indians and Coloureds as oppressed minorities. This alliance was, however, to undergo change, both in substance and definition, in subsequent decades. When the ANC and other organisations were banned in 1960, the SACP became part of the formation of Umkhonto we Sizwe ('Spear of the Nation' or simply MK), an organisation established to launch the armed struggle.[2]

During the first phase of its underground existence, between 1953 and 1963, the SACP was able, at least partially, to resolve the race-class debate that had occupied the organisation since its formation and in the 1930s in particular. The relationship between the struggle for socialism and the struggle against colonialism was resolved thanks to the development in the 1950s of the thesis that came to be known as Colonialism of a Special Type (CST). CST was not simply an elaboration of the 'native republic' resolution, but was in fact a response to the relationship that the Party, especially in the Transvaal, had developed with the nationalist movement during the course of the struggles of the 1940s and 1950s. According to this theory, advanced most prominently by Michael Harmel and Rusty Bernstein who were then the Party's leading theoreticians, South Africa had a form of settler colonialism where the coloniser and the colonised lived side-by-side; the coloniser enjoyed first world privileges while the colonised were subjected to conditions typical of other third world countries.

The CST thesis would be incorporated into the programme adopted at the SACP's 5th Congress, held underground in 1962. The new programme, *The Road to South African Freedom*, contained a very detailed development of the CST as a theory on which basis the Party could fight for socialism, exercise its vanguard role as conceived by Lenin, and, at the same time, take part in the struggle against colonialism under the leadership of the ANC. Accordingly, a 'two-stage' theory was developed which distinguished between the national democratic phase which was led by the ANC and the second phase aimed at building socialism.

The 5th Congress elected a Central Committee the life-span of which was to be very short as many would either flee the country or end up in prison. The general secretary, Moses Kotane, and the national chairperson, JB Marks, both highly respected within the Congress alliance, also occupied influential positions in the ANC. Other Central Committee members who were to play an important role after 1963 included Joe Slovo, Michael Harmel, Rusty Bernstein, Brian Bunting, Marimuthu Pragalathan (MP) Naicker, Joe Matthews, Bram Fischer, Duma Nokwe and Mark Shope.

What is covered in this book is the story of the SACP during the exile years through the unbanning in 1990, the 1990–94 negotiated transition, and the immediate period after the 1994 first democratic elections which brought into being post-apartheid South Africa.

## Historiography and Methodology

There are a number of ways that the literature on the SACP can be categorised; one can distinguish between polemical and scholarly writings, or between different sources (for example, memoirs as opposed to secondary literature). Both can be employed in the writing of this history. However, this study will divide the literature in question into three chronologically-determined categories. There is a substantial literature dedicated to the period prior to the 1950 banning, thanks to the availability of oral and written sources as the CPSA operated as a legal organisation during that period.[3] The literature on the underground years (1953–63) and the exile period (1963–90), the second category, is very limited due to the problem of the availability of sources. This problem notwithstanding, the literature in this category is dominated by the Cold War and *rooigevaar* schools, whose main preoccupation was Soviet influence and strategy in southern Africa and the extent to which the ANC was controlled by the SACP.[4] The third category of the literature emerged following the unbanning of the Party in 1990, some as academic works and others as autobiographies, as well as the history written by the Party itself. The Cold War and *rooigevaar* perspectives can also be found in this literature, but so too are efforts by the SACP and some members aimed at exonerating and defending the Party.[5]

This study, as an attempt to reconstruct the periods 1963–90 and 1990–98, is, however, not without its own limitations. What makes this effort so important is the fact that, from the literature that is available, it is clear that the exile period history of the SACP is not adequately known. Even the history produced by the SACP itself reflects the lack of a more comprehensive knowledge that is being proposed in this study. The South African Democracy Education Trust (SADET) volumes covering the period 1960–94 of the liberation struggle is an important contribution in the right direction.[6]

It is also hoped that the material that is discussed in this study will provoke those who are interested in building on the first edition of this book as well as the path-breaking work already done by Vladimir Shubin in his *ANC: A View from Moscow*.[7] Shubin's book is invaluable. It was one of the first attempts to use the archives of the liberation movements in order to reconstruct their exile history; the other advantage is that Shubin had the privilege of meeting and interacting with many ANC and SACP figures, some of whom are discussed in this study. However, Shubin, because of the macroscopic focus of his project and possibly also due to a lack of sources, could not give the SACP the attention that it is accorded in this study. For its part, this second edition brings new material to enrich and even correct some accounts of the story proposed in the first.

There are some methodological and comparative questions that must be asked upfront. A history of a communist party (CP) ought to attempt to tackle issues of ideology, strategy and tactics, internal organisational dynamics, and the relations between the party and other important role players. This is what this study attempts to do. But it must also be emphasised that the SACP's experience is an exception if other African cases are to be taken into consideration.

Africa's responses to the influence of communism have varied from period to period, and the greatest difficulty has always concerned how the communist party, or a like-minded organisation, conceptualised and related to colonial oppression as opposed to class exploitation.

The first generation of post-colonial African leaders displayed mixed attitudes towards Marxism-Leninism, preferring instead their African Socialism. To African leaders like Julius Nyerere of Tanzania, Modibo Keïta of Mali, Sékou Touré of Guinea and Léopold Senghor of Senegal, pre-colonial Africa was an egalitarian society where the means of production, especially land, were communally owned. Colonialism represented a counter logic to these societies, introducing private property and inequality. The solution then, to these leaders, was to rebuild post-colonial Africa on the basis of the political economy logic and values system of traditional societies. Senghor elaborated his African Socialism thesis with his Negritude philosophy. Kwame Nkrumah's philosophy Consciencism was also based on similar assumptions about pre-colonial African society, and so was Nyerere's Ujamaa thought and villagisation programme. Kenneth Kaunda churned out books on 'humanism', also a brand of African Socialism.

Some of these leaders, such as Kwame Nkrumah towards the end of his rule in Ghana, and Sékou Touré, would opt for what David and Marina Ottaway called 'transitional' socialism – a brand of socialism that drew inspiration from both Marxism-Leninism and African Socialism.[8]

As to countries with established communist parties, in particular Morocco, Sudan, Algeria, Egypt and Tunisia, the relationship between these parties and the anti-colonial political movements was untenable. The tendency was for communist parties in those countries to opt for a narrow concept of Marxism at the expense of the 'national question'. Their relationship with the nationalist movement therefore became conflictual. In the case of Algeria, for example, where the communist party was established as an extension of the French Communist Party, the "nationalists never forgave Communists for consistently putting the interests of France or Frenchmen above those of their own community".[9] In some of these countries the communist parties became targets of repression after independence.

In some cases, such as in Senegal, Marxist-inclined parties emerged after independence as an opposition to the nationalist government. There are also cases, between the late 1960s and the mid-1970s, where military regimes assumed power and thereafter opted for Marxism-Leninism. In such cases, for example in Ethiopia under Mengistu Haile-Mariam, Marxism was imposed from the top. The final category was of countries, notably Mozambique and Angola, where, as in the case of Cuba, a nationalist movement converted itself into a communist party after independence and tried to implement socialism.[10] Keeping these cases in mind, it is clear that the SACP is the only communist party in Africa which resolved the ideological tension between national liberation and socialist struggle, and managed to develop a dynamic working relationship with the nationalist movement.

Indeed, the then ANC president, Oliver Tambo, was to observe in his address on the occasion of the 60th anniversary of the SACP in July 1981 that: "The relationship between the ANC and the SACP is not an accident of history, nor is it a natural and inevitable development. For, as we can see, similar relationships have not emerged in the course of liberation struggles in other parts of Africa".[11]

Another comparative point refers to how the Cold War affected the SACP and the whole African communist movement. The SACP, like other like-minded parties on the African continent, was affected not only by the conflict between the Soviet Union and Western powers, but also by the political and ideological dispute between the former and the People's Republic of China (the Sino-Soviet split) of the period 1960 to 1989 over divergent interpretations of classical Marxism. In both cases, the SACP sided with the Soviet Union.

The story of this history of the SACP begins with the arrest of the first generation of MK commanders under the leadership of Nelson Mandela, following the police ambush on their hideout at Liliesleaf Farm in Rivonia, thus leading to the famous Rivonia Trial which resulted in life sentences for some members of the group.

# 1
# The Reconstruction Period

IN THE AFTERMATH OF THE Rivonia arrests, coupled with the 90-day detention law, many SACP leaders, together with those from the ANC, were forced to flee the country and go into exile. Yusuf Dadoo, a prominent leader of the SACP and president of the South African Indian Congress, was among the first to leave, making his contribution to the Party's underground 5th Congress from exile; Moses Kotane, JB Marks, Joe Slovo, Ronnie Kasrils and Duma Nokwe were all among the group that left in 1963, and others, such as Ruth First and Rusty Bernstein followed suit in 1964. London and Dar es Salaam subsequently emerged as two important political centres of the exiled movement, with the Party establishing its headquarters in the former, and the ANC settling in the latter. Kotane, Marks and Nokwe settled in Dar es Salaam with the ANC's acting president, Oliver Tambo, and London became a home for other Party leaders, notably Harmel, Slovo and Dadoo. The challenge of keeping the internal Party machinery running was left in the hands of Bram Fischer.

The Party, after almost a decade of underground experience, had developed a more sophisticated structure and recruitment system which suited the conditions at the time. Party cells, consisting generally of three to five members, were the foundation of the underground Party; Area Committees coordinated Party structures within their jurisdiction, and in their turn, reported to the District Committee, which for its part was responsible to the Central Committee. Members could be recruited to a cell on the recommendation of other cell members, but the final decision was referred to a higher level, such as the District or Central Committee. This structure and recruitment system was to be put into practice in exile. However, in spite of this underground experience, the Party's style of work had not, in many respects, fully adapted to new security conditions. According to one contemporary assessment:

Partly as a hangover from the long years of legality, and partly because of the failure of police methods between 1950 and 1963 to achieve any major victory, bad habits developed. Our organization up to 1950 and the Congresses up to 1960 worked openly and conducted their affairs without any secrecy. When we were banned certain precautions were taken, but we never really adapted ourselves to illegal conditions.[1]

It was such complacency, among other things, that made it relatively easy for the apartheid spy, Gerard Ludi, to infiltrate the Party's Johannesburg structures in 1963. Thanks to Ludi's work, the apartheid security forces were able to prepare for an offensive in 1964, which resulted in one of the biggest blows to the Party structures.

Bram Fischer, a long-time Party activist and a member of the Central Committee since 1945, gained prominence during the 1956–60 Treason Trial, where he served as a member of the defence team, and later led the defence in the infamous Rivonia Trial. Fischer, a well-educated Afrikaner with family ties deep into the Afrikaner political elite, was arrested in September 1964 – a year and two months after the police raid on Rivonia – and charged under the Suppression of Communism Act. Fischer was charged together with 13 other Party members including Eli Weinberg, Jean Strachan and Norman Levy. However, in January 1965, Fischer skipped bail and went underground for about ten months, leaving his lawyer a letter of explanation, which was read to the court. Some of his co-accused, such as Weinberg, were found guilty and imprisoned until their released in 1970. In order to survive in the underground, Fischer retreated to Rustenburg where he changed his disguise before returning to Johannesburg to operate from Waverly and Bramley, using the names Douglas Black, C Thompson and Peter West.[2]

Between January and November 1965, Fischer became the most wanted person in the country, with a reward of £3 000 hanging over his head. Fischer was in contact with an embryonic Secretariat of the external mission of the SACP that was being established in London, from a small office on Goodge Street, under the leadership of Slovo and Dadoo. Some four months into the underground, Fischer recommended to the Secretariat that the leadership of the Party shift to the external mission. The Central Committee had met at least twice in exile, first in December 1963 and again in July 1964, but it would appear that the first major Central Committee meeting sat in May 1965 in Prague, to deliberate on the reconstruction of the Party in exile, against the background of Fischer's recommendation. At the meeting, a Secretariat, which came to be known as the Central Executive Committee (CEC), was formally established with headquarters in London, and "given full authority to approach fraternal parties for any assistance it deem necessary". Dadoo was appointed assistant secretary to Kotane "with personal authority to make these approaches on behalf of the CEC".[3]

With the Central Committee (or CC) reconstituted by the Prague meeting, comprising leaders elected at the 5th Congress, its responsibilities were to give political leadership and exercise all the powers of a central committee provided for in the constitution adopted at the 5th Congress; to work in close liaison and consultation with Party apparatus inside the country; to draft and circulate to all members, both in and out of the country, general political directives from time to time, if necessary; and to build the Party. Principles for operating under the new conditions were also approved, which called for the adoption of new identities by members who were known to the security police; those who were known and could not change their identities "must as soon as possible, be excluded from any contact with any organized segment of the Party".[4]

With the general secretary and the chairperson of the Party based in Africa, the meeting had to deliberate on the relationship between the CEC and those CC members based in Dar es Salaam – then known as 'Hull' in Party underground correspondence – as well as their role in the reconstruction of the Party in exile:

> We must be on the alert to seek out and take every opportunity to have more regular personal contact between Hull and the CEC to exchange information and discuss mutual problems. This may, if necessary, include the sending of representatives under security conditions to Hull when the occasion demands.[5]

The meeting was also concerned about the racial composition of the CEC and the leadership of the underground mission in the country. Thus, it was decided that CC members in Africa were to "do everything possible to obtain the allocation of leading African comrades to work on the CEC and in Jane [ANC] Office" in London. With regard to underground work in the country, "it is agreed that amongst those to be returned home for the purpose of reconstructing the party must be some drawn from the African membership". Equally important was the relationship with the ANC, and not least because Kotane and Marks were based at ANC headquarters.

> To enable the CC to provide adequate political leadership and guidance, the comrades from Hull will keep the CEC informed on the main outline of what Jane is doing both inside and outside the country.[6]

Financing the external mission also required attention. Accordingly, in August 1965, the London Aid Committee, a charity organisation with Dadoo and Julius First as founding members, was established as a front for the management of Party finances, including opening bank accounts and leasing buildings. Members of the Aid Committee were to change and increase in later years due to changes at the leadership level. An important source of funding for the Party was the Soviet Union's international fund, which was composed of contributions from several socialist countries, whose annual allocation to the SACP caused certain difficulties in the 1970s which I deal with in Chapter Three.

## The External Mission Takes Over

The decisions of the Prague meeting were communicated to Fischer, referred to as Noel in the correspondence, in particular the role of the Central Committee and guidelines for operating in underground conditions, however, with the understanding that:

You (the CC man on the spot) and the true beginning of our new structure must, in the spirit of the above [security guidelines], decide what steps are practical at the moment to begin their implementation.[7]

Fischer's work in reconstructing the Party and building units in various parts of the country was cut short by his arrest in November, after which he was sentenced to life imprisonment. Awarded the Lenin Peace Prize (with the sum of £12 500) in 1967, Fischer became a symbol of the international campaign for the release of political prisoners in South Africa – a campaign which gained momentum until his death from cancer in 1975.

The arrest of Fischer presented the external mission with a new challenge. The CEC, in a report handed to Marks for Hull, conceded:

With the capture of Bram and then of Fred [unidentified], the Party has ceased to exist as an organized force in SA [South Africa]. We are no longer in touch with any member at home. Many members, including several who served on the CC at one time or another, have broken down under police interrogation. This has resulted in the disclosure of the workings of the Party and the identity of nearly all our members, even many now in exile.[8]

As if that was not enough, the CEC was also hampered in its work by problems, including "poor communication with leading comrades in Hull"; little contact with members scattered all over the world, including those in MK camps; and "lack of contact with any leading bodies of the ANC and, in consequence, complete ignorance of the policy and plans of the most vital sector of the liberation movement in which the bulk of our membership is involved". Because of the weaknesses facing the CEC, whose work had been reduced to 'technical functions', to the extent that many of the Prague decisions could not even be implemented, the Party "failed to arrive at a collective perspective which would be a guide to all our members wherever they are". According to this CEC report, because of these weaknesses, "the absence of collective political guidance of the Party in the most important spheres must reflect itself in ideological gaps in the policy and work of the whole national liberation movement, with negative effects on the struggle we are engaged in". The report, therefore, proposed another CC meeting to address these problems.[9]

The CEC was consistent, during the course of 1966, in its effort to resuscitate the CC and the remaining Party membership. Critical weaknesses were in three areas, namely the very workings of the CC itself; the relationship between the CC and the Party membership; and the relationship between the Party and the ANC. The CEC proposed an augmented CC meeting for 30 November 1966, to include members such as MP Naicker, Flag Boshielo, Ray Alexander Simons, Chris Hani, Ben Turok, Moses Mabhida, Ruth Matsoane (to be known later as Ruth Mompati) and Dan Tloome. The "basis for this suggestion [for an augmented CC] is that the leadership could well benefit from a certain amount of renewal, replacement (of those on Robben Island) and more direct contact with personnel on key areas and posts".[10] In order to strengthen its efforts for the resuscitation of the Party, the CEC also undertook a road show to meet Party groups based mainly in London, to report on the current crisis and the efforts underway. The report touched on the state of the Party and international relations without, of course, disclosing details about the workings of the Party, for obvious security reasons.[11] Furthermore, the CEC also prepared the Party for participation at the Consultative Conference organised for November by the ANC, as the first formal meeting of Congress alliance partners in exile. One important decision of this meeting was to open ANC membership in exile to non-Africans, which rendered the existence of the South African Indian Congress and the Coloured People's Congress as separate organisations redundant.

As for the organisation of membership, by 1966, only London had an ordered Party formation in exile. This was due, on the one hand, to the presence of the CEC and the headquarters in London, and, on the other, to the fact that London probably had the largest concentration of South African exiles outside Africa, many of whom had been active Party members at home. The main tasks of the London Party groups were identified as solidarity work, especially in the Anti-Apartheid Movement; political and educational work aimed at strengthening the understating of Marxism within the ranks of the liberation movement; work in the organs of the liberation movement, especially the ANC and SACTU; and "technical work for the Party"[12] such as the distribution of propaganda material. These groups, though considered by the CEC as "not a permanent or 'normal' organizational form… [but] as a temporary measure to assist certain aspects of Party work at this stage",[13] were to be coordinated by a 'London committee' consisting of two representatives elected by each group. The committee was not to be "purely an administrative committee to collect dues and supervise the routine functioning of the groups",[14] but was also to have a political function. Apart from deliberating on political developments and discussing the workings of entities such as the Anti-Apartheid Movement, the committee was to give political leadership to the groups by setting an agenda for them and ensuring that their meetings had dynamic contact with the issues that were of interest to the Party.[15]

International relations, as shown in Chapter Six, were also important. In the past, and as with other European colonies, the Communist Party of the Soviet Union kept in contact with the SACP via the Communist Party of Great Britain. However, from 1960, with the Party and ANC shifting towards armed struggle, it became necessary to establish direct contact with the Soviet Union, and this was initiated by Dadoo in July 1960. The following year in October, Dadoo visited Moscow again, but this time with Kotane who had just arrived in exile. Thanks to these contacts, the Soviet Union initiated the practice of making annual allocations to the SACP, beginning with US$30 000 in 1960. Fraternal meetings were also held by the Secretariat with European communist parties, notably those in France, Britain and Italy. And in 1966, the SACP twice brought together African like-minded parties based in Algeria, Sudan, Tunisia, Morocco, Nigeria and Senegal to discuss a socialist agenda for the continent.

The next CC meeting after Prague took place in January 1967 in Moscow, but with attendance not augmented as had been suggested by the CEC. The following CC members were present: Kotane, Dadoo,

Slovo, Marks, Mark Shope, Brian Bunting and Michael Harmel. The meeting, with a CEC report presented by Slovo (referred to as Alex in the minutes) and a political report by Harmel (entered as Tony in the minutes), deliberated on, among other things, the reconstruction of the Party, propaganda work, relations with the ANC, and the workings of the CEC. All CC members based in London were to be part of the CEC, now conceived as a structure similar to a working committee or a politburo, but with a Secretariat made up of Slovo, Dadoo and Harmel. Besides decisions taken with regard to communication with the Party membership (to establish an inner-party bulletin) and matters pertaining to propaganda, the meeting was particularly concerned with the outcome of the ANC Consultative Conference of November of the previous year. The Consultative Conference had resulted in the establishment of the Consultative Congress Committee as a mechanism for including minorities in the work of the ANC in exile and coordinating work among the Congress alliance partners, but the Party was excluded from the Committee. Thus a resolution was passed reiterating the Party's "policy of support for the ANC in the national liberation struggle", but with the concern that "as an independent organization, with its own established machinery, journal, activities and plans, we feel that our Party too should be included in the proposals for greater co-operation of the liberation movement" in exile. The Party, according to the resolution, was prepared to share its technical facilities and resources, and exchange organisational information concerning its underground work "to avoid working at cross-purposes and needless duplication of efforts".[16]

In communicating this resolution to the ANC, a letter was written to Tambo to request a meeting with the ANC. A draft of this letter, prepared by the Secretariat and with comments and corrections by Kotane, reflects the differences that existed between London and Kotane on how the Party should be reconstructed in exile. Kotane, treasurer general of the ANC and based in Dar es Salaam, was of the view that the Party should keep a low profile in the liberation movement so as to avoid offending states such as Zambia and Tanzania which had more of an affinity with the politics of the PAC than that of the ANC. For example, Kotane deleted a sentence in the letter to

Tambo that referred to "express pride in the contribution made by our [Party] members at every level in the National movement", and signed off: "Please accept this amendment and I shall be happy"![17]

By the time of the CC meeting of February 1968 – attended by Kotane, Dadoo, Slovo, Rusty Bernstein, Harmel, Shope and Bunting, with apologies from Marks, Ruth First and Joe Matthews – it was clear that the Party was beginning to function as a collective. Not only was the CC beginning to develop an identity as a collective, but also the CEC, as a working committee, was making it possible for decisions to be implemented and the whole Party machinery to begin functioning. In fact, some of the issues discussed at the 1968 CC meeting, such as propaganda, were referred to the CEC.

The deliberations at the 1968 CC meeting centred on the reconstruction of the Party and relations with the ANC. Among important decisions regarding the reconstruction of the Party, was to resolve "to organize members into units [in exile] whenever this is not inconsistent with security and the need to preserve the unity of mass organizations"; and to consider co-opting some members into the CC. Equally important, and with the purpose of resuscitating the Party inside the country, a decision was taken to send "one or two of its [Party] personnel for a temporary period to assess on the spot the situation and the possibilities of activity in South Africa". With regard to propaganda, an underground edition of the *African Communist* was to be prepared for distribution inside the country under innocent covers.

Even though the decision of the 1967 CC to request the ANC to include the Party in the alliance coordination mechanism had been implemented, resulting in a Party member being invited to sit on the Consultative Congress Committee, relations with the ANC still needed to be strengthened. Thus a decision was taken for "an opportunity [to] be sought for a formal meeting between representatives of the CC and of the ANC leadership for discussion of common problems". In spite of this problem, however, the meeting approved a donation of £5 000 to the ANC. A resolution was also adopted to the effect that "the central aim of our Party at this time is to promote the further unity of the national democratic movement, for the liberation of our country, as a step towards socialism. It recognises that this aim can only be achieved on the basis of close cooperation between our Party and the ANC"; the Party "believes that the strengthening of the socialist outlook in the movement can be a source of strength for the whole movement and for the future of our country in combating racialistic, tribal and other divisive and reactionary influences".[18] Of course, this resolution was a reinstatement and elaboration of elements of the CST theory as developed in the 1962 programme, but its implementation, as shown later, was not to be without problems.

As part of establishing an effective external mission, a propaganda machinery had to be put in place. The Party's main propaganda organs during this period were pamphlets – the first distributed in the country in 1967 in support of the Wankie campaign. One of the important steps to take to get this project off the ground was the decision taken at the 1968 CC meeting to prepare an illegal edition of the *African Communist* for distribution inside the country (but this was only implemented in 1970), and to establish the journal's headquarters in London. The *African Communist* was to appear in the country under innocent covers such as 'The Good Food Guide' and 'Landscape Gardening'. The journal was headed, for example in 1967, by a six-person editorial board that included Rusty Bernstein, Brian Bunting and Harmel – with Harmel as the editor. Duma Nokwe and another person that the author was unable to identify represented Hull on this editorial board.

The 1968 CC meeting laid the basis for the Party's approach not only to the 1970s, but also for participation at the ANC's Morogoro conference of 1969. The 1970s were to witness the reconstruction, in the real sense of the word, of the Party both in exile and in the country.

In spite of the progress achieved in the 1960s, there were, however, a number of issues that still had to be resolved. First was the fact that some members were unhappy with the style and how the Party was reconstructed during this period, especially with regard to the role of the Secretariat in London. For instance, the London Committee was to report to the Secretariat that: "There have been reports circulating about the liquidationist tendencies that existed in the Party from about 1964 to 1968 or thereabout. It is felt that the historical reasons for this (if accurate) and the way in which it came about should be made known or researched".[19] 'Liquidationist tendencies' is a term which was used to refer to political purges and the suppression of internal debates within the Party.

Secondly, the role of the London Committee was still not clearly defined, something that was to be the case with other regions as they became established. Key to this question was the role regions should play in the recruitment of cadres and in the establishment of the underground inside the country. The Secretariat had tight control and a monopoly over this issue, and this was to create tensions later in the 1970s.

Finally, the recruitment policy was also unclear. For example, in June 1967, Kotane wrote to Dadoo about a South African in Moscow who wanted to join the Party: "I am not familiar with the correct procedure in these matters having for so many years been dealing with the abstract theoretical side of the organisation".[20] The Secretariat was also unclear, preferring to leave the decision to the discretion of Kotane, but with some advice: "He must of course be prepared to conform to the requirement for new recruits laid down by our last [1967 CC] meeting which as you know demands readiness if called upon and required to do so, to undertake illegal activity within South Africa".[21] A recruitment policy was only to be put in place in the 1980s, and still was not without problems.

# 2
# The Morogoro Aftermath

THE END OF THE 1960s WAS another important phase in the history of the entire exiled liberation movement. The ANC, with the experience of the 1961–63 MK sabotage campaigns behind them, tried again between 1967 and 1968 to infiltrate MK fighters into the country through Rhodesia via the Wankie Game Reserve, supported by the Zimbabwe African Peoples Union (ZAPU). The SACP Secretariat in London only learnt about the Wankie campaign in the press. Nonetheless, the Wankie Campaign resulted in a number of problems, especially with MK soldiers. This resulted in the ANC convening the historic Morogoro conference which, according to one SACP contemporary report, "was the first occasion of an extended consultative conference at which the Party and other sections of the liberation movement were represented by delegates with full participation and voting rights".[1]

The ANC's Morogoro conference of 1969 was a watershed in the history of the liberation movement in exile. The conference solidified the ANC as an organisation and an ideological force, and formalised the process of including other oppressed groups and organs such as the SACP into the liberation alliance under the leadership of the ANC. A Revolutionary Council, with representatives from other Congress alliance partners – including Dadoo (as the vice-chair) and Slovo – was established for the coordination of the struggle inside the country. Thus the Congress alliance as conceived in the 1950s underwent a change as the South African Indian Congress and the Coloured People's Congress virtually disappeared in exile; the 'alliance' was now to refer to the ANC, SACTU and the SACP. The conference adopted a programme, *Strategy and Tactics*. Its analysis of South African society was informed by the SACP's theory of Colonialism of a Special Type.

The Party celebrated the achievements of the Morogoro conference in its document 'The Results of the Consultative Conference of the ANC and the Tasks of the Party'. According to the document, "there was unanimous support for the integration of all national groups and revolutionary forces including our Party in the revolutionary struggle led by the ANC". Therefore, "the consultative conference was historic. If its decisions are carried out in the letter and spirit of the deliberations in the conference much progress will be made in the revolutionary struggle." The document also issued an eight-point list of principles that were to guide Party members on the ground which, among other things, called on Party cadres to "always set an example of devotion to the people and respect for their interests and traditions", and noted that "Party members wherever they are represent the high ideals of Communism and the liberation of mankind from the bonds of oppression".[2] Indeed, Tambo wrote to Slovo about the Conference: "...much water has flown under the bridge since I last saw you... a whole year has ended... But nothing yet has happened to... the memory of that great meeting we all had. Looking back to it, I cannot help feeling it was the starting point of a new phase in our strategy – at the very least, a new and welcome element".[3]

However, the outcome of the conference was not without controversy. Some members of the ANC who were unhappy with the outcome organised themselves into a dissident group because, according to them, the conference had resulted in the ANC being taken over by minorities, and the SACP in particular. This view has been accepted and popularised by some academics.[4] The dissidents' view was based on the fact that the ANC, on the basis of the process initiated at the 1967 Consultative Conference, formally opened its ranks to non-African groups, but only insofar as the latter could not be elected to the National Executive Committee. Secondly, the dissidents were concerned that non-Africans, including leading SACP members such as Slovo and Dadoo, had been elected to the Revolutionary Council.[5] The dissidents' struggle persisted until the expulsion of what was known as the Group of Eight in October 1975 under the leadership of Tennyson Makiwane. The view of this Group was that: "The SACP white leadership who oppose the political philosophy embodied in the concept of African nationalism and who oppose the

African image of the ANC reflect their social and class roots as petty-bourgeois whites…"⁶

The emergence of the dissident group was a reflection of the difficult transition that the liberation movement had to make organisationally and ideologically in order to incorporate non-African groups, including the SACP, into an integrated fighting force. Parallel to this transition were efforts in Africa, led by the Organisation of African Unity (OAU) Liberation Committee, to urge the ANC and the PAC to form a United Front, and the SACP was seen as a stumbling block towards that goal. The view on the continent among orthodox Pan-Africanists was that the ANC was not pursuing a proper nationalist struggle because of its non-racialism and the influence of communists.

Indeed, some in the Party, whose position was contained in a confidential 'Report by a Group of Comrades' dated March 1972, were of the view that "the present effort by the OAU Liberation Committee to force the organization into a United Front would also be viewed seriously by the Party". According to this document the main focus of which was on the dissident group, the Party's response should be to "strive to draw membership from the ordinary MK members – those who deserve it even if their standard of education is low" as these were the main targets of the dissidents' message. "Furthermore," the document continued, "members of the Party who are in the RC [Revolutionary Council] should try by all means to strengthen the underground Party machinery at home so that when the armed struggle starts at home, the Party should be in a strong position in the ranks of those who will take an active part" so as to frustrate the efforts of the "rabid nationalists who will want to give the revolution a different direction".⁷ The attitude towards the OAU was to persist right into the 1980s. For example, in a Party document produced in the mid-1980s, a concern was raised: "More and more, the tendency to reactionary policies in the African States is hampering our struggle. This is reflected in the attitudes and actions of the Liberation Committee and in particular its executive machinery in Tanzania"; and as to Tanzania and Zambia, "our relationship with these two countries… [is] complicated by the attitude, role and influence of China".⁸

But these problems were also a reflection of the transition that the Party itself was undergoing in the early 1970s at the ideological and leadership level. Ideologically, the Party was struggling to situate the Leninist notion of vanguardism within a liberation movement led by the ANC. The Party's 1962 programme, *Road to South African Freedom*, had tried to distinguish between one position where the "Communist Party unreservedly supports and participates in the struggle for national liberation *headed* [my emphasis]" by the ANC, and the belief that the "immediate task of the Communist Party is to *lead* the fight for the national liberation of the non-White people [my emphasis]".[9] The 'headed' and 'lead' issue aside, there was confusion within the Party's ranks, especially in London, on what constituted the vanguard role of the Party; others argued that such a role implies that the Party was, in effect, a leader of the national democratic struggle. This interpretation, as shown later, created problems with the ANC.

A further issue which was related to this, and reflected in the citation above, was how a socialist agenda was to be pursued during the course of the national liberation struggle; how should the Party engage "rabid nationalists" and defend the resolution of its 1968 CC meeting on the subject? At the leadership level, the hospitalisation in Moscow of Kotane in January 1969 and Marks in July 1971, and his death in 1972, deprived the Party not only of its general secretary and chairperson, someone who had had very strong and intimate relations with the ANC in general and with Tambo in particular, but also deprived the SACP of an African leadership in the literal sense. With the absence of Kotane and Marks, Slovo and Dadoo became the face of the Party, and this presented the organisation with a difficult challenge. In fact, even though Marks was replaced by Dadoo after his death, Kotane remained the general secretary of the Party until his death in 1978, despite the fact that he had been physically incapacitated by a stroke in 1968. Kotane was conscious of this fact, and thus requested Marks in 1971 to raise the matter with the Secretariat on his behalf: "Comrade Moses has… approached me… that in view of the nature of his present illness coupled with his relatively advanced age he be relieved of all leading positions held by him including that of General Secretary and that you consider the election or appointment of a suitable person as General Secretary".[10] However, a replacement was only appointed in 1979.

Nonetheless, the Morogoro conference ushered in a new era for the Party. For the first time in exile, a meeting took place immediately after the conference between the Party and the ANC. Present at the meeting, chaired by Marks, were nine persons including Tambo, Dadoo, Slovo, Harmel and Joe Matthews. Dadoo, who invited Slovo to put forward the CC position, led the Party input. Areas of disagreement revolved around three points, namely whether the Party should establish its units in the army; lack of contact between the Party and ANC leadership; and confusing interpretations of the Party's vanguardist role. Regarding the first point, the decision was that the Party could not establish units within the army, but could appoint a CC representative in each of the major exile centres to maintain discreet contact with the soldiers. Outside the army, however, the Party was free to set up its collectives. As to contact with the ANC, Tambo's view was that he had always understood the contact he had with Kotane, Marks and Nokwe constituted contact with the Party: "Some of us, including myself, have been unaware of the gap which appears to have existed between the two bodies as collectives. We have not always felt the need for joint discussions of this character because we had thought that the party was a collective and operates as a collective." It was, however, resolved that a CC member, to be designated, was to act as a link with Tambo. On the issue of the Party's vanguardism, Marks raised a concern: "...the isolation of our members from the SACP has created wrong attitudes even towards some basic problems of the South African revolution. There is even a questioning of the wisdom of the present democratic phase of our revolution led by the ANC".[11] Marks was here referring to a view current within some circles in the Party's London groups which confused the Party's vanguard role with the issue of leadership within the liberation movement. All in all, the meeting was a success in as far as the opening of channels of communication between the two leaderships was concerned. The Party moved into the 1970s determined to establish units and regional committees.

## Reviving the Underground

The Party Secretariat in London had never abandoned the hope of rebuilding the underground in the country after the arrest of Fischer, and this factor contributed significantly to the growth of the Party in the 1970s and 1980s. One of the exercises conducted by the Secretariat for this purpose was to conduct a survey, in the late 1960s, among its members, mostly those based in London, to determine their state of preparedness for deployment inside South Africa for illegal work.

Between around 1969 and 1971, the Secretariat dispatched a number of cadres, mainly individuals who had been to London for a variety of reasons, to re-establish the Party presence inside the country by creating units and engaging in propaganda work. Communication with these operatives required a specialised technique that was sophisticated for its time: using an invisible ink to hide a message behind an innocent text addressed to a friend, for example. A developing chemical would then be used to retrieve the hidden message following a variety of formulae, some of which were described by Ronnie Kasrils in his autobiography: "Developers for our operatives inside South Africa could be as simple as an oven-cleaner lightly sprayed over the page. Within seconds, the secret writing would emerge. Other developers included a caustic soda solution and even a drop of blood dissolved in a few millilitres of distilled water. Soaked in a piece of cotton wool and lightly wiped over the page, the developer would reveal a vivid orange or yellow message".[12] The innocent letter would be organised around a relationship between the sender and the recipient – be it, for example, a relationship between a boy and a girl or between old friends – and would contain, within the text, conventional signs, such as 'my dear' or 'sincerely yours' in order to indicate to the recipient what chemical formula to use for the retrieval of the hidden message.

The operatives used different code names, such as Cobra, Patrick, Fred, Stephen, Rufus and Herbert. One of the first operatives of this phase, named Patrick, was active in Johannesburg from around 1969 to at least the end of 1971. As early as 1969, Patrick was trying to establish his own units, and received a positive reply from the Secretariat in London:

The Committee favours the idea of your forming a unit with the two people you named and propose that, as a preliminary to this, you organize a meeting with them and, in the context of the tasks already given to you, you discuss with them what you and they can do about them. Report to us on these discussions *and await* further directives [emphasis original].[13]

Other operatives, such as 'Rufus', who was active around 1970–71 in Cape Town, were more successful in their endeavours, even recruiting individuals some of whom were later to play a prominent role in the Party, such as Jeremy Cronin and Rob Davies.

The central brief of operatives during this phase was limited to propaganda work. They distributed Party propaganda material received from the Secretariat, but some were innovative enough to develop their own pamphlets and journals. For example, Rufus, thanks to his journalistic skills, could produce his journal *Revolt* for distribution in Cape Town. While the operatives had to get permission from the Secretariat before they could recruit any person, potential recruits were nonetheless put into three categories, namely those to be recruited for Party work; those to be recruited for general national liberation work; and those to be monitored and assessed. If the available correspondence file on the subject is anything to go by, operatives were largely based in Natal, Cape Town and Johannesburg. Finally, the operatives were kept informed about Party developments, and some were even sent reports of CC meetings.

The Party tried to explore other innovative ways of resuscitating the underground inside the country. One of the attempts, for example, was to try to use white 'tourists' to carry arms and fighters from the Zambia-Botswana border to Francistown. Indeed, there is no doubt that Party underground work during this period was a seriously risky undertaking. Not only was the level of political mobilisation of the people low, but the activities of the security forces, especially the Special Branch, further complicated the terrain for the operatives. Some of the Party operatives of this phase were arrested and, like Ahmed Timol, were killed by the apartheid security forces.

As the Secretariat was busy attempting to deploy operatives inside the country primarily for propaganda work, another big initiative involving the ANC was underway. The idea of landing MK troops inside the country by sea was considered as early as 1963, but was only formally raised when Slovo tabled a formal request to the Soviet Union for support in August 1967. The initiative was known as Operation J. Both the ANC and the Party were very optimistic about the operation, according to correspondence between Tambo and Slovo on the matter, between 1969 and the period before implementation.[14] The Soviet Union, which decided in favour of Operation J in October 1970, was to focus its support in three areas: financially, including the £75 000 required for the purchase of the vessel which was to be used for the shipment of the MK soldiers; training of the soldiers in the necessary, specialised techniques; and continuous technical and security support by Soviet personnel.[15]

Operation J involved landing MK soldiers on the Transkei coast for infiltration into the hinterland. This was an attempt aimed at circumventing problems with land-bound infiltrations, such as the Wankie campaign. Preparations for Operation J were not limited to finding a country from which to dispatch the vessel, but also involved sending reconnaissance missions into the country to study the landing sites; immigration, customs and other border controls; the movement and vigilance of the security forces; and the state of readiness of the people.

The vessel finally left for South Africa on 6 March 1972 from Kisimayo, Somalia, but within 24 hours had to return to shore at Mogadishu, following a message sent by the captain that the radar had failed. However, as the Party was to report later, it turned out that the crew, recruited from Greece with the help of the Greek Communist Party, had a hand in the problems that were encountered by the ship: "…we have now strong reason to believe that both the generator and the electric steering motor [of the ship] may have been deliberately tampered with in order to give more substance to the rather thin excuse of a return based on a slight deterioration in the clarity of the radar".[16]

Within two weeks, having lost hope in persuading the Greek crew even with the intervention of the leadership of the Greek Communist

Party, another crew arrived from England "which not only combined a great deal of scientific and technical talent but which proved to be a model in devotion to work and revolutionary commitment and courage".[17] Thus on 13 April the ship departed, but, within one and a half hours, experienced a mechanical failure, forcing it to return to the shore again: "In the light of all [this]… we had no option but to abandon the whole mission, whose basic failure we believe to have been caused by sabotage on the part of the cowardly Greek crew".[18] The failure of Operation J was to affect the confidence that the Soviet Union had in the SACP.

Soon after the failure of Operation J, another new method was explored in order to "return all or most of our men to our country"; the new plan was based "on the provision of 'valid' travel documents for each of the men who will travel individually to points close to our borders and then illegally make their way across".[19] However, as shown by Shubin, this new method also suffered a setback, even resulting in nation-wide arrests: "A number of people were arrested, all Umkhonto fighters, who had already reached different destinations inside South Africa".[20]

The external mission never lost hope. One of the important moves taken in this regard was to send Chris Hani into the country in 1974 to undertake both SACP and ANC underground work. Hani, code-named Phoenix in correspondence with the Party Secretariat, entered the country using the name Lawrence Socishe, accompanied by another operative, known as Thomas. Hani carried £500 and Thomas £300, with £5 000 scheduled to be delivered by a courier.

Hani later moved to Lesotho, opening, with the help of his father Gilbert, a shop as a front for underground work. However, because of lapses in security Hani was arrested in June 1975 under the Lesotho Security Act of 1974. It emerged later that the Lesotho government was particularly concerned that the foreign currencies Hani was cashing were being used for the activities of the then banned Basotho Congress Party. On his release from prison after 60 days, he was re-arrested, tortured and even put in solitary confinement. He, however, continued to operate in that country until he was recalled by the ANC in 1981.

Hani's mission was nonetheless a great success. First of all, and unlike other operatives who were being sent into the country by the Party, Hani and Thomas had both the political and military mandate. They established a Party, ANC and SACTU underground presence in various parts of the Eastern Cape, Western Cape, Natal, the Free State and the Transvaal. For this reason, Lesotho, to be known later as the Island in the underground vocabulary, became an important centre of operations of the external missions of both the ANC and the Party, and this was to be the case until the Maseru massacre of December 1982. Finally, because of his seniority in both the Party (already a CC member) and the ANC, Hani did not need to get the permission of the Secretariat before he could recruit cadres into his machinery.

It was thanks to efforts such as these – operatives of the period 1969–71, Operation J, and the work of Hani and Thomas – that the Party, and the whole liberation movement, was on the ground at the time of the eruption of the June 1976 students' riots. A number of Party and ANC units became engulfed in the struggles of this period, and the apartheid regime responded with the determination to dislodge these organisations as it had done in the 1960s. For example, the fruits of the work of operatives such as Rufus received a blow when in July 1977 a number of Party activists in Cape Town, among them Jeremy Cronin and David Rabkin (Rufus), were arrested. However, Cape Town was to remain one of the important centres of the Party's underground presence inside the country. Whatever the setback, the external mission of both the ANC and the Party had now, in the 1970s, accumulated enough experience to be able to sustain the momentum throughout the decade, into the 1980s.

# 3
# The Soldiers of Luthuli

A FEW MONTHS AFTER THE first formal ANC-SACP meeting in exile, in June 1970, the Party organised its first augmented or extended CC meeting in Moscow, along the lines the CEC had suggested in 1966. The meeting, attended by 19 people, was the first formal gathering to bring together the CC and some rank-and-file members. With Kotane entered in the attendance register as present when he was in fact in hospital, non-CC members present included Ray Alexander Simons, Ruth First, Moses Mabhida and Eric Mtshali; representation covered exile members in the USSR, East Africa and London. Most of those present had joined the Party between the 1930s and 1950s (the bulk of these having joined in the 1940s), with only two having joined the Party in the 1960s. The meeting benefitted from the depth of experience that most of those present had with the Party, running from the legal period to the post-1953 underground years as well as the 1961–63 military campaigns. The racial composition of those present was eleven Africans, five whites, two Indians and one Coloured person. For the elections to the nine CC positions, 26 nominations were received, and with Kotane and Marks retaining their positions, new members on the CC included Josiah Jele, Moses Mabhida and Chris Hani.

Resolutions were taken on a number of issues, in particular on relations with the ANC, the armed struggle and organisational work. With regard to the latter, an important decision aimed at strengthening the work of the CC and establishing units. The resolution on the armed struggle, while reflecting a shift from the sabotage thesis that informed the 1961–63 MK campaign, was still based on the belief that guerrilla warfare in South Africa had to be waged from the rural areas – a position that was to lie behind some of the operations that were to be undertaken later in the 1970s such as Operation J. The augmented meeting not only saw the emergence of a new breed of African leaders for the Party, some of whom were later to play a prominent role, but also prepared the Party to root itself among the exile community based in Africa.

However, the September 1972 CC meeting took place against the background of the attacks on the Party led by 'dissidents', this even overshadowing Operation J. In fact, earlier on, at the ANC meeting organised in Lusaka in 1971 to discuss "strategic questions connected with new developments inside the country", the Party was not invited; the meeting "was the first of its kind since 1966 in which brother organizations, including the Party, were not asked to send a participant or an observer".[1]

Slovo's verbal report to the 1972 CC meeting is also telling in this regard. According to Slovo: "A pattern has been set that the Party has call only on its white, Indian and Coloured members and [that] all Africans are the almost exclusive property of the ANC... Yet the fact that it [the Party] was restricted essentially to minority groups has caused and is continuing to cause enormous political damage"; an "impression has become even more entrenched that we are a minority organization. Loss of Moses [Kotane] and JB [Marks]... And no public African figure of stature seen to be at the top". Furthermore, "...a view has become entrenched that we have only a qualified right to mobilize people at home under the Party's banner". Nor was the independent profile of the Party exempted from this challenge: "We hear attacks against us every time it leaks out that we take a collective stand on an important issue even in support of the ANC Executive... In other words we are expected to accept a position which makes a complete mockery of our independence." If this trend were to continue, argued Slovo, "we might as well decide here and now to liquidate the Party".[2]

Therefore, Slovo's report suggests that critical issues, some of which were discussed at the ANC-SACP meeting of 1969, were still unresolved. First was the right of the Party to organise among the exile community; there was still some resistance to allowing the Party to have an organised presence, especially in MK camps. Secondly, the Party was not expected to have its own independent profile; Tambo even raised concerns about the Party having to meet before the meetings of the Revolutionary Council. Finally, that the Party was perceived to be an organisation of minorities was indeed a serious stumbling block. So, instead of a Party that was triumphing, and even taking over the ANC in the post-Morogoro period as some scholars have suggested, we see a Party that is struggling for its own survival as a political force both in exile and within the liberation movement.

The response of the Party to this crisis was to strengthen its presence among the exile community based in Africa. The plan was to create more capacity to support CC members based in Africa, in the form of Eric Mtshali, appointed as a full-time functionary for Hull. In addition, the Party increased its efforts aimed at creating units in East Africa. Importantly, the process of creating a new layer of African leadership was initiated in appointing Hani as assistant secretary at the 1972 CC meeting. The SACP then agreed to support the establishment of an organised, exile-based SACTU. Finally, the Party's propaganda work within the liberation movement intensified (as demonstrated in Table 1 on the following page), thanks to the establishment, in 1970, of an *Inner-Party Bulletin* for distribution among Party members, and in 1971, of *Inkululeko-Freedom* as the Party's mouthpiece. With Dadoo elected chairperson at the November 1973 CC meeting following the death of Marks the previous year and two Africans co-opted into the CC at the same meeting, the Party continued its resolve to root itself in Africa. By the time of the October 1975 CC meeting, the affairs of Hull were now a standing item on the agenda of CC meetings. In fact, the business of the CC was becoming more and more regularised; meetings would begin with a political and organisational report, then proceed to a discussion, and end with resolutions and a public statement.

**Table 1: Party Propaganda, 1966–72**

| Year/Date | Material | Distribution |
|---|---|---|
| Mid-1966 | 'Freedom' leaflet to celebrate the 45th anniversary of the Party | Mass internal posting |
| November 1967 | 'Freedom' leaflet on Russia's October Revolution | Mass internal posting |
| Mid-1968 | 'Freedom' leaflet on the Wankie Campaign | Mass internal posting |
| Mid-1968 | Yusuf Dadoo's leaflet to the Indian people | Posted from London |
| August 1969 | Pamphlet with speech by JB Marks | Posted from London |
| April 1970 | Leaflet on the centenary of Lenin | Mass internal posting |
| July 1971 | First special illegal edition of the African Communist (no 46, 3rd Quarter) to coincide with the Party's 50th anniversary | Posted from abroad |
| July 1971 | Launch of Inkululeko | Internal distribution |
| July 1971 | 50th anniversary stickers | Internal distribution |
| End of 1971 | 'Little Lenins'; six titles and one Xhosa edition | Over 2 000 of each edition posted, and 1 000 of the Xhosa edition |
| February 1972 | Special publication on the history of the Party | Internal posting of 500 issues |

However, in spite of this, difficulties in relations with the ANC were far from over. A report sent after the 1975 CC meeting by the Secretariat to Hani who was then operating in Lesotho, raised some concern:

OR's [Tambo] attitude remains an extremely complex one. At the RC [Revolutionary Council] meeting itself he paid tribute to the Party but in his own rather complicated way, he emphasized the need for the Party to work in the tradition of Malume [Kotane] by which he understands that it should not really be organized as an independent force.³

Nor were relations with the Communist Party of the Soviet Union (CPSU) unaffected, especially after the failure of Operation J. With the 1971 annual allocation from the CPSU reduced by £10 000 to £30 000, the CC had to appeal:

> This reduction [of the 1971 allocation] has had serious consequences for the capacity of our Party to maintain and expand our various efforts in the extremely difficult conditions which face us... [T]he new problems which arose in connection with the attempted implementation of Operation J have seriously aggravated our financial position. To date there has been an expenditure of £25 000 over and above the total amount which had been allocated for this project by you... The additional amounts involved in pursuing Operation J has had to be found solely by our Party and has denuded our reserves to a critical point and we face the coming period with wholly inadequate resources.⁴

However, by the end of the 1970s, relations had improved; the CC could thank its Soviet counterpart for the 1977 allocation:

> It is needless to stress that without this solidarity aid it would not have been possible for our Party organization to make the substantial progress it has been able to achieve during the last twelve months. In this period we have not only consolidated but also increased the number of our units functioning inside the country. Also, the network connecting the internal machinery with the Centre [CC] is working more satisfactorily through the regional committees established in the bordering States including Lesotho [referring to Hani's work].⁵

As for the London Committee, later renamed a district, it had grown since its restructuring in 1966. The Committee and its groups were continuing to meet regularly, keeping in constant communication with the Secretariat, and often even sending suggestions on people to recruit and material to produce. In fact, the eight London Committee members of the mid-1970s were figures who had a rich experience with the Party – the members included Brian Bunting, Rusty Bernstein and Reg September. But London's problems were far from over. Firstly, the groups, because of their distance from home and their general isolation from the frontline, would sometimes lose purpose and direction. Important too was the turf battle between the London groups and the Secretariat. Many members of the London groups wanted to do more than solidarity work, propaganda work and political education; they wanted to interact with the underground inside the country. Much of the correspondence between the Secretariat and the London Committee during the 1970s centred on this issue. The Secretariat tried, on at least two occasions, to spell out the tasks of the London Committee and its groups with the hope of closing the debate on the matter.

But the lack of clarity in this area persisted, even leading to the expulsion of Ben Turok from the Party in March 1976, after he had taken the initiative to raise funds from Oxfam (Canada) for assistance to certain underground formations inside the country. The Secretariat asked Turok to provide the names of his contacts in the country, but he refused. The London Committee deliberated on the matter at its meeting of January 1976, and concluded that the Turok affair was largely due to the fact that the Party lacked clear guidelines on the matter – even instructing Bernstein to develop guidelines for discussion. Thus, the Committee recommended that Turok be suspended for six months, but the Secretariat opted for expulsion instead. This is how Turok finds himself outside the Party to this day. Inevitably, the racial composition of the London groups was also a concern:

> ...by an historical accident the racial composition of our membership in London is overwhelmingly white and, until recently... the other levels of our movement have not been effectively integrated... care has to be taken to guard against the

temptation of entrenching our top-level apparatus in a basically unsuitable area and with a predominance of personnel who do not reflect the real character of our social structure. It is not a question of lower grade participation by those who belong to the minority groups, but rather one of guarding against what could become a harmful distortion in the true character of our movement with all the negative consequences which would flow from such an arrangement.[6]

These problems notwithstanding, the 1970s presented the Party with both opportunities and new challenges, which were linked to developments inside the country. Following the re-emergence of trade unionism and the student uprising in the mid-1970s in the country, a flood of young people crossed South Africa's borders to swell the ranks of the ANC resulting in the establishment of MK's Luthuli Detachment. Thanks to the independence of Mozambique and Angola in 1974, the latter even providing the ANC with facilities for the establishment of MK training camps, the apartheid regime felt exposed and insecure, possibly for the first time.

When the CC met with the membership at its second augmented meeting in 1979 in the German Democratic Republic, Party regions and units were now in existence in Africa, and the new CC included more leaders who were based there. The issue was no longer that of 'reconstructing' the Party but rather of 'strengthening and extending' Party regions and units. More powers were devolved to the regions, including London, on matters relating to Party building inside the country: "Regional committees in the forward areas bordering on our country and the London region must devote uninterrupted attention to the task of creating internal Party units and contacts". This decision may have helped in moderating the turf battle that had been taking place between the London Committee and the Secretariat, but the problem was far from over. Another issue, which was still outstanding, was the development of a comprehensive cadre recruitment policy: "The incoming CC shall issue a guide on cadre policy based on the discussions on this topic [at this extended meeting]".[7]

# 4
# People's War

THE 1980s SAW THE CULMINATION of the mass popular uprising, which had been sparked in the 1970s. These developments, including the emergence of the United Democratic Front (UDF) and the Congress of South African Trade Unions (COSATU), required more creativity on the part of the exiled organisations.

With the CEC restructured to become a Politburo in 1977 and Mabhida elected as the new general secretary at the 1979 augmented meeting, the headquarters of the Party was shifted to Luanda. There a permanent Secretariat was created to work with the general secretary. The Secretariat was "to attend to the whole range of problems around the internal organisation of the Party, its growth inside as well as proper guidance to the working class and the Trade Unions".[1] The Politburo (PB), at one of its meetings in 1981, established three sub-committees to focus on propaganda; trade union work; and 'internal' work in the forward areas and inside the country. Unlike in the 1960s when the Party existed in an organised form only in London, or in the 1970s when Party collectives outside London could only be found in Lusaka, Dar es Salaam and Moscow, by 1981, the Party's organised presence had spread to Angola, Lesotho, Mozambique, Swaziland, Botswana, and, inside the country, to Cape Town. Therefore, in the 1980s, the Party's strategy focused on building a strong underground presence inside the country, and amongst the working class in particular. For this purpose, relations with SACTU and the trade unions emerging inside the country became very important. In order to strengthen CC leadership on the ground, at the CC meeting of September 1981, some CC members were deployed to Party regions. John Nkadimeng was made responsible for Mozambique and Swaziland, Dan Tloome for Botswana, Slovo for Zimbabwe, Hani for Lesotho, Bunting for London and the *African Communist*, and

Mabhida for Angola and East Africa. And equally important was the demarcation of responsibilities between the general secretary and the chairperson, with the latter given international work, and the former internal Party building.

The period leading to the mid-1980s also saw the stabilisation of the workings of the Party in a number of areas. Firstly, the PB, as a recent phenomenon, began to sit regularly with a well-structured agenda. The proceedings of the meetings focused on minutes of the previous meeting, regional reports, deployment and transfers of cadres (including those sent to the Lenin School), and concluded with a discussion of the international situation. Secondly, a full-time secretariat also became necessary. Thus in June 1982, Hani and Slovo were appointed by the PB to serve in the three-person Secretariat; in 1984, with permission from Tambo, Josiah Jele was released for full-time work in the Secretariat. Later in the mid-1980s, also with permission from Tambo, Slovo was released for full-time work as the Party's chairperson. Thirdly, CC members based in Lusaka, at the ANC's headquarters, constituted themselves into a core whose minutes were discussed at PB meetings. New approaches were introduced to establish the underground in the country. Of particular interest was the PB decision in January 1984 to, on the one hand, activate Party stalwarts in the Transvaal, Natal, Western Cape, Eastern Cape and the Transkei, and, on the other, to allocate the Western Cape to Ray Alexander Simons and Hani, the Transvaal to John Nkadimeng and Dan Tloome, the Eastern Cape to Josiah Jele and Hani, and Natal to Mac Maharaj.

Party finances gradually improved. By 1980, the London Aid Committee, now with a membership which included Slovo, Dan Tloome and Moses Mabhida, had money in various London-based banks in three currencies (pounds, dollars and rands), totalling £130 000, US$249 000 and R29 000. So demanding was the work that in 1984 the Party had to ask its Soviet partners to increase their existing annual allocation of US$60 000, US$40 000 of which was spent on administrative expenses and the production of the *African Communist*. The Party appealed for an increase not only because of inflation and the demands of the struggle, but also due to the fact that "we have no other income and underground conditions make it virtually impossible to raise our financial needs from public collections amongst our people".[2]

The propaganda machinery was stabilising, thanks to a number of steps taken during the 1970s. Important in this regard was the development of the practice of distributing Party pamphlets in various African indigenous languages inside the country. (See Table 1 on page 38.) Furthermore, the launch in July 1971 of *Inkululeko-Freedom*, which was renamed *Umsebenzi* in 1985, as a mouthpiece of the Party was vital. The circulation of the *African Communist* continued to increase, between 1967 and 1972 almost doubling from 3 500 to 6 300 copies. The distribution of party propaganda material, including publications such as Michael Harmel's *Fifty Fighting Years*, Brian Bunting's *Moses Kotane*, and *South African Communists Speak*, was facilitated through special outlet stores, universities, political parties, trade unions, the Anti-Apartheid Movement and other solidarity networks. What also strengthened these efforts was the development of a mailing list of influential individuals based in the country who were sent Party publications automatically.

A number of factors also contributed towards steadying relations between the Party and the ANC. First, the intensity of the struggle inside the country in the aftermath of the workers' strikes, and student riots of the mid-1970s made increased cooperation among the various organs of the exiled movement necessary. Secondly, with Mabhida at the head of the Party, given his strong footing within the ANC, it promised a return to the days of Kotane. If the latter's legacy in the Party was the indigenisation and Africanisation of the organisation, Mabhida's was that he integrated the Party's external mission into Africa. The relocation of the Party's headquarters from London to Luanda in 1981, and the following year to Maputo, and following the Nkomati Accord, to Lusaka (where the ANC headquarters was located), was another factor in improving the chemistry between the Party and the ANC. Not only was the Party now taking part in meetings between the ANC and SACTU aimed at strengthening the labour movement inside the country, but the Party and ANC, in one instance, "had exhaustive discussions on the internal situation and future co-operation".³ The meeting was probably one of the first formal encounters between the ANC and the Party since the 1969 meeting. At a subsequent meeting with the ANC held in 1982, it was agreed that the two organisations should meet at least twice a year. It was agreed, too, that the Party could now establish units among MK soldiers in Angola. Tambo conceded in his address on the occasion of the 60th anniversary of the Party in July 1981:

> To be true to history, we must concede that there have been difficulties as well as triumphs along our path, as, traversing many decades, our two organizations have converged towards a shared strategy of struggle. Ours is not merely a paper alliance, created at conference tables and formalized through the signing of documents and representing only an agreement of leaders. Our alliance is a living organism that has grown out of struggle. We have built it out of our separate and common experiences.⁴

The relationship between the two organisations was still not without its contradictions. The issue was no longer whether the Party should establish its units or not, but what the Party expected of its members in the ANC and other organs of the liberation movement. In this context, at its meeting of September 1981, the CC passed its famous resolution on "Party Work in Fraternal Organisations". According to this resolution: "It is the right and duty of communists working in the national movement to discuss and decide collectively on their common approach to all matters which affect the basic direction and content of the revolutionary struggle, and to ensure that they advance and support such decision in any organ in which the matter arises". Furthermore, "every Party cadre who is active at any level of a fraternal organization is accountable to the Party collective to which he or she is a member for his or her work and conduct in that organization". Party members in the latter position were to be regularly assessed and guided by their units and regions, and "it is the duty of every Party collective to recommend appropriate disciplinary measures against any comrade who has been judged to have acted in breach of this resolution".⁵

Similarly, in 1985, the CC noted in one of its documents that "it is vital... that already at this stage our Party should be able, with the full cooperation and agreement of the national liberation movement, to function in close and accepted forms so as to bring to the fore the noble aspirations of the labouring people in our country for socialism". The document continued:

> But it is not only a matter of co-operation and co-ordination at the policy and decision-making level that is of immediate interest to all Party members. It is also vital that the Party should be in a position to exercise discipline and control over all Party members, wherever they may be in the world or in whatever organization – military or otherwise – they may be active. It is important that our partners in the struggle must see this as something in the interest of the entire struggle, as it will enable a higher ideological level to be maintained as well as higher standards of unity and discipline all round.[6]

Nor was the problem with the London Committee on its role in internal work resolved. For example, in January 1983, the London Committee wrote a strongly-worded report to the PB, seeking "more precise directives" on the matter:

> Is the LC to be the main center responsible for internal work, or do we get instructions from the PB? What are we to concentrate on – internal reconstruction and the formation of units etc, or propaganda, leaflet bombs etc.? The LC feels that our most important task is political, not technical – that it is more important to get a unit functioning as part of the local population in, say, CT [Cape Town], than to set off a leaflet bomb.[7]

## A People's War

As the liberation movement mounted its offensive in the 1980s, a number of tactical questions came to the fore. One answer to these tactical questions was the development of the concept of a 'people's war' thanks to the ANC's Politico-Military Strategy Commission which came up with the famous *Green Book: Thesis on our Strategic Line*. It argued that "the armed struggle must be based on, and grow out of, mass political support and it must eventually involve all our people". Eventually, thanks to the Kwabe ANC Conference of June 1985, which revised the thesis of classical guerrilla warfare launched from the rural areas, the ANC's new perspective came to be based on the belief that the organisation "should step up the all-round political and military offensive sharply, and prepare for protracted people's war. A general insurrection was seen [by the ANC] as the logical culmination of this struggle."[8]

But the ANC had to deal with another phenomenon. In 1981, a network of apartheid spies was uncovered, and subsequently a number of cadres were arrested. However, as the ANC would acknowledge later, some of the organisation's security personnel resorted to the abuse of prisoners in their effort to extract information from the alleged spies. This caused serious problems within the exile community. The Party's response was two-fold: the first was to take internal security measures that included developing security guidelines for the members, and revising communication codes. At the second level, the Party took a political position on the matter, including the treatment of prisoners. The Party warned against the "movement" being "panicked into a wild and groundless witch-hunt against innocent members", and "felt that it is the duty of the Party to ensure that those who are used for interrogation purpose do not unnecessarily adopt methods which undermine revolutionary morality".[9] These new security concerns were to be deliberated upon at the Party's 6th Congress.

As the Party's exile structures stabilised, with the number of regions and units growing, it no longer made sense to convene augmented CC meetings as a forum for contact with the membership and the election of the new leadership. Thus the 6th Congress (the 5th was in 1962), conceived initially as an 'augmented' or extended meeting of the CC, was convened in Moscow to deliberate, in particular, on the Party constitution, the approach to a people's war, and the relevance of the *Road to South African Freedom* as a programme.

The organisation of the 6th Congress was necessitated not only by the shift to a people's war, but also by the fact that, following the Vaal uprising of September 1984 in the country, the apartheid regime was faced with one of its most serious crises ever. The crisis was further entrenched with the emergence of the Mass Democratic Movement (MDM) in the form of the UDF and COSATU.

Finally, there is no doubt that the Party wanted to use the 6th Congress to prepare for the ANC's Kwabe Conference in Zambia, scheduled to take place in June 1985. It was there that non-African groups were allowed to stand for leadership positions in the ANC. The Party, in anticipation of this decision, had taken a view that:

> The revolution must move forward on a realistic basis. It should also be borne in mind that the African majority group in our country suffers vicious national oppression and that the natural desire for national resurgence expressed in their own organization and leadership of the struggle for democracy is something we support in principle. This has to be placed alongside the equally important principle that the interests of oppressed national minorities and of revolutionary forces are fully recognized. We communists are not national nihilists. But we insist that national aspirations should be democratic and progressive. [Thus] ... we are convinced that the time has come for a big step forwards that can result in a qualitative change in the relations between revolutionary organizations with the resultant increase in the mobilizing power and effectiveness of the liberation struggle.[10]

Attendance at the 6th Congress was initially set at 35, including both delegates and CC members, but was later changed. Representation by region was as follows: two delegates for Dar es Salaam; one for Zimbabwe; one for Botswana; four for Lusaka; one for Swaziland; one for Mozambique; one for Lesotho; three for London; and three for Angola. Indeed, representation of regions reflected the uneven strength of the Party. Lusaka, with the highest number of delegates, had the highest concentration of CC members in Africa because of the location of the ANC headquarters there, and even had its own Party school. This factor placed the region in a much better position, and it was probably one of the most organised regions. London, the oldest region, was also numerically strong in terms of membership, and Angola was where the MK camps were located.

As expected, the 6th Congress focused on organisational and ideological matters. Among the most dominant debates was the notion of a people's war. As shown above, by the 1980s, with the experience of the 1960s and 1970s, it had become clear to the liberation movement that the success of the struggle against apartheid lay in rooting the 'war' among the 'people', and that guerrilla warfare in South Africa would have to be conducted under non-traditional conditions of the city as opposed to the rural areas where known, successful guerrilla wars had taken place. The 6th Congress, thanks to the new Constitution, also laid to rest the contradictory definition of the Party's understanding of its vanguard role. While the Constitution's Preamble, under 'Aims', reaffirmed that the SACP "is a leading political force of the South African working class and is the vanguard in the struggle for national liberation, socialism and peace in our time", this is, however, qualified later under the same section: the Party was "to participate in and strengthen the liberation alliance of all classes and strata whose interests are served by the immediate aims of the national democratic revolution. This alliance is expressed through the liberation front headed by the ANC."[11] The 6th Congress expressed concern about criticism of the Colonialism of a Special Type thesis and the so-called two-stage theory, by what was regarded as a Trotskyite grouping. To counter this, between the 6th Congress and the 7th Congress (held in April 1989), the Party's propaganda organs, especially the *African Communist*, were to concentrate on this debate.

Organisational matters centred around discussion on the new constitution and the workings of the CC and other Party structures. For the first time in exile, the Party, in adopting a constitution, formalised its structures and elaborated its recruitment policy based on the system of probation. A congress, to be organised every four years, was also agreed. Furthermore, now that the challenge of establishing regions and units had been realised, efforts were redirected into improving the quality of the operations of these Party structures. For example, some delegates raised concerns about the effectiveness of both the PB and CC: "It appears that the PB seldom meets, and the CC is simply a prestige organ". As to the units, an observation was made that they "tend to think that they are a 'talking shop'; they ought to be functional and CC should pay attention to the structure of the units".[12] Nonetheless, Slovo, who had been acting chairperson since January 1984 following the death of Dadoo in 1983, was elected to that position, with Mabhida retaining his position as general secretary. Mabhida was to fall ill soon after the Congress, and spent most of the time thereafter in and out of hospital until his death in March 1986.

Following the 6th Congress, the PB, given new challenges, established sub-committees based on the following areas: propaganda; education, research and training; industrial work; internal reconstruction; work in mass organisations; military affairs; international work; and security and intelligence. Because of increased security concerns, the CC, at its meeting in 1985, adopted a policy on the "imposition of maximum sentence" at the instruction of the 6th Congress, and established a three-person tribunal which was accountable to the PB. Subsequently, in September 1985, the CC issued a circular to regions and units on "Security Measures to be Taken".[13]

The formalisation of a cadre policy in the constitution that was adopted at the 6th Congress was an attempt to clear the confusion that existed on the matter. First of all, it must be pointed out that the Party's emphasis on cadre policy was consistent with what was practised by other communist parties. By and large, all communist parties were very clear about their ideological beliefs as well as their membership policy, which included admission requirements such as probation, oath-taking and social status criteria.[14]

The SACP's cadre policy came to be based on a number of important elements. First there was the system of probation, which had been part of the Party's history for decades, but which took a clearer shape in the 1980s. The 1984 Constitution opened the Party to "all South Africans over the age of 18 who accept the programme and policy" of the Party. But recruitment was to be undertaken by regional committees: "the recruiting of a member requires the unanimous decision of a Regional Committee, or, where no such committee exists, of the Central Committee". Importantly, "the Central Committee shall from time to time lay down rules and regulations which oblige applicants for party membership, unless specially exempted, to serve a probationary period under the supervision of a Party structure prior to being accepted as full members".[15]

But the CC meeting of 1985 was to observe that "a great deal of confusion has arisen in connection with probation", and eventually, the PB circulated an "Elaboration of Rules of Membership" in 1987 in the hope of addressing the confusion.[16] Probation was to be for a period of six months, the probationer being supervised by one of the members so designated by the unit, and the latter was to send its recommendation to the regional committee for decision. However, confusion persisted, and another document, 'Probation' had to be circulated by the PB in January 1988, with an illustration of how the probation system should work in practice.

The second element of the cadre policy was the requirement that "no member shall, without the permission of the CC, directly or indirectly divulge the facts of his or her membership to the Party or the identity of any other member to any unauthorized person".[17] This, linked to the September 1981 CC resolution on 'Party Work in Fraternal Organisations', which required Party members to account for their activities in the ANC, was a very complex issue and politically not without problems. Throughout the exile period the Party leadership tried to exercise control over their members and have them account for their activities in 'fraternal' organisations such as the ANC.

However, some interpreted this stance to mean that the Party was a caucus within the liberation movement. Hence, in one of its meetings, the PB received a report from one of its regions that "it was felt that there is not sufficient accounting to the Party and that not enough Party directives are given in relation to fundamental questions… [O]ur Party must maintain its traditional approach of not undermining the integrity and independence of the ANC and that it would be wrong for the Party to act as a caucus on every issue which arises in the fraternal organization. Nevertheless it is the duty of the Party to give guidance on major fundamental questions of political principle".[18] Not surprisingly, the Lusaka Region, in its report of August 1982 to the PB, noted that "our Party life in exile, and the stunted style of work to which we have become accustomed, has resulted in", among other things, "the development of conspiratorial characteristics in our style of work" not least because of "our reluctance to show our Party face to other members of the family [the liberation movement]".[19]

Indeed, getting Party members to account for their work in the ANC was not that easy. For example, the Lusaka Regional Committee, in its circular of 1 January 1983, called on its members in this manner:

> In keeping with previous directives from the CC, the Regional Committee would like to have reports from units on the activities of members in the various sectors in which they are working. The PB remarks that there are serious weaknesses in the work of members in the NLM [national liberation movement], such as an absence of leadership by Party units on important questions of our revolution...[20]

Thirdly, a Party member was entitled to participate in decision-making within the framework of democratic centralism, which was described in *Umsebenzi* as "the living tissue which binds our party together – organizationally and ideologically".[21] Democracy, the Party argued in its definition of democratic centralism, "does not mean endless discussion and debate but rather serious examination of burning problems of the day. Nor does democracy mean that the secrets of our party are known to all members". And "centralism means that all majority decisions democratically adopted by our Party, the constitution and rules, the broad parameters of its theoretical standpoint and instructions given to members and units by higher collectives, are binding and compulsory".[22]

Thus documents prepared for major gatherings, such as congresses, were circulated to regions and units for comments, as were discussion documents, which were developed on major themes preoccupying the liberation movement. As mentioned previously an *Inner-Party*

*Bulletin* was also introduced in the 1970s to "strengthen the political and organizational unity and cohesion of the Party as a whole, to rally the rank-and-file around the leadership, and draw the leadership into closer contact with the rank-and-file, and to improve the effectiveness of the political activity of Party members". The *Bulletin*, as a political organ, "must be of an *inner-party* character, neither intended nor allowed to be seen by non-members, nor quoted or published" (emphasis original); therefore "the distribution of the bulletin would have to be organized in accordance with the principle of conspiracy".[23]

Thus, issues of the *Bulletin* carried a clear directive: "Regions and Units must ensure that this Bulletin does not circulate to any person who is not a Party member"; or "every copy of this issue must be accounted for and returned to the respective regions after study and comments". However, the production of the *Bulletin* was not as regular as the leadership would have wanted.

In addition, Party members were required to undertake continuous political and ideological training. Units were important in this regard, and so were some regions, such as Lusaka and Angola, which conducted their own political schools. However, more prestigious was the Lenin School in the USSR. On their return from the Lenin School, the graduates were deployed in various structures of the Party and the liberation movement as a whole. With its membership growing, in the 1980s the Party was offered a quota by the School, but the PB decided, as part of the development of the probation system, that "only comrades who have already been tested in the Party and in the struggle should be considered" for the School.[24] So important was political education at the School that in May 1984 the PB decided to send four CC members there for refresher courses. Cuba also became an important centre in the 1980s, not least because of the one- to three-year courses that it offered to Party members.

Moreover, by the 1980s, the Party leadership, through the PB and the Secretariat, had devised a system of monitoring and keeping track of the movement of Party members in exile. Permission was sometimes even sought from the PB for movement elsewhere in exile. Finally, subscription fees for members was also an important element, especially in regions where a significant component of the membership had the means of generating their own income. For example, the London Committee could report in May 1972 that "we have £500 available from our collection of subscriptions".[25] Similarly, in 1981, the region in Lesotho had a subscription policy based on 1% of a member's earnings. But this was not easy to implement. Thus in 1985 the CC made an appeal to its members:

> It is important that payment of such dues be seen by our members not only as a means for the Party to raise funds for the work that it has to do but also as an act of political commitment and dedication... We therefore urge all regions to examine the rule and rates of dues imposed upon membership in their respective regions. We are mindful that there are many cases where the membership is unable to pay any regular subscription. On the other hand we have members who are in full-time employment, we therefore urge that when regions look into this question they should consider the possibility of imposing flexible scales which take into account the ability of each comrade to make the necessary financial contribution.[26]

All in all, therefore, these developments in the consolidation of the Party's cadre policy were necessitated not only by the quantitative growth in membership, but also by generational shifts in the total composition of the membership as more and more youth joined the Party.

The period following the 6th Congress witnessed further growth in the Party, both in terms of membership and profile. While Party structures had collapsed in Lesotho, Swaziland and Mozambique after the mid-1980s due to an increase in the activity of apartheid security forces in those countries, combined with deportations and the Nkomati Accord (in the case of Mozambique), the Party experienced growth in other areas, and a new region was even established in Zimbabwe. Thanks to the heightening of the struggle inside the country and an increased flow of cadres into the exile community, the number of members and units increased from 241 in 40 units in November 1986 to 267 in 45 units in November 1987. By the time of the 7th Congress, in April 1989, the Party could boast of 340 members distributed in 48 units that were located in eight regions: London, Lusaka, Angola, Swaziland, Mozambique, Dar es Salaam, Zimbabwe and Botswana. Lusaka, with 67 members and 10 units, was still the largest region, followed by Angola with 59 members and eleven units, and London with 45 members and four units. Botswana and Dar es Salaam, each with 18 members, were among the medium-sized regions. While the average size of regional committees ranged from three to six members, that of units varied from three in medium-sized regions, such as Dar es Salaam, to about eight in larger regions, such as Angola.

The breakdown of the 340 members was as follows: 84% male and 16% female; 60% above the age of 35; and 70% African as opposed to 16% whites, 10% Indian, and 4% Coloured. In addition to the 340 members, there were 53 'unaccounted members', 66 probationers, twelve who were in prison, and some 23 who were either on mission abroad or students at the Lenin School. Therefore, this figure of about 494 members of the Party in 1989 in exile, is far below the 5 000 suggested by Tom Lodge and others.[27] The inflation of SACP membership figures by Lodge was not deliberate, but simply guess-work and a function of the exaggerated view that prevailed about the influence the Party wielded over the ANC.

The membership of the Party in exile was deliberately kept small not just for reasons of security and quality of cadres, but also to enable the leadership to exercise control over the membership. In fact, the PB, in the face of this substantial growth of the Party from the mid-1980s, was to express a concern in 1989 whether the recruitment "has not been too fast".[28]

As to the workings of the PB and the CC, these also experienced improvement in the period after the mid-1980s. The meetings of the PB became more regular – the structure met on average every three weeks, as opposed to meeting only every three or four months as was the case before the 6th Congress. By the time of the 7th Congress in April 1989, the PB had met 76 times since the 6th Congress, with the CC meeting thrice during the same period. Furthermore, with the influx of the internal leadership and the youth into exile, the CC, in its meeting of 1986, co-opted six members but without voting rights, in order to accommodate the latter two sectors. Since "the anonymity of most Party leaders continues to be a serious obstacle to Party organization and to our political impact", the "gradual exposure" of six CC members was effected from December 1985 (up to then only the general secretary and the chairperson were known publicly), thanks to the decision of the 6th Congress.[29] The purpose of this move was not only to maintain the profile of the Party, but also because of the need for day-to-day contact with regions and their units. Related to this was the intensification of the practice introduced by Mabhida of regularly visiting regions and units. When Slovo became the chairperson, he too joined in this practice.

The underground movement was also growing. *Umsebenzi* even ran series in the late 1980s aimed at supporting units inside the country, with, for example, 'Notes from the Underground' wherein operatives gave first-hand account of their works and shared experiences; 'How to Master Secret Work' which served as a manual; 'Party Life' which focused on the dynamics and internal workings of units and Regional Committees, as well as other organisational matters, such as membership and the running of meetings; and political education material on Marxism-Leninism, including providing guidance to members on studying the programme of the Party.[30] Units were organised and guided in their work by principles of accountability, self-criticism, assignment of task to each member in accordance with one's strengths and ability, and 'territorial' and 'production' considerations in their distribution and location. The latter principle was defined in *Umsebenzi*: "…a network of units must be built in the very midst of the working people – in the factories and townships. Particularly in conditions of cruel persecution and repression our Party structures must combine the principle of organization at a 'territorial and production level'".[31]

Thanks to the hard work of the internal sub-committee and other related structures as well as the legacy of the hard work discussed in Chapter Two, by the end of 1988, the Party had functioning structures in the Western Cape, Transvaal, the Border region in the Eastern Cape, and Natal, with 99 members in 35 units, and 19 probationers. The racial breakdown (in terms of numbers) of members was 55 Africans, 20 Indians, 13 Coloureds and eleven whites. Therefore, in total, including the 494 based in exile, the Party had about 609 members at the time of the 7th Congress in April 1989.

However, there was still no effective Party presence in the Free State because "one comrade was given the task to begin [Party work in the province] but apparently moved over to the enemy".[32] The Western Cape was the most advanced of all Party underground structures, having established its district in 1985 with its full-time organiser, earning a monthly allowance of R250, but it was still faced with an equally important challenge: "Even at its height this region was underrepresented in the African townships".[33] The membership of units in the Border and Transvaal areas was drawn largely from the trade union leadership and factory-based workers in those areas. Indeed, these underground outfits focused their work on propaganda, 'interventions' in the trade union and the mass democratic movement, and intelligence and security matters. None of them played a combat role, at least in so far as their Party brief was concerned.

Nor was the contribution of regions the same with regard to internal work. The degree of involvement in internal work by regions varied from Zimbabwe which was making an "outstanding contribution", through Botswana, Mozambique and Swaziland which were "doing very little in relation to internal work", to London which was making a good contribution on matters of propaganda "but disappointing in organizational field in relation to the potential which exists in this area". According to the PB, the region had great potential even though "no single unit [had been] created by this region" by the end of 1988, and this was "completely insupportable and unacceptable".[34]

Indeed, units, described, as it were, as "the foundation of a party – its operational arm – without which democratic centralism cannot function, without which it cannot grow and without which we cannot perform our ideological and organizational tasks",[35] played a particular role in the total architecture of the Party. Units, explained *Umsebenzi*, "must be formed at the factories, on the mines and farms and in the townships at street level across the length and breadth of our land. Units must be small, completely unknown to all but the members of the unit and the comrade to whom they report and they must observe strict secrecy in all their work. Units have a variety of tasks to perform – they must recruit to the Party's ranks the best and most committed militant fighters; they must work to build and strengthen the trade unions and the mass democratic movement; they must spread the ideas of socialism and they must be active in our people's army, MK".[36] Furthermore, each unit was expected to "set itself a strict programme of ideological work – study and discussion of theory and the relating of this to the day-to-day struggle and the tasks of the moment".[37] The units, as suggested already, operated under the supervision of the Regional/District Committees which "are the executive arm of the PB and CC without which the many units would remain directionless and un-coordinated". The task of the RC included deciding "upon the make-up of the various units under its authority. In other words it must decide in which unit members should be placed".[38]

But units performed their tasks within a complex environment on the ground. According to one Party operative:

> Building an underground network needs a plan. Too often we build new units without any guiding idea. If you are given the task of recruiting, the first thing that jumps into your mind is simply to approach your closest friends. But a vanguard Party is not just a circle of friends. It has to be built with a clear, revolutionary plan. The first question we discussed in the unit was if I should concentrate in my township, or on the industrial area where I work. We agreed that I must concentrate on the industrial zone... Next, I drew the comrades a map of the industrial zone, showing which factories are placed where. Then we asked ourselves how many workers did each factory employ? Which factories had strong trade union organization? What factories had the greatest strategic importance? Does any of them supply SADF [South African Defence Force]? Which make essential goods for other factories? We also asked ourselves which factories were involved in the production of chemicals. We must investigate whether there are chemicals supplies that

can be used for the manufacturing of explosives for our combat work. Then there were a whole number of questions connected with the physical layout of the zone. What are the main access roads and rail-lines to the industrial zone? Where is the nearest police station and army camp? How possible would it be to barricade the whole zone with delivery lorries? If yes, where should these lorries be located? Where would be good storage places for arms within the zone itself?[39]

Another operative gave a first-hand account:

I have been assigned to coordinate a new Party unit operating somewhere in South Africa... There are three of us in this unit, and the other two comrades, a worker and a young intellectual, are quite new Party members. In sharing our experiences I would like to place stress on the crucially important human element in underground work. Our first meeting as a unit was a few weeks ago... Every unit is different. But I think that there are also some general common features. For instance, in all the units in which I have served, there is always some tenseness and uncertainty at the beginning. You are wondering – "Will I prove capable of fulfilling the tasks that will come up? Who are these other comrades, are they reliable?" etc. Coming together as a unit is a serious step; each one is literally placing his or her life in the hands of the others.

The role of the unit leader is always of great importance, most especially at the beginning. The leader must help to overcome this tenseness and uncertainty. In the first place this means careful planning before each meeting.

At our first meeting, we began by establishing very clear security procedures, the date and time for the next meeting, the legend (that is, the cover-up story for this meeting), fall-back procedures, and personal security reports from each of us... While being firm about security, a unit must not become harsh or ultra-critical. I say this because I have been in units where there was sometimes a tendency not just to correct and criticize security errors, but to humiliate the comrade who has made the error. This kind of harshness can actually worsen security. Comrades can become too afraid to admit errors and simply report that "everything is okay".[40]

As to relations with the ANC, these reached a new level in the period post the mid-1980s, thanks to the institution of the practice of regular meetings between the two organisations. By 1985, the concept of a Tripartite Alliance – involving the ANC, SACP and SACTU – had entered the vocabulary of the liberation movement. Between the 6th Congress and September 1985, at least two formal Tripartite meetings sat, and this figure increased to eight by the time of the 7th Congress in April 1989.[41] However, caution was still needed in the management of the relations between the two organisations. For example, at one PB meeting in December 1984, a concern was raised that "we should be careful how we launch the new phase aimed at seeing that our Party functions and that in doing so the Party should avoid beginning to present itself as a leader of the current stage of the revolution; that we understand the phase we are in and that we keep a balance which will ensure that both [the] Party and [the] ANC grow stronger".[42] Tambo was still central to the management of relations between the two organisations, even developing a practice of approving the list of Party members being sent to the Lenin School.

However, a resolution which was to be adopted by the 7th Congress on the alliance, reflected weaknesses in the relationship between the two organisations that still needed attention. The resolution centred on the representation of the Party at meetings held between the ANC and SACTU and the MDM; on the need for more regular and frequent alliance meetings; and on the need to "ensure that members of the tripartite Alliance share information about their programmes and problems".[43]

The relations with labour, both in the form of SACTU and trade union formations that had emerged inside the country since the 1970s, became one of the Party's main themes for the 1980s, the CC even circulating a discussion document, 'The Party and the Trade Unions'. An Industrial Sub-Committee (ISC), a structure established by the PB in the 1970s, was the entity responsible for the work. Since its inception, the ISC focused on giving leadership to SACTU, even meeting with the latter probably for the first time in December 1979. In June the following year, the meeting between the PB and the ISC which developed guidelines for Party work in the trade union sector in the country, resolved to "build a powerful revolutionary trade union movement and charged those organs and cadres of the Party specifically charged with trade union organization to make significant progress in this central front of our struggle".[44] Thus in May 1983, an extended PB meeting including ISC members was convened to deliberate on the subject, including the direction that trade unions in the country should take. Subsequently, more attention was given to SACTU with the aim of repositioning it for the internal union work, including making contacts with unionists inside the country. As trade union work inside the country gained momentum, thanks to the formation of COSATU in 1985, and contacts made with trade unionists, another extended PB meeting was convened in May 1987, to focus on these developments and what was seen as the ineffectiveness of SACTU in this field. Of course, COSATU gained prominence, putting the role of SACTU into question, and thus the CC circulated, in August 1988, a discussion paper on 'The Role of SACTU in the National Democratic Struggle'. The view of the Party leadership was that SACTU still had a role to play as "a liberation arm in the trade union movement".

The Party was also interacting intimately with the MDM structures based in the country, notably the UDF and COSATU, especially from 1986. In fact, between May 1986 and January 1987, at least two 'formal' meetings were held with COSATU representatives. Parallel to this trend, at least from 1985, the PB started deliberating on 'talks' and the possibilities of reaching a negotiated settlement in the country. This development was partly a response to meetings that certain sections of South Africa's white community were holding with the ANC leadership.

The Party underground inside the country was active in MDM structures. One SACP operative recounted the experience and challenges of working underground in MDM structures:

> I am working at ABC factory (of course, that's not its real name). In our party unit we have discussed some areas of daily party work for myself. This includes general work in the trade union. On this front my first task is to give reports on the trade union for the district committee to develop a clear political strategy for our region. My party task in the trade union is also to work from the bottom to help strengthen the organisation. At first I was not sure how a communist works inside a mass democratic organisation like a trade union. In looking into this question I have been very much affected by the words of the late comrade Moses Kotane. He says a communist gives leadership in a mass democratic organisation not with orders from the top, like a boss, but through hard work, personal example and political clarity. You must be prepared to argue a point – yes. But you must also stick with the decisions made by the mass democratic collective. The party and its cadres respect the inner democracy of the trade union. I am not saying that this can be easy in every case. For a person it can be frustrating to see what you think is a wrong decision being taken. But once there is a collective decision you must work harder than anyone to try to implement it, even if you disagreed. This is not just a moral principle. It is correct organisational politics. The broad mass of the workers must learn from their own experiences. No underground cadre must take short-cuts, hi-jacking a mass organisation and forcing a personal view by using the authority of our underground movement. You might have a quick success, but you are making a long-term problem. Revolutions are not made by small groups of advanced revolutionaries. They are made by millions and millions of working people – guided by a vanguard party, yes – but who actively and willingly engaged themselves.
>
> There is another particular problem in my work in the trade union at present. It is a problem that is happening in many mass democratic organisations. One of the workers in

our branch is giving us trouble. It is a guy who speaks in very revolutionary words. He is always challenging everybody. He likes to label people as 'reformist', as 'opportunist' and such things. Now, either this guy is just very undisciplined, or he is an agent provocateur – I mean somebody working for the police who poses as a militant. He tries to provoke comrades into reckless actions, or into revealing sensitive information. At our last branch meeting this guy's talk was especially irritating. He turned on me to say I was a reactionary. He even called me an 'anti-communist'! My tongue was burning to show who is the real revolutionary. I wanted to show the meeting that it was me that knows about communism, about Marxism-Leninism and about our Party. I nearly allowed my pride to uncover me. It was a close thing, *maqabane*. *Ja*, this work sometimes calls for revolutionary patience.[45]

Other units helped MDM structures deal with agents. According to one operative:

Comrades in an MDM structure have someone they are sure is an agent. Suppose these suspicions are correct. But the comrades don't know how to proceed. The matter is discussed loosely, the story spreads. But still the suspect lingers on in MDM structures. Soon enough he gets to hear the stories about himself. Being a clever agent, he then gathers to his side members who have personal grudges against the leadership. He wins over new members who are flattered a more experienced 'comrade' shares information with them. The agent starts to spread a counter story. He says the suspicions were started by people in the organisation who are 'sectarian', who don't want their 'undemocratic style' challenged. Eventually the organisation is divided.

Even if the enemy has failed to introduce a totally unsuspected agent, they have succeeded in paralysing the organisation. The situation has become so messy it is now virtually impossible to get to the bottom of it all. But if basic steps are followed, none of this needs to happen. In our region we are helping MDM organisations set up small, three-person security and discipline committees. These committees can be entirely under underground discipline. Or they can be confidential structures answerable to the leadership of the relevant MDM organisation. It depends on the circumstances. Only the most trusted and mature comrades must be pulled into such a committee. Such a committee can be used to check on individuals where the need arises. There are basic things to check:

- Personal history – childhood, schooling, relatives, friends. What to look for is any possible connections with the police. Or any gaps, any unexplained and sudden changes.
- Money – does the person have more money than can be explained by their job or family situation?
- Absences – are there regular or unexplained absences from work? from home? These could be times when the person is being instructed by the police. Sometimes false detentions are used for the same purpose.
- Behaviour in the MDM organisation – is the person sectarian, or provocative (always suggesting ultra-revolutionary action)? Does the person get involved in loose sexual behaviour, or drinking sessions with key individuals in the organisation?

Such investigations must be conducted quietly. With well-disguised questions to friends and former school-mates plenty of information can be gathered. Under no circumstances must the person under investigation become suspicious. These investigations should not drag out too long. Sometimes the person is clearly innocent. Sometimes there is hard evidence of direct work for the enemy. But often things are uncertain. How then do we proceed?

Extreme measures are not always necessary or appropriate. An MDM structure will seldom have the resources to complete a full secret investigation, or withstand an intense enemy counter-attack. But other effective measures can be taken to neutralise an infiltrator. Already in our region we have had success with these measures. After a careful investigation by a security committee, other members of the MDM leadership are informed of the result. If needed, a surprise session with the individual is set up with five or six MDM leadership people. He or she is then confronted with a mass of information, with contradictions and unexplained facts. It is surprising how often this kind of confrontation has led to a confession. In other cases questions remain unclear and unanswered. In the first case the individual must be expelled. In the second case he or she must be suspended from the organisation. The general membership and the MDM as a whole must be informed with the general reasons given. At all times these cases must be handled efficiently, confidently and with minimum disruption.[46]

And, of course, Party units could recruit members from MDM structures, but this was not always without difficulties, some of which were captured in the account by one of the operatives:

...[I] had identified one comrade, 'Tom', who was on the branch executive of his trade union. He works in a factory with great strategic importance. And another thing, his trade union is under backward leadership, and it is not in Cosatu. In short, Tom has opened a way to both a key factory, and to a union that has been closed to us. I had recruited Tom, with clearance from my unit and from the Party centre. He is still a probationer, a somebody who is being trained to become a full Party member. I have been working with him for some time. We have been reading and discussing. I have also given him some small tasks.

About two months ago, the comrade was forced to resign from his elected position in the union on charges of 'theft'. Trade union money had disappeared and Tom was held responsible. Now let me straight away say I do not believe for one moment that this charge is true. This is a comrade who would give his last cent away for the struggle. It is Tom's view that he was deliberately framed by the reactionary leadership in the union. They fear his militancy and popularity with the workers. Within our unit we discussed this case. My view agreed completely with Tom. I said we must continue with his Party probation. One of the other comrades in the unit took the opposite view. She argued that even if the case was almost certainly rigged, it didn't matter. The Party must consist of only the most outstanding comrades. There must be not the slightest doubt or stain on any of them. The comrade went on to ask what would happen if Tom's Party connection eventually became public – maybe through a trial? What would workers in his union think of someone their union leadership had suspended? The comrade ended by saying: "Even if Tom didn't take the money, he was careless to give his enemies the gap to suspend him." We had a heated debate in the unit, but we could not reach agreement. Finally, we referred the matter to our Party district centre. This is how they advised us on the matter: They said Tom's probation must be suspended as long as there is any doubt about the money issue. It does not matter that Tom is still well placed in a key factory. There can be no shortcuts. At the same time, the district committee instructed that I must remain in closest contact with Tom. At a time when the leadership of his union had launched a heavy campaign against him, it would be a great blow to his morale (and possibly to our own security) if his Party contact just suddenly cut him. The district committee advised that the situation must be explained honestly to Tom. So, that is how we are proceeding.[47]

The management of Party finances was also improving, thanks to the establishment of a Finance Committee – a structure that was also incorporated into the 1984 Constitution. With the annual allocation from the Communist Party of the Soviet Union having increased to US$100 000 by the end of the 1980s and the Party headquarters now based in Africa, more transparency became necessary. Not only was the functioning of the Finance Committee to be improved, but also, as part of preparations for the 7th Congress, a finance administrator was to be appointed to attend to the "day to day finance matters and proper recording of financial matters". Furthermore, "all foreign currency funds should be sent to [a] London bank account so that they can give us profit, and only 40 000 US Dollars should remain in our bank vaults in Lusaka".[48] A sum of US$5 500 from these funds was to be used for the travel allowance and airport tax for delegates to the 7th Congress.

# 5
# Ideological Hegemony

ONE QUESTION OFTEN ASKED IS, how did the Party gain the influence it enjoyed within the ANC and the whole MDM during the period under discussion when its membership was so small? *Rooigevaar* ideologues reduced this complex dynamic to the influence of the Soviet. The appeal and influence of Marxism within the ranks of the ANC and MDM constituencies is arguably the factor that can best explain this complex situation. The Party, since the days of the CPSA in the 1920s, used political education, sometimes even through formal political classes, to spread the influence of Marxism within the ranks of the nationalist movement. Eddie Roux, one of the members of the CPSA, described their first night school: "This had been started in 1925 in the Ferreirastown slum, in a Native Church building hired on week nights for the purpose. The building had no electric light. There enthusiastic white communists bent their energies to teaching by candle-light, semi-literate Africans to read involved passages in Bukharin's ABC of Communism".[1] The ANC also organised its political education programme, especially in the 1950s, but even this could not escape the influence of Marxism as Nelson Mandela was to recount later:

> As part of the M-plan, the ANC introduced an elementary course of political lectures for its members throughout the country. These lectures were meant not only to educate but to hold the organisation together. They were given in secret by branch leaders. Those members in attendance would in turn give the same lectures to others in their homes and communities. In the beginning, the lectures were not systematised, but within a number of months there was a set curriculum.
> 
> There were three courses, 'The World We Live In', 'How We

Are Governed' and 'The Need for Change'. In the first course, we discussed the different types of political and economic systems around the world as well as in South Africa. It was an overview of the growth of capitalism as well as socialism. We discussed, for example, how blacks in South Africa were oppressed both as a race and an economic class. The lecturers were mostly banned members, and I myself frequently gave lectures in the evening. This arrangement had the virtue of keeping banned individuals active as well as keeping the membership in touch with these leaders.[2]

With the shift to armed struggle and exile, political education gained more prominence in the ANC and the commissariat system was introduced into MK, thanks to the Soviet influence and, by extension, into the Party. Raymond Suttner explained in his study of political education in the ANC-led liberation movement: "Even where soldiers were expected to be returned [home] quickly, the emphasis had always been that the political should dominate the military and that what mattered was not holding a gun but who was behind the gun, what understanding that person had. This is a repeated theme in political education and seems to have almost been a cliché, that the ANC's army was not merely soldiers in a conventional sense, but bearers of a message, ambassadors for a particular vision of society".[3]

With the youth exodus of the 1970s and the ANC establishing camps in Angola, key Party cadres came to play important roles in political education in the ranks of the MK. In fact, it was Jack Simons, one of the Party's leading scholars, who moulded the ideological architecture and syllabus for the political education in MK camps, when he was deployed to Novo Catengue as a political instructor in September 1977. Simons' task was not only to conduct political education, but also to train and produce a new crop of commissars for MK. January Masilela, a member of the June 16 Detachment of MK and one of the early products of Simons' work, recalled: "We faced this really monumental task of organising the commissariat, organising the political instructors and at the same time imparting instruction to the detachment. At the time we had about four companies which constituted the detachment. Comrade Jack's task was to prepare lectures; lecture the companies during the day; in the afternoon assemble those who were already commissars and also deliver lectures to them; also circulate with the instructors; and he also had a set of lectures for the administration".[4]

Reggie Mhlongo, another member of the June 16 Detachment, gave an overview of the impact that Simons had on them: "Most of us had never stood in front of a big class to teach people – and worse, people who you were training with today, and then the next day you wake up and they're starting to look on you as a person to provide all the answers. That's where one really valued the approach that Jack tried to inculcate in us: the need to approach and prepare your lectures; to try first and foremost to understand the people you are dealing with; and without making people feel bad, try to ascertain their educational level. And all the time getting them to participate before you introduce a subject in detail, so that people can feel they are beginning to discover things for themselves".[5] For Christian Pepani, another product of Simons who later became one of the regional commissars in the 1980s: "It was very very important for us that for the first time we were learning politics and of course removing all the distortions. When you are from South Africa you have a complete different picture, first of communism – that when you meet communists they are going to be people with horns and tail! There are all sorts of distortions. First we met Jack Simons, himself a communist, but of course he's a very simple person with a great sense of humour".[6]

Joel Netshitenzhe, also a member of the June 16 Detachment, illustrated the effectiveness of Simons' teaching methodology:

> To give some examples: Comrade Jack would simplify things like examples of the relationship between objective conditions and subjective factors, things that some of us had read and thought we understood. And his approach would be like: "We are sitting here under a tree and there is the river there and the mountains there, which are the obstacles as an army if you wanted to cross the river and go over the mountains? There

would be the difficulty of crossing the river, the mountains are steep, and problems of that nature. What would you then do to resolve those problems?" And people would come with ideas on how to cross that river and how to climb over the mountain, then Jack would say: "That is the essence of understanding the difference between the objective conditions and subjective factors. Objective conditions are those things that we face in life which are not created by you; they exist on their own and in order to overcome them, you have to devise." That simple way of explaining things made things very easy to understand for everybody, both those who had been to school and those who had not been.[7]

So, even though the bulk of MK soldiers were never formally part of Party structures, their political education and orientation was communist, not least because of the role played by commissars in the life of soldiers and the structure of the commissariat at camp level. As Christian Pepani explained, the commissariat was part of the political department at camp level:

> The political department was the comrades responsible for the political education of the camp; political instructors were trained in the camp under those difficult conditions by Jack Simons himself, and among them he chose the head of the political department. I happened to be head of the political department and we also had a secretary. We divided up tasks: each of us dealt with so many platoons (a platoon is 30 to 32 comrades) and gave them political instruction. It was easier because with smaller numbers we had access to individual comrades. You know exactly whether they understand, you go at their pace and you arrange studies for those comrades who don't comprehend the subject matter, and then they arrange additional classes for themselves. In the political department at that time were myself, Ché Ogara [O'Gara], Vuyisile Mati, Raymond Nkuku, Dan Cingi… and others.[8]

Moreover, commissars were at the centre of a soldier's life. Pepani elaborated:

> Commissars, what are they? Their task is to look into the general life of people in the army, political life, morale, spirit, to develop their commitment, pride and love for their people, hatred of the enemy and brotherhood amongst comrades. Commissars are also responsible for the culture and welfare of comrades. We also had cultural evenings where comrades prepared plays, sang, danced. We arranged days to have presentations and of course we were also responsible for commemorative days, January 8, June 16, June 26, August 9, December 16.[9]

Simons was not the only Party figure dispatched to MK camps in Angola for political education; Ronnie Kasrils arrived in October 1977 for the same purpose. Kasrils reminisced about his students: "The topic they were most interested to learn about was communism, which undoubtedly stemmed from the pathological attacks on everything to do with communism that emanated from South Africa's apartheid masters. The leadership of the ANC had decided to introduce Marxism as a subject because there was such a demand to know about it. I pointed out that you did not have to be a Marxist to belong to the ANC".[10] Similarly, at the ANC Kwabe Conference of 1985, the Commission on Ideological and Political Work, recommended for inclusion in the political education syllabus of the organisation, among other things, "Marxist-Leninist Revolutionary Theory. This to [sic] be taught in such a way that comrades do not regitate [regurgitate] the theory, but apply it to the concrete South African situation". Furthermore, the Commission recommended, also for inclusion in the syllabus, the inculcation among the ANC cadres of the "ideological and theoretical understanding of the relationship between the concept of National Liberation, class struggle and the emancipation of women".[11]

Indeed, Party intervention in the area of political education in the ANC was not limited to the camps. Ray Alexander Simons – another seasoned communist and wife to Jack Simons – recalls her experience when she visited Chris Hani in Lesotho in the late 1970s:

> ...Comrade Chris Hani invited me to work with him in Lesotho, so we conducted study classes together in Maseru. I was well received by the workers there, many of whom I knew, and they attended a number of classes in my home. Comrade Chris, a member of the ANC, MK and the SACP, had left South Africa in 1963. He served as MK Commissar at this time and became Chief of Staff in 1987. He was elected General Secretary of the Communist Party at its first Congress after legalisation, in 1991, and was at the time also a member of the ANC National Executive Committee...
>
> Comrade Chris introduced me to a number of comrades... One evening while I was staying with Dr May Maclean, Chris was giving me a lift home from a study class when the Lesotho Liberation Army stopped us. Chris had his baby with him in the car and I was sitting next to him, so he quickly pushed me down and placed the baby on top of me so the army wouldn't see me. The next morning Chris warned that we could not risk another such incident, and decided that I needed another place to stay, so I went to Phyllis Naidoo and held the underground study classes at her place.[12]

For its part, the ANC was not only comfortable with the prevalence of Marxism within its ranks, but the nationalist organisation also considered itself part of the global anti-imperialist movement. In its *Strategy and Tactics* adopted at the Morogoro Conference in 1969, the ANC, with a class-oriented analysis, observed: "The struggle of the oppressed people of South Africa is taking place within an international context of transition to the Socialist system, of the breakdown of the colonial system as a result of national liberation and socialist revolutions, and the fight for social and economic progress by the people of the whole world". The working class had a role in the thesis of national democratic struggle elaborated in *Strategy and Tactics*: "This perspective of a speedy progression from formal liberation to genuine and lasting emancipation is made more real by the existence in our country of a large and growing working class whose class consciousness complements national consciousness... It is historically understandable that the doubly oppressed and doubly exploited working class constitutes a distinct and reinforcing layer of our liberation and Socialism..."[13] Similarly, the ANC journal, *Sechaba*, carried an article in its issue of February 1970 written by then secretary general, Alfred Nzo, entitled 'Our Anti-Imperialist Commitment'. Nzo argued in the article:

> ...the South African racists who cling to apartheid are an integral and key part of the sinister plot of exploitation by the imperialists on an international scale... There is no other country in the world in which the imperialists have been prepared to relegate their differences to the background and unite their efforts economically, technically and militarily as they have done in South Africa... the African National Congress of South Africa will not be found wanting in the forums of anti-imperialist movements nor in action in its own sector, South Africa and Southern Africa... With the massive assistance of the mighty and invincible anti-imperialist forces, victory will be ours and fascism, racism and imperialism will rapidly approach their day of doom.[14]

*Sechaba* itself also carried an editorial in its July issue entitled 'Anti-Communism in South Africa'; other themes published in the journal included debates which were taking place in the SACP, such as that on the 'national question' and the role of the working class in the national liberation struggle.[15] This anti-imperialist outlook and a class-oriented understanding and approach to the national liberation struggle permeated the thinking within the ANC throughout the exile period.

Robben Island prison was another important space for SACP engagement. Although the Party never established a formal organisational presence in the prison, it was virtually present there thanks to three factors: personal influence of known SACP figures; political education activities in the prison; and debates among prisoners on issues relating to the place of communism in the liberation movement and the future dispensation of the country. Mac

Maharaj, incarcerated on the Island in the early 1970s, was among the SACP members who wanted to establish formal Party structures among the prisoners. This was discouraged, particularly by Nelson Mandela on the grounds that this could lead to divisions among ANC members on the Island. But, recalled Maharaj: "Certain Comrades, including Harry Gwala, a longtime hard-line Communist, formed a group called Mpabanga [sic], which means 'we the poor'. Harry gave lectures on things like 'the labour theory of value'. That became cover for some comrades to organize themselves into a Communist cell".[16] But not all communists on the island favoured Gwala's approach. For example, Andrew Masondo who spent eleven years on the island was part of those who not only discouraged the establishment of Party units but was also not for the idea of establishing political education classes open only to communists:

> I became a member of the Communist Party in 1961, that's when I joined. I joined it when I was at Fort Hare and I used to be the secretary of my party group. But we members of the party within the island decided that we were not going to have the party as an organisation. The reason being that it would create far more problems if it were discovered because the authorities would clamp down on us in a very vicious way. The paranoia about communist was very serious. So, that's why whilst I was in the main sections I had suggested that we teach Marxism to everybody. The reason being that, one's view was that if a person is not a Marxist he should know what he's not and if he is he should know what he is because in some cases you would find people who become Marxist as a religion rather without the proper theoretical basis. Ishmael Ibrahim, he was one of the people who was selected to give lectures on Marxism.[17]

The fear of dividing ANC members on the Island led to the discouraging of the establishment of Party units, and those who were of this view were to be vindicated later when problems arose as a result of Gwala's Party unit. Masondo recalls:

[A]fter I've left the section, the main section to go to the segregation, they [Gwala's group] then started a study group for young people. They taught what was called labour theory, which was Marxist. But then they didn't do it the way we had agreed, to offer it to everybody. That created a problem... they chose specific young people and they gave them this thing. It was like a separate programme from the normal programme of the Congress Movement... So, with the question of Gwala and Steve starting this particular thing, even people like Ntsangane were not very happy about this situation. Maybe precisely because when I left that section we had agreed that Marxism should be taught to everybody. The labour theory classes would not have created any serious problem, had it not been for the fact that you are introducing younger people into the labour theory and the question of the bourgeoisie and the working class seemed to be put very sharply. People started talking of some leaders of the ANC petty bourgeoisie and that was something which created a problem, to an extent that this group, the Marxist oriented, or shall I say the labour theory oriented group... after a time they began to have a name called *Izimpabanga*. They became *Izimpabanga*. It created a very serious rift within the main sections, to the extent that this matter was then taken to us at the segregation because it was now becoming a serious matter. And we needed to look into it and try to make sure that we handle it in such a way that at the end the ANC comes out stronger. Within the segregation section itself, we had the normal programme, everybody. We had our programme.[18]

Besides divisions that an organised Party presence among ANC prisoners could cause, there was also another concern as explained by Ahmed Kathrada in his *Memoirs*: "Security considerations also had to be taken into account. It was difficult enough to maintain contact between the different sections of the prison, and any additional organization would place undue strain on the tenuous communication channels".[19] The High Organ[20] then took up the matter with Gwala:

"The leadership informed Harry", according to Kathrada, "that there was no objection to his classes, and suggested that he could include them in the ANC's political education syllabus. However, the formation of Communist Party cells would not be advisable, as this would merely duplicate the ANC's functions within the closed community, and might even prove divisive." Gwala accepted, "albeit reluctantly".[21]

Nonetheless, Gwala's influence among younger ANC prison cadres who arrived on the Island in the course of the 1970s was significant. Naledi Ntsiki recalled that Section E of the prison where Gwala was incarcerated "was the most like the Soviet Republic in South Africa".[22]

Political education, as illustrated above, was one turf which the SACP contested to exert its influence on the Island. Jacob Zuma recounted his experience in this regard:

> About five of us who had attended those political discussions here [Durban] found ourselves on Robben Island… and felt we needed to have some political discussions among ourselves [on the Island] to revise what we used to discuss [before prison]. We… began… political lectures for everybody during lunch time, which was an hour, we used that [time] to revise and discuss if there were news items… So when we were joined by particularly Comrade Stephen Dlamini, who was our leader, [and] Harry Gwala… [who] was actually our political instructor outside… we started having discussions with them every day at lunch time and we were gradually joined by other people, whoever was interested. Revising political lectures or discussions that we'd had over the weekend, analysing news items, discussing about labour theory in particular and enriching our knowledge, that became in fact the nucleus of the culture on Robben Island, the culture of political education.[23]

Debates of an ideological nature contributed to deepening the influence of the SACP outlook amongst the ANC prisoners on the Island. These debates would be very heated, to the extent of even dividing the prisoners between "nationalists" and "communists";

these divisions sometimes took the form of a tension among members of the High Organ, notably between Nelson Mandela, believed to be the leader of the "nationalists", and Govan Mbeki, the "communist".[24] Wilton Mkwayi, who spent over two decades on the Island, gave his interpretation of these divisions, particular the contribution of some known Party personalities.

> Our leadership was arrested. There was tension amongst us. We were divided. Whilst frankly discussing issues that affect us, some people would say: "That is nonsense. You can go to hell." But if you were affected you were compelled to remain calm rather than sulk so as to maintain peace. You should avoid such situations. In my view constructive criticism is welcome because it makes you a better person. Some of us were not on talking terms with the PAC. Sometimes Oom Gov and Madiba would be engaged in very serious disputes, the two of them. We would avoid taking sides. In most cases I would be summoned and asked to try and resolve the disputes between the two. They use to say: "*Makubizwe* 'uMakade' – that was my nickname in prison – must try and solve the problem between the two." This was always the case concerning disputes between the ANC and PAC on Robben Island. We had to engage with each other constructively and try and resolve the disputes. Amongst the ANC on Robben Island, Harry Gwala, 'uMntomdala', was the most uncompromising. He was really a difficult character to deal with. I used to say to both Mntomdala and Oom Gov: "You are staunch communists who are intolerant, impatient and cannot hold discussions with other people who differ with the two of you. You always surround yourselves with young people who do not know anything as your supporters. Usually these young people have the impression and conclude that you are the only leaders that matter." I told Harry Gwala that I am aware that on his arrival at Robben he told the younger generation that "*umuntu ongathengisi munye lapha eRobben Island, ngu Oom Gov*" (loosely translated to mean that – amongst the old leadership, Oom Gov was the only one who

was not a sell-out, the rest were). Gwala claimed that everybody else is a sell-out, including myself, Joe Gqabi, and so on. There were also disputes and rivalries between different sections, for example, Section A and Section B. These were some of the frustrations.[25]

Some debates, such as the one on the Bantustan system and whether Mandela should be elected ANC 'leader' on the Island, contributed to the 'communist' versus 'nationalist' divide; at some point Gwala, according to Kathrada in his *Memoirs*, became a "central figure around whom 'communists' rallied". Fortunately, these divisions did not crystallise into an organisational form; they remained largely ideological and political. And at least for Kathrada, it was only the Mandela 'leadership' debate that depressed him to the point of taking a break from his ANC communion to spend some time with PAC company.

There is, however, one debate that should be singled out here. Around 1978, thanks to the growing number in prison of the youth who had passed through the programme of the commissariat in MK camps and had been to former socialist countries, a debate began on the 'ANC and Marxism'. The debate, known among the prisoners as 'Marxism and Inqindi' ('fist', or the ANC), not only interrogated the role and orientation of the ANC vis-à-vis the struggle for socialism; it also focused on the interpretation of the Freedom Charter in relation to 'people's democracy' as opposed to 'bourgeois democracy'. Prisoners in B Section of the prison where members of the High Organ were incarcerated developed a consensus paper around January 1980 which was drafted by Kathrada for circulation to other ANC prisoners on the Island with the view to calming the storm over the debate. Kathrada assumed that the document had been received by the intended recipients only to discover on his release from the Island in 1989 that it had been intercepted and kept by prison authorities.[26] The document was given to him with his personal possessions when he was released.

'Marxism and Inqindi' discusses the following seven areas in some detail: the history of the Congress of the People of the 1950s and the Freedom Charter; the relationship between national oppression and class exploitation; the place and role of the working class in a national liberation struggle; the international and regional context of the South African struggle, and the impact of these on the latter; the position of the Freedom Charter on the ownership of the means of production and nationalisation; the agenda of the Freedom Charter and the transition to socialism; and whether the 'national liberation movement' included other organisations (such as the PAC) other than the Congress Movement led by the ANC. Admittedly, the document, as a consensus framework, attempted to present a balanced view of the debate:

> The polemics arising from 'Inq-M' ['Inqindi-Marxism'] constitute an important milestone in our political education and enlightenment. It certainly was timely. The two basic aims of 'Inq-M' were to encourage comrades to study M [Marxism], and to remind them of the distinction between a national struggle and a class struggle. We were happy to note that both viewpoints that were sparked off by 'Inq-M' rely on the dialectical method. They try to tackle the problem scientifically and at grass roots – something unique in a broad national movement.
>
> The polemic is also evidence of the dynamic nature of the FC [Freedom Charter] which is capable of being interpreted in the light of the developing situation. Neither critics nor supporters of 'Inq-M' suggest that it envisages a 'pd' [people's democracy] with a dictatorship of the proletariat. That is significant and shows that FC is flexible to allow for different interpretations in accordance with changing conditions.[27]

The document acknowledged that: "The sharply differing viewpoints that emerged emphasize the inconvenience, and even harm that is caused to our work by our isolation from one another. Had we been housed together, and discussing daily some of the differences would have been either avoided or easily smoothed out". Moreover, noted the document, "Some of us have not seen the CP Program [SACP's

*Road to South Africa Freedom*] for 15 years, and again we concede that our recollection of the actual words used in that document was wrong..." In the end, the document summarised the core consensus areas as follows:

- The oppressed people of SA face the dual problem of class and national oppression. In striving to solve this twin problem the CM [Congress Movement] and the CP [SACP] have each worked out a definite strategy which they have consistently followed. Although the long term objectives of the Congress coincide with the short term aims of the CP, the Congress leads the national struggle while the CP leads the class struggle.
- The SA revolution is basically an African Revolution and nationalism is the inspiration of the Congresses. But the preponderance of the wc [working class] in our membership, and the wide acceptance of Marxist ideology serve as a guarantee that a victorious people's revolution will give birth to a democratic state.
- In conducting the struggle the people of SA are influenced by the international situation, the experience of rev [revolutionary] movements throughout the world and by events on our borders. But it is the concrete conditions in our own country that are decisive and that determine our strategy and tactics from time to time.
- Although the FC [Freedom Charter] does not abolish private property in land, industry and commerce, it is an excellent programme of equilibrium and peace, and it reconciles the interest of various classes and social groups. The nationalization clause as well as the controls on land, industry and commerce will break the power of monopoly capital and lay the basis for even more radical economic and social development.
- The FC is a dynamic programme since under certain conditions it might be regarded as a qualitative leap towards socialism. But strictly speaking it visualizes a national democracy...

The national liberation movement in SA includes other political organizations outside the Congress Movement.

This debate, nonetheless, continued during most of the 1980s as was the case among the Congress Movement and the SACP in exile. The details of this debate in exile and, of course, among the MDM formations, are covered in the pages of the *African Communist*, *Umsebenzi* and *Sechaba*. However, those on the Island, because of prison conditions which evidently limited their access to SACP, ANC and other relevant literature, found themselves having to improvise to stay on top of this debate. Thanks to this debate, the SACP ideology was influential among the prisoners on the Island.

# 6
# Internationalism

INTERNATIONALISM IS A CORE component of the activities of any communist party, and, accordingly, the SACP established fraternal relations with like-minded parties all over the world, particularly in Africa and the former socialist bloc. As suggested already, the Communist Party of the Soviet Union was a key partner, but so too were other communist parties. Some of these relations were even formalised into an agreement of cooperation, such as the one the Party signed with the Socialist Unity Party of (East) Germany (SED) for the period 1980 to 1981. This agreement covered bilateral meetings between the two parties, invitation to each party's congresses, as well as the exchange of information and publications. Furthermore, in terms of the agreement, the SED was to "support the SACP in printing party materials and publications", "accept cadres from the SACP for training at party institutions and institutions of higher education", "provide facilities for medical treatment in the GDR [East Germany] for four comrades from the SACP annually", and "invite 2 [two] senior comrades of the SACP annually to spend a four-week holiday in the GDR".[1]

Fraternal parties would send (and vice versa) the SACP messages of support for Party events, such as anniversary celebrations and congresses, as well as statements of condolences for some Party figures when they passed on. Even some birthdays were celebrated with fraternal parties, such as when the Communist Party of the Soviet Union congratulated Kotane on his 70th birthday, describing him as "an outstanding representative of the communist, working class and national liberation movement of Africa... [thus] you are known in the Soviet Union as a dedicated internationalist".[2] Some SACP figures even received orders and other types of recognition from fraternal parties. For instance, Dadoo and Harmel were awarded a Memorial

Medal by the *World Marxist Review* in 1978 on the occasion of the 20th anniversary of the journal. Dadoo also received, among others, the Order of Karl Marx awarded by East Germany, the Order of Georgi Dimitrov of Bulgaria, and the Order of the Friendship of the Peoples of the former USSR.

Thanks to these fraternal relations, the Party could hold some events in the socialist bloc, with the host providing – but not always – conference and translation facilities, accommodation, and travel for the participants. The Party would issue a request, for example: "The Central Committee of our Party is desirous of holding its next plenary session in Bulgaria in September of the current year [1983]. I, therefore, have been directed to make this formal, fraternal request to you to allow us the necessary facilities for the holding of the proposed meeting… In the event of our request being granted including the provision of travel facilities for our members participating in the session, we could then proceed to fix the exact dates…"[3] But this was not always without challenges. For instance, Mabhida could write to Dadoo about the request that had been addressed to the Bulgarian CP: "Arising from your telephonic discussion with JS [Joe Slovo] where you said that the Bulgarians have not responded, we have since approached Czeck [sic], but just until now [there] is no reply".[4] Essop Pahad later reported to Dadoo about the response from Czechoslovakia: "Your request for venue and other connected facilities has been granted. *But they cannot pay for the tickets…*" (emphasis original).[5]

But the Party's exchanges with fraternal parties were not limited to messages of support. The parties also exchanged publications, contributed to each other's journal and magazine, exchanged speakers, engaged in solidarity work for mutual benefit, and shared information on developments evolving in each other's sphere of operation.[6] For example, in July 1976 the Party approached the Communist Party of Israel "with the view to securing closer co-operation between our two parties. In the light of the recent visit of Premier [John] Vorster to Israel and the agreement then reached for co-operation between the two governments, we feel it is essential that our two parties should discuss the joint action which we can undertake to defend the interests of the peoples of the Middle East, Africa and the world at large against the machinations of Israel-South Africa Axis, and against world imperialism for which they stand as local bastions".[7] The Israeli counterpart then acted on this approach: "We have asked a knowledgeable Member of the Central Committee to write the article on the 'Israeli-South Africa axis' and hope that he will be able to fulfill the task on time".[8] In December 1976, Dadoo attended the 4th National Congress of the Vietnam Workers' Party: "Whenever he [Dadoo] went from Hanoi to Ho Chi Minh City" wrote Essop Pahad in the unpublished *Dr YM Dadoo, A People's Leader: A Political Biography*, "he was received with great warmth and comradeship. The Vietnamese consistently expressed their support and solidarity for our revolutionary struggle, and the ANC and SACP".[9]

Furthermore, the Communist Party of Jamaica expressed its gratitude to the Party in September 1982 "for your consistent Complimentary Copies of the African Communist which is serving a most wonderful and indispensable cause to the struggle of the African and Jamaican people for freedom".[10] For its part, the Iraqi Communist Party invited the Party "to write to our magazine and share in our efforts to further the cause of peace and socialism". The magazine "concentrates on subjects dealing with problems facing the peoples of Arab countries, and the national liberation movements…"[11]

The Party also participated in activities of the international communist movement, such as the congresses of fraternal parties, celebrations of the October Revolution, and the International Conference of Communist and Workers' Parties. Nor was the Party passive at these events. For instance, "throughout the preparatory meetings", reported the Party about its involvement in the International Conference of Communist and Workers' Parties of June 1969, "we tried to play a positive and constructive role. We introduced a number of proposals and amendments at various stages, all of which found a reflection in some form or another in the final documents". Furthermore, "it was fortunate indeed that we had on this occasion [of the Conference] a delegation of sufficient numbers [i.e. four members] to take part in the work of the conference at various levels – secretariat, editorial commission, and sub-committees including the important 13-member commission to study the convocation of a world anti-imperialist conference".[12] The Party delegation also used the Conference to meet a number of parties, including the German Communist Party, to mobilise them for anti-apartheid work in West Germany; the French Communist Party where "a wide-ranging discussion took place on the possibilities in Africa to build Marxist-Leninist Parties... [and] it was agreed that both our parties should cooperate more closely in this task"; and delegations of Sudan, Reunion, Nigeria and Algeria.[13] Discussions with African delegations were to result, as shown later, in a process towards organising African communist and other like-minded parties into a conference.

Like some communist parties, the Party was represented on the 15-member Editorial Board of the journal of the international communist movement, the *World Marxist Review: Problems of Peace and Socialism*, by Michael Harmel and, following his death, Essop Pahad. The journal was the successor to the Cominform's newspaper – *For Lasting Peace, For Lasting Democracy* – and based as it was in Prague, was an important platform and mouthpiece for the generation and dissemination of Marxist-Leninist ideas globally, and, indeed, carried a number of articles on various aspects of the South African struggle. When the journal was being reviewed, the Party also made its contribution to, among other things, the governance, staffing and editorial issues related to the publication.[14] The journal, established in 1958, went under in 1989 with the collapse of the socialist bloc.

Relations between the SACP and the Communitst Part of China (CPC) could not escape the effect of the Sino-Soviet dispute. For example, when Dadoo visited the People's Republic of China in 1960, he underwent an experience which he described as "extraordinary, perhaps even bizarre". Explained Pahad in the unpublished political biography of Dadoo:

> For three days, after their [SACP delegation] arrival, they were ensconced in a guest house and lectured to by a team of three or four, for two to three sessions of about 30 minutes each. The main burden of these lectures was to convince the delegation that the CPSU was revisionist; and that everything

they had in China was thanks to Mao Tse-Tung; they also elevated into a law-governed principle of revolutionary struggle the Chinese experience of the long march and forms of armed struggle... Having patiently listened to these lectures, with which they did not agree, Dadoo reminded the officials that since their arrival they had not seen anything of the city let alone the country. Only thereafter were they taken to visit some communes..."[15]

Relations between the SACP and the CPC remained sour throughout the 1970s, the parties even exchanging blows in public forums. For instance, in his address to the Emergency International Conference in Support of Vietnam in Helsinki in March 1979, Dadoo declared: "In Chile, Angola, Ethiopia, wherever the people are fighting against imperialism and reaction, they find ranged against them the Peking leadership. Our people can never forget the perfidious activities of the Chinese leadership in supporting Savimbi and Holden – imperialist puppets – and the racist dictatorship of Vorster and Botha against the People's Republic of Angola". For their part, the Chinese, among others, dismissed the ANC as a "running dog of Moscow" for siding with the USSR in the dispute, and opted for providing the PAC with material and political assistance. However, towards the end of 1982 the CP of China approached the SACP: "The CPC wishes to set up and restore Party to Party relations on the basis of equality, autonomy, mutual respect and non-interference in each other's affairs... We would propose that the SACP consider ending all public attacks on the CPC in order that this may create a favourable atmosphere for the restoration of relations".[16] The SACP agreed: "In principle we agree that both Parties must work towards creating a climate in which there can be a restoration of relations between the two Parties... As part of this process we also agree that both Parties must cease, directly or indirectly, from engaging in any public attacks on one another."[17]

Communication between the two parties continued with the SACP consulting the Communist Party of the Soviet Union early in 1983. The process of the restoration of the relations subsequently gained momentum, and a delegation of the SACP was even invited to China in September 1986: "The visit", reported the SACP delegation, "can be said to be [sic] successful in that it was able to bring closer our two Parties after a long separation". The two parties not only exchanged views during the visit on China's 'Open Doors Policy', but they also "agreed to bury the past, refrain from public attacks from both sides and to work towards strengthening our forces in the interests of the working class movement".[18] The following year, 1987, the CPC gave the SACP US$9 000 for the purchase of two vehicles.

There were also efforts by the Party to create a platform for cooperation with like-minded parties in Africa. The process began in 1967 at an occasion celebrating the 50th anniversary of the October Revolution[19] in the form of meetings "between Nigeria and South Africa, between Nigeria, Senegal and South Africa etc".[20] Another meeting took place on the margins of the International Conference of Communist and Workers' Parties in June 1969, attended by representatives of the Communist Party of Lesotho, Socialist Vanguard Party of Algeria, the Party of Liberation and Socialism of Morocco, the SACP, the Marxist-Leninists of Nigeria, the Communist Party of Reunion, the Sudanese Communist Party and the Communist Party of Tunisia. The meeting not only "unanimously recognized the need for closer co-operation" among the parties, but also "agreed in principle on the holding of a well-prepared Conference of African Marxist-Leninists in 1970". A standing committee, comprised of the SACP and the Socialist Vanguard Party of Algeria, was to oversee the coordination towards this conference whose theme was to be: "The imperialist and reactionary offensive in Africa and steps necessary to bring about a new upsurge in the revolution for national and social liberation". The SACP was to coordinate and liaise with like-minded Anglophone parties, with the Algerians focusing on Francophone Africa.[21] The conference, however, never materialised as planned.

Attempts to convene this all-Africa conference continued in the 1970s, but three major questions served as an obstacle. First, was the venue; "the question is still with us today", was reported to the Party in a document of the mid-1970s. "It is generally agreed", continued the document, "that the venue for any and all open conferences of African Communist Parties and for all other revolutionary forces in

Africa must, in principle be a spot inside the continent and not outside it". Secondly, was participation to be confined to parties south of the Sahara? "This question arises because already many of the parties inside the continent belong to the Arab regional groupings, namely, the parties of Algeria, Morocco, Tunisia and Egypt". As to the third and final question, the issue was: "Which are the true Marxist-Leninist parties in Africa? Which are non-Marxist Socialist parties? What should be our attitude to the Revolutionary Democrats... the National Democratic parties?"[22] These three questions were to continue to arise into the 1980s.

Subsequent to another consultative meeting of African communist parties held in Berlin in May 1976, a secretariat[23] for the process for what was to be a meeting of "Communist and Workers' Parties of Tropical and Southern Africa", was established. This secretariat, charged, among others, with preparing documentation for the meeting, was comprised of representatives to the *World Marxist Review* of the SACP (Essop Pahad), the Communist Party of Sudan (Ahmed Salim), and the African Independence Party of Senegal (Amath Dansoko).[24] The membership of the secretariat was to be increased to four in the 1980s to include the Workers Party of Ethiopia through the ambassador of Ethiopia in Prague.

What became known as the 'Summit Meeting of the Communist and Workers' Parties of Tropical and Southern Africa' was held in Moscow in May 1978, but without the participation of the Mozambique Liberation Front (FRELIMO) and the People's Movement for the Liberation of Angola (MPLA). This summit was a meeting where a 'Communist Call to Africa' was issued by the seven parties – namely: the SACP, CP of Sudan, CP of Reunion, CP of Lesotho, Socialist Party of Working People (Nigeria), the African Independence Party of Senegal, and Party of Congress for the Independence of Madagascar. However, the correspondence file of the secretariat suggests that the MPLA and FRELIMO were not happy with their exclusion, to the extent that Amath Dansoko had to be dispatched to Luanda and Maputo "to familiarize MPLA and FRELIMO with the main [Summit] document prior to its publication".[25] Additionally, the secretariat approached the Portuguese Communist Party because "all the participants [at the Summit] stressed the great importance of translating it [Summit document] into the Portuguese language and also its distribution in the Portuguese speaking countries of Africa particularly Angola and Mozambique".[26]

But, still, another meeting of African parties had to be convened, and this time on the margins of the International Scientific Conference in Berlin in October 1980, after Sérgio Vieira of FRELIMO approached Dadoo and "raised the question as to why certain parties were not consulted when drawing up the [Communist] Call [to Africa]".[27] Participants at the meeting comprised the seven parties that had issued the "Communist Call", plus FRELIMO, MPLA, the Congolese Party of Labour, and the Commission for Organizing the Party of the Working People of Ethiopia. The gathering deliberated on Vieira's concerns, and at the next meeting, in Moscow in April 1981, with participation having increased to twelve parties, including representation from the Party of the Popular Revolution of Benin (PRP) of Mathieu Kerekou, the participants agreed to "organize a conference or seminar in Africa as soon as it is possible". The meeting also established a Preparatory Committee comprised of FRELIMO, the SACP, and the Congolese Party of Labour with a brief, among other things, to "prepare a draft outline of a document which would take into account the main theoretical and practical issues which should be elaborated, as well as examine new phenomena... and could use the document 'A Call to Africa' as a basis for their work".[28]

There was still another outstanding issue however: "Insofar as the conference is concerned, two interrelated but distinct views emerged. That is, should our first conference consist only of those Parties which have opted [for] the science of Marxism-Leninism, or should it be of a broad character in which we should invite other revolutionary Parties and the National Liberation Movements?"[29] North African parties, key players in this process in the 1960s, were no longer part of this all-Africa network. This could have been because of a view held at the time by some African communist parties, especially the Sudanese CP, that their Arab counterparts in the Middle East and North Africa were ideologically rigid to the point of failing to understand the national question,[30] let alone the plight of Palestinians. The Sudanese CP was also of the view that Arab communist parties were appendages of the

CPSU to the extent that they even deferred some of their international issues to the latter for decision or arbitration.[31] One can add to these issues that of the affiliation of North African communist parties to the Arab-Middle East communist network.

Following a meeting of the three-party Preparatory Committee in Maputo in July 1981 where the SACP sent a high-powered delegation comprised of Dadoo, Mabhida and Slovo with that of FRELIMO led by Armando Guebuza (the current president of Mozambique), the process towards an all-Africa conference, to be held in Maputo, gained momentum, with Vieira generating correspondence to the twelve-member network of the parties.[32] The main theme of the conference was to be: "African communist and the present tasks of the continent in the struggle against imperialism, colonialism, neo-colonialism, racism and underdevelopment: for peace, national independence, democracy, progress and socialism". It was expected that the conference, which was to be partially open for publicity, would adopt what was prepared as the "Maputo Manifesto" as well as a "Protocol of Cooperation".[33] The Manifesto covered in detail the class character of Africa, challenges of the transition from capitalism to socialism on the continent, and the latter's position in the global context. For its part, the Protocol of Cooperation envisaged, among other things, annual inter-party seminars and meetings and biennial "Summit meetings of the Parties". "In addition", wrote Vieira on behalf of the Preparatory Committee on whether invitation should be extended to non-African fraternal parties, "the presence of outside parties may be exploited by those who wish to undermine the conference and its follow-up, to spread allegations and innuendos that, at its birth, it was a direct or indirect creation of forces outside the continent of Africa".[34]

But six years down the line, nothing had come out of these efforts, and at a meeting of the Preparatory Committee in Moscow in November 1987, a date of May 1988 was set for what was to be a five-day conference to take place not in Africa but in Berlin. It is unclear why the venue was changed from Maputo; perhaps this could have been due to financial considerations as the host was expected to foot the bill for travel and related expenses. And as to the Manifesto and the Protocol of Cooperation, these were taken off the radar screen as the conference, when it eventually took place, became mainly a discussion and information-sharing forum. Slovo explained in his opening address to the conference:

> The first [of our efforts towards this conference] was a stage of very intense activities with a perspective which seems to have been extremely ambitious. The first stage involved the idea of convening a summit in Africa of all the parties, to be attended by the heads of all the parties some of whom, as we know, are also heads of state. The idea was that the summit would discuss and adopt a manifesto which would contain a characterization of the continent-wide revolutionary processes and which would declare socialism to be the way forward. It was also envisaged in the first stage that a protocol of cooperation should be signed between all the parties, and that this protocol should, among other things, provide for the holding of regular inter-party summit meetings, for publication of a joint African Marxist journal and for the setting-up of some standing machinery for promoting cooperation at all levels, which, it was envisaged, would include other parties in Africa who are not part of the original group.[35]

Because the conference was now to be held in secret, the East Germans suggested that the title of the event be changed, as Pahad's report to Slovo reveals: "For purpose of open communication they [East German counterparts] suggested that we use a neutral title 'The African Seminar'. We agreed".[36] But other participating parties, without this background, seemed to have treated the gathering as simply a seminar. In a report of the SACP of the seminar it was indeed noted that "most of the prepared papers [by the parties] were informative rather than analytical. The most interesting aspects were the answers to questions".[37] As to participation from non-African fraternal parties, Pahad suggested to Slovo: "Perhaps we should consider inviting the GDR, Soviet Union and Cuba to send one observer to our meeting. As you may recall for [sic] our previous meeting we had agreed on this".[38] Indeed, Mzala, who had replaced

Pahad as SACP representative at the *World Marxist Review*, was at pain in his report to the Preparatory Committee to explain the role of the SED: "Throughout this report I have incorrectly referred to the Cdes [Comrades] in Berlin as the hosts of the seminar. They insist that they are only the organizers and not hosts".[39] And even though measures were taken to ensure that the seminar was a secret, an article appeared in the *Ethiopian Herald* of 11 May 1988 revealing that a delegation of the Workers Party of Ethiopia was to participate in the "1st Congress of Progressive African Parties" which "will be opened in Berlin, GDR on Saturday".[40]

Nonetheless, the conference, now an open secret in the Ethiopian media, was attended by eleven parties (the CP of Reunion was absent), comprised of 38 delegates, a number much smaller than was initially envisaged, including five general secretaries, seven politburo and twelve central committee members. And as for Dadoo and Mabhida, two people who had been part of this conference initiative for years, they had since passed away; indeed Slovo used his opening address to the conference to request delegates to observe a moment of silence for his two comrades. The four-person SACP delegation to the conference included Slovo himself and Essop Pahad.

Deliberation at the conference concentrated on three areas: "an outline by each Party of the situation in its own country and the nature and role of the Party"; a presentation by the SACP of the situation in southern Africa, including the destabilization activities of the apartheid regime; and "future bilateral and multilateral cooperation and programme of activities".[41] As an outcome of the conference, "it is agreed to promote among the participants different forms of bilateral cooperation"; "that different meetings at appropriate levels will be organized on themes of common interest with the broadest possible participation according to the contents of the themes"; and "that consideration should be given to the possibilities of enlarging the initiating group with the consent of the Central Committees". The Preparatory Committee, still convened by the SACP, was to continue as a "contact group", with the support of the Prague contingent led by the Sudanese CP.[42] In effect, the outcome of the conference was formulated in a manner such that the concerns of participating parties could be accommodated: no reference is made to 'multilateral cooperation', the parties simply being encouraged to explore bilateral relations outside the conference; and "the broadest possible participation according to the contents of the themes" was the best way to avoid the thorny issue of 'who' should be part of the network.

When Slovo wrote his letter of 6 November 1989 to the two other member parties of the Contact Group suggesting the holding of another seminar – and this time in Africa – "towards the middle of 1990" and for the Group to meet "sometime in the middle of January to exchange views and take decisions on the process", he could not have predicted that his initiative would be overrun by events.[43] Three days subsequent to his letter, events were to unfold in the socialist bloc which were to result in the fall of the Berlin Wall. And within three months, not only was the USSR to experience the chaos occasioned by its disintegration and eventual collapse, but the ANC and the SACP were also unbanned by the apartheid government. The focus of the Party now shifted towards heading back home.

# 7
# Towards Home

THE 7ᵀᴴ CONGRESS, ORGANISED in Havana in April 1989, and attended by 49 delegates, was the highest point the Party could reach in exile. With some 70% of delegates above 35 years of age, the Party had, nevertheless, experienced a significant growth in the number of members under the age of 35. The 7th Congress was also significant in the sense that, for the first time in exile, the underground was represented at a meeting of the highest decision-making body of the Party. The Congress, conducted in the spirit of 'glasnost', reviewed the 1962 programme and adopted a new programme, *Path to Power*. The decision of the CC meeting of November/December 1988 was also confirmed: Dan Tloome rose to the position of chairperson, and Slovo was elected general secretary. Other important decisions of the 7th Congress included the tightening of security measures, appointment of full-timers for regions, and the establishment of an integrated underground leadership inside the country (Operation Vula was an attempt in this regard).[1]

The review of the *Road to South African Freedom*, which resulted in the *Path to Power*, was necessitated, in particular, by the deepening crisis with the apartheid regime, the heightened mass struggle, and global changes in the wake of Mikhail Gorbachev's 'perestroika'. Thanks to the practice of democratic centralism, the process of the review of the *Road to South African Freedom* was very thorough, as was explained to delegates at the Congress:

> The draft programme before you is the climax of a most thorough-going and democratic process allowed by our conditions. It can truly be said that every member of our organisation, both inside and outside our country, has had a say in determining its shape and contents. The process began in

1983. A sub-committee was appointed to go into the question of whether, and to what extent, the programme [*Road to South African Freedom*] needs to be rewritten. The sub-committee recommended a series of additional theses which would appear as an addendum to the 1962 programme, *The Road to South African Freedom*. These recommendations were circulated to all party units. The overwhelming response was that it was necessary to prepare a completely new draft.

The plenary session of the Central Committee in 1987 accepted this approach. It appointed a Programme Commission, chaired by the General Secretary. The first step taken by this Commission was to ask all units to undertake an intensive examination of the 1962 programme and to submit concrete proposals on the contents and shape of the new draft. These proposals formed the basis for the initial discussions by the Commission. The Commission met a number of times both in plenary sessions and in separate groups. A draft was prepared which, with some amendments by the Political Bureau, was circulated for discussion. An enormous number of comments came in from the membership. Taking these comments into account, the Commission then prepared an amended draft which, after additional changes by the PB, is the document before Congress.

Approximately 1 250 amendments, suggestions and additions came from the units. Only a negligible minority considered the draft unacceptable. The overwhelming majority accepted the main theses contained in the chapters with varying degrees of enthusiasm. On questions of formulation, emphasis, omissions, style, additions, etc., the structures responded critically, constructively and most thoughtfully. You have before you a summary of those comments that came on time. The verbatim comments are too mountainous to circulate to each of you, but they are available for perusal by delegates. You also have before you the original draft. If you examine the specific criticisms, suggestions and amendments and compare the two drafts, you will see how the PB and its Commission

*Yusuf Dadoo and unidentified others with a Soviet Union army officer who fought against the Nazi invasion of the Soviet Union*

*Yusuf Dadoo, OR Tambo and unidentified others*

*Bram Fischer*

*Moses Kotane and Oliver Tambo on presenting the Isitwalandwe medal from the ANC to Moses Kotane*

*Chris Hani disguises for underground operation inside the country*

*Yusuf Dadoo in Vietnam*

*Yusuf Dadoo in India*

*Yusuf Dadoo in Mongolia*

*Yusuf Dadoo in India*

*Yusuf Dadoo addressing a meeting of the Transvaal Indian Congress*

*SACP delegation at a meeting with Congolese counterparts; amongst this group are Moses Mabhida, Yusuf Dadoo and Joe Slovo*

*Yusuf Dadoo in GDR (East Germany)*

*Yusuf Dadoo with Eric Mtshali and unidentified others in Iran*

*Yusuf Dadoo addressing a meeting of the South African Indian Congress with a poster of Dr Moroka in the foreground*

*Chris Hani passport for Operation J*

*James West, Central Committee of the Communist Party of the USA; Raul Valdes Vivo, Central Committee of the Communist Party of Cuba; Essop Pahad, South African Communist Party representative, the World Marxist Review, among others at a conference in Moscow*

*Essop Pahad, James West and Raul Valdes Vivo at a ceremony in Red Square, Moscow*

*Yusuf Dadoo in India*

1. NAME :

2. ADDRESS : ~~Khotso Halle,~~   /~~Dr Gilbert Hani~~/ London
              ~~P.O.Box 558,~~      ~~PO Box 18~~      Address.
              ~~Maseru, Lesotho.~~  ~~Mafeteng~~       Peter S
                                    ~~Lesotho~~        (see RK)

3. CONVENTIONAL SIGNS :
    To indicate a secret text, date on innocent letter will be written thus : "2/3/70"

4. Secret text will be on back of innocent letter and is numbered and dated thus ih secret text :"1/2/3/70".
    Word "Ends" completes message.

5. The date will be written at top right corner of innocent letter but no address will be given.

6. RELATIONSHIP IN INNOCENT LETTER : Friends.

7. METHOD : Dry method using carbon Z – book provided.
    Use sharp HB pencil, Bold capital letters, down strokes only, press on smooth backing,; when complete steam for 2-3 minutes.

8. TO DEVELOP : Mix one-third eggspoon Dithizone, one-quarter eggspoon Carbonate of Soda in two ounces of distilled water; bring to boil to dissolve –

    Steam side with secret text for 30 seconds and apply solution lightly with tampon of cottong wool.

    Note : Developer will keep in dark bottle for 2-3 weeks

9. BOOK CODE :
    To be used only as a reserve.
    Penguin "Over the River" by Galsworthy.

    Colon indicates page; semi-colon indicates line; comma indicates letter –
    e.g. 10: 8; 3, 5, 7, 15,  indicates page 10, line 8, letters 3,5,7 & 1
    Count lines from top to bottom and letters left to right.
    Ignore page and Chapter titles.

*Note*
*Copy of Instructions above*
*Sent to our contacts with*
*Third Party (Feb- March 1970)*

10. We write to – "Dear John"
             From – "Peter"

Guidelines for underground letter-writing

> 30/3/69
>
> DEAR J.S.,
>
> 1) WHAT ON EARTH HAS BECAME OF THE CABLE I SENT ASKING FOR THE OPERATION J REPORT YOU TOLD ME OF? THERE'S NO WORD FROM LUSAKA – FOR SOME ODD REASON.
>
> 2) WE NEED A NEW BOOK HERE. DID JH NOT GET MY MESSAGE?
>
> 3) LONDON IS "SILENTER" THAN A TOMB. WHAT'S ON?
>
> amandla!
>
> OR

*Letter from Tambo to Slovo hidden inside an innocent-looking letter through a chemical process*

OR Tambo, Joe Slovo, Yusuf Dadoo, Moses Mabhida, Eric Mtshali and unidentified others at an ANC–SACP alliance meeting in Lusaka

Walter Sisulu, JB Marks, David Bopape, Dr Moroka, James Philips, Yusuf Dadoo, Molvi Cachalia and unidentified others

incorporated so much of what came out in the collective discussions at grassroots level. In this sense we can truly claim that the draft before you is an attempt to express the collective thinking of... [the] whole membership. The process is an example of democracy in action.[2]

The *Path to Power*, like the 1962 programme, was still based on the belief that the world was going through an era of transition from capitalism to socialism. Thus, the programme reaffirmed, with some elaboration, the Party's thesis of Colonialism of a Special Type. The theory of the national democratic revolution was also elaborated, especially with regard to the so-called 'two-stage' theory, and the role of the working class. With the experience accumulated during the preceding decades, the programme revised the earlier conception of guerrilla warfare, acknowledging that a war may have to be fought under non-traditional conditions, as part of a 'people's war' for the 'seizure of power'. Nonetheless a negotiated 'transfer of power', as with the case of the 1962 programme, was never ruled out.

The PB report to the 7th Congress was indeed prophetic in declaring:

[The] 8th Congress will be on our own soil... This is not a pipedream... It is a clarion call whose fulfillment will depend upon each and every one of us and those who have sent us here. We must regard ourselves not only as delegates of structures but as delegates of history.

In February 1990, the apartheid president FW de Klerk announced the unbanning of the ANC, SACP and other organisations. The announcement may have caught the Party's leadership unprepared, but nonetheless a few days later in the same month, an extended PB meeting was organised to deliberate on the new situation.

## The Unbanning

The unbanning of the SACP in February 1990 brought to an end almost 40 years of the Party's life of illegality and underground existence. Unlike in the 1950s before the exile years, or during the exile period spanning the 1960s to February 1990, the Party now had to deal with the challenges of existing in the open, as a mass Party with branches all over the country. Following the unbanning, a more important challenge would confront the Party at the ideological level. How was the struggle for socialism to be executed during the transition to a post-apartheid dispensation, and then, what and how should socialism be constructed in the 21$^{st}$ century especially in the light of the collapse of the Soviet Union and other former socialist countries? These questions were to persist after the first democratic elections of April 1994, and stand at the heart of the substance of the role of the Party in the post-1994 transition, and the relationship between the Party and the ANC as both a liberation movement and a governing party. The Party, like its communist counterparts in some post-colonial African countries, was faced with the difficulty of having to survive as a socialist force within an alliance led by a nationalist movement whose government is presiding over a capitalist economy.

There is a related issue which is linked to the Party's two-stage theory as articulated in its programmes of 1962 and 1989, and that was how to ensure that the post-apartheid transition resulted in the establishment of socialism and eventually communism, and whether domestic and external constraints on this transition are real, imagined or even exaggerated. This debate is not new. It preoccupied Karl Marx and Friedrich Engels after the abortive Paris Commune of 1871, Vladimir Lenin after the 1917 Russian Revolution, and indeed set Joseph Stalin against Leon Trotsky. Therefore, the Party had to adjust to new conditions brought about by the negotiations for a new post-apartheid dispensation, and the establishment of a government led by its ally, the ANC, after the first democratic elections of April 1994. What follows in this chapter is how the Party dealt with all these new challenges, including ideological and organisational changes it had to undergo.

In assessing the SACP's role during the pre-1994 and post-1994 transition, it has to be borne in mind that the Party could exercise its influence indirectly, but with impact, without being directly involved as an organisation, thanks to its 'vanguard' method of work within the ANC and the alliance in general:[3] it participated directly as one of the parties to the negotiations; its cadres were deployed in strategic positions in the ANC's negotiations structures; through some of these cadres, it made strategic interventions at different points of the negotiations to give the process momentum; and its presence in the process put pressure on the government to find a peaceful settlement with the ANC, quickly, or face a more radical alternative.

Following the unbanning of the Party, an extended Politburo convened later in the same month of February 1990 to take stock of the new developments and formulate the Party's response. The meeting "agreed that the outcome, the speed and social content of the democratic revolution necessitates the existence of the Party as a legal, public and independent political vanguard of the working people. The reconstitution of the legal Party will need speed and bold steps".[4]

The meeting resolved to establish an 'internal leadership core' to be selected from a list of names including Andrew Mlangeni, Ahmed Kathrada, Govan Mbeki, Billy Nair, Sydney Mufamadi, Chris Dlamini and Elias Motsoaledi. This list was to be consolidated at subsequent meetings inside the country towards the July launch of the Party. When it came to 'who' and 'how' many of the CC members should publicly declare their Party membership, there were differences of opinion in the meeting. One group, led by Slovo and Chris Hani, argued that all CC memberships should be known to the public; while the other side including Thabo Mbeki, Jacob Zuma and Aziz Pahad, felt that this would expose the ANC to anti-communist attacks as many ANC National Executive Committee (NEC) members were on the CC. Zuma's biographer, Jeremy Gordin, wrote about the problem the latter group had with serving 'two masters', that is, the difficulties that would be encountered with serving at the top leadership of two legal organisations – the Party and the ANC.[5] In the end, the meeting developed a list of twelve CC members (out of the total of 20) who were to surface and publicly acknowledge their CC status, and three CC members who were not to 'expose' their CC status. These three were Mbeki, Zuma and Aziz Pahad. However, this issue was to prove to be no easy matter as differences on it were to continue into the country and lead to some CC members leaving the Party.[6]

Other decisions taken at the meeting revolved around issues such as the establishment of districts and the return of certain exiles such as Ray and Jack Simons. Following this meeting, the Party propaganda organs, the *African Communist* and *Umsebenzi*, carried responses which cautiously welcomed the unbanning, and called for the intensification of the struggle against the apartheid regime. Indeed, the CC statement, published in the *African Communist*, acknowledged that "today our Party is emerging from the underground with massive prestige and popularity. The CC is fully aware of the weighty responsibilities this prestige and popularity place upon our Party and upon each one of our militants", and declared that "a major objective of the coming months will be the building of a strong, legal SACP, rooted among the working masses of our people".[7]

On the part of the ANC, its NEC meeting of 15 February also reflected on the unbanning of the organisation. The attendees received a briefing from Mbeki about a meeting he had held with the government's intelligence elements about how the two sides could work together towards a peaceful settlement of the country's problems, particularly getting the negotiations off the ground. The NEC meeting agreed to "publicly acknowledge that we are prepared to proceed with talks [with the apartheid government] for the purpose of getting the implementation of the balance of the preconditions of [the] Harare Declaration".[8] A drafting committee comprised of Mbeki, Aziz Pahad, Hani and a non-Party member, Pallo Jordan, was put together to compose a statement to communicate this position. When it came to the discussion of the future of the SACP, the consensus at the meeting was that the Party "should continue to exist and the Alliance should continue, perhaps in a slightly new form". The change to the alliance was to be in the form of the dissolution of SACTU and the inclusion of COSATU in the tripartite mechanism.

As will be shown later, Party cadres would play a strategic role at different levels of the negotiations machinery of the ANC, making critical interventions that gave momentum to the negotiations process. Mbeki, Slovo, Zuma, Aziz Pahad, Essop Pahad, and Mac Maharaj were all among Party figures who played this role in the transition to negotiations and during the negotiations. In fact, Mbeki and Zuma were designated to serve as the ANC's contact point with the government during the transition to the negotiations, the latter even smuggled into the country with a team to prepare the ground for the return of the exiled leadership. The Party would be visibly present at the Groote Schuur meeting of May which was the first formal contact between the ANC and the government, and at one which took place in Pretoria in August where the ANC unilaterally suspended the armed struggle. As Slovo symbolised the Party in the eyes of the regime, his presence at both the Groote Schuur and Pretoria meetings would be a source of tension between the ANC and the apartheid government.

Following the extended PB and NEC meetings, a three-day historic SACP-COSATU gathering sat at the end of March 1990 in Harare to deliberate on the respective roles of the SACP, COSATU, SACTU and the ANC, as well as "the general character of a future socialist South Africa, to which both the SACP and COSATU are actively committed". And "considerable stress was placed by both parties on the necessity of ensuring a thorough democratic socialism".[9] From COSATU's perspective, this meeting was viewed as a forum to take forward the discussion that had been taking place within the organisation on the Workers Charter as a basis for a programme of action on which to base the alliance then and beyond into the post-apartheid dispensation. Jay Naidoo, then secretary general of COSATU, explained: "Now that we were on the verge of defeating apartheid, the question was: what should be the programme for constructing a new South Africa".[10] The other issue that the meeting had to ponder was the future of SACTU. "The role of COSATU was one of the key questions after the unbanning of the liberation movement", recalled Naidoo. "To begin with, we had to sort out our relationship with SACTU, which had been closely allied to the ANC since 1953... There was pressure from some quarters for COSATU to merge into SACTU. In my view that was absolutely out of question, and I argued very strongly against the idea".[11] It would take a series of meetings between Naidoo and SACTU general secretary John Nkadimeng for a decision to be taken in favour of COSATU when it was agreed that SACTU would fold and its cadreship be absorbed into the former.[12] The other pre-unbanning organisation which suffered the same fate as SACTU was the UDF which was disbanded in August 1991. With SACTU gone, COSATU then became the third member of the Tripartite Alliance which had been consolidated in exile in the course of the 1980s.[13] In the 1990s and beyond, the tripartite was to mean the ANC-SACP-COSATU relationship, but its working modalities as a mechanism were to become a matter of dispute especially once the ANC became the country's ruling party after the 1994 democratic elections.

Towards the end of May 1990, the extended PB took a decision to hold an underground consultative conference of the Party in Tongaat, a coastal town in what is now called KwaZulu-Natal, to deliberate on the organisational and political implications of establishing a legal SACP or, as they put it, "the Party of a new type". The conference, known as Operation Eagle, was convened through the machinery of Operation Vula which had been initiated by the ANC before the unbanning to deploy a section of its leadership inside the country. Many of Vula's operatives were Party members, and its head, Mac Maharaj, was on both the CC and PB.

The 20-odd participants at the Tongaat meeting were a mix of the exile group, MDM activists, trade unionists, and veterans, such as Billy Nair and Govan Mbeki. The meeting had to take place without a written agenda because, as its chairperson explained, "unfortunately we had planned for you to have the agenda last night but the comrade who received it for photocopying did not realise that this was to be photocopied and so burnt it". This was not an act of stupidity on the part of the participant who burnt the agenda, but a function of security precautions that were required for underground work. The commencement of the meeting itself had to be delayed because, as was explained later, participants "had to wait, were taken from one place to another... because we wanted to ensure that you had no tail". If apartheid security elements were to make an appearance, precautions had been taken for participants from the underground or exile to disappear, the removal of sensitive documents, and for the meeting to be converted into an innocent type of a gathering.[14]

Among the issues that were discussed at the conference was the need to revisit the membership and recruitment policy of the Party with a view to doing away with the system of probation; issues of internal democracy and democratic centralism; the need to interrogate the Party programme *Path to Power* (which had been adopted at the 7th Congress in 1989) and its relevance in light of the new situation; the future of *Umsebenzi* and the *African Communist*; and a programme of action towards the public launch of the legal SACP. The recommendation of the extended PB of establishing an interim leadership was endorsed and names even suggested.[15] Govan Mbeki's reaction was: "If my name is there I think I should be excluded. I am the oldest person in the movement and I already have too heavy a load and find it difficult to be packing my bag all the time". Billy Nair's summary of the conclusions of the discussions on challenges facing the Party gives a good sense of the mood at the meeting:

> The errors of socialism of alienating the masses we must avoid. Where organisation itself becomes alienated from the people and people don't know what is going on we run into danger. Unbanning is not demobilising the people; it is the leadership ourselves who have become demobilised and have been caught in euphoria. Mass struggle has to be intensified so that pressure is brought to bear on the state to ensure that people's power comes about. Central to our demand is calling for an interim government and a constituent assembly so that this becomes the focal point so that the present regime does not have the capacity to effect real change. To this end comrades have emphasised the need for the establishment of dual power and organs of people's power to be effectively translated into focal points of action so that when there is a transition there is a base. There is a need for education and intensive propaganda.[16]

This conclusion did not mean that the Tongaat meeting was not in favour of the negotiations as the apartheid regime would allege later in the year. What the meeting called for in essence was for the Party to be vigilant and maintain a strong and effective organisational presence among the people during the negotiations. The outcomes of the Tongaat conference, running into about three hundred pages, were in Lusaka at the Party headquarters within hours after the conclusion of the meeting.[17]

Within weeks of the Tongaat meeting, in July, the government swooped on the Vula machinery, arresting Mac Maharaj and forcing Ronnie Kasrils on the run. As part of this offensive, five days before the public launch of the Party, the regime, through foreign minister Pik Botha, briefed ambassadors accredited to the country on what was presented as a communist ploy to scuttle the negotiations. Botha, according to an intelligence cable of the United States State Department, "gave ambassadors background information on a secret May 19–20 SACP politburo meeting concerning tactics for 'seizure/ transfer' of state power, reading extensively from selected computer printouts of meeting's opening remarks, speeches, discussion and minutes".[18]

The meeting in question was the Tongaat conference. Contrary to what the regime propagated, the meeting was not a Politburo gathering, and nor were Zuma and Slovo present at the meeting as was alleged. The only proof the government had of Slovo's presence at the Tongaat conference was the reference to 'Joe' in Tongaat documents that were seized in Vula safe-houses. Yet the Joe in question was not Slovo but a code name for Siphiwe Nyanda. Not only was Botha "convinced that Nelson Mandela and most of the ANC senior leadership were unaware of the SACP meeting, tactics or plans", it was also suggested there were even SACP plans to assassinate Mandela. Botha "appealed to ambassadors and the ANC to sever ties with the SACP, or at least distance themselves from these actions. He also expressed the hope that foreign governments would publicly condemn the SACP's latest actions".[19]

The media, through particularly their editorial and opinion articles, did not miss the opportunity to feast on this 'Red Plot' conspiracy theory.[20] The saga was also manipulated by the apartheid state to call for the exclusion of Slovo from the Pretoria meeting between the ANC and government; FW de Klerk, the apartheid president, only gave in when spoken to by Mandela and presented with proof that Slovo was not in the country at the time of the Tongaat meeting.[21] The launch rally of the Party took place at the height of this Red Plot frenzy which hovered over the negotiations well into March 1991 when charges against Maharaj and other Vula operatives were dropped.

The unbanning of the Party was not the only new factor that the SACP leadership had to tackle, another was the collapse of the Soviet Union and other former socialist countries. One of the responses by the Party was Slovo's highly debated pamphlet, 'Has Socialism Failed?'[22] Slovo, in his attempt to reaffirm the validity of Marxism, dealt not only with how Marxists globally had responded to the crisis in the Soviet Union, but also with factors which to him contributed to the distortion of Marxism and the eventual failure of socialism in those countries. These factors included the bureaucratisation of Marxism and the economic backwardness of Russia itself. He then argued for his 'democratic socialism' as a solution. Subsequent to 'Has Socialism Failed?', Slovo delivered other lectures and speeches on the same theme, acknowledging mistakes and excesses committed over the years.[23]

Slovo's pamphlet received a flood of responses from within the ranks of the liberation movement and outside, especially among academics. Within the liberation movement, Pallo Jordan's response attracted the most attention. For Jordan, departing from the premise that Slovo's pamphlet only dealt with symptoms and not the causes, the source of the crisis that led to the collapse of the former socialist countries had to be sought in both structural factors and in how dissenting views and voices were dealt with in those countries. As for the SACP itself, Jordan argued:

> One cannot lightly accept at face value Comrade Joe Slovo's protestations about the SACP's non-Stalinist credentials. Firstly, there is too much evidence to the contrary. Any regular reader

of the SACP's publications can point to a consistent pattern of praise and support for every violation of freedom perpetrated by the Soviet leadership, both before and after the death of Stalin. It is all too easy in the context of Soviet criticism of this past for Comrade Slovo to boldly come forward. Secondly, the political culture nurtured by the SACP's leadership over the years has produced a spirit of intolerance, petty intellectual thuggery and political dissembling among its members which regularly emerges in the pages of both the *African Communist* and *Umsebenzi*.[24]

There were other responses. Some people, such as Harry Gwala, attempted to defend Stalin. Others even took issue with Lenin himself and the notion of 'democratic socialism'.[25]

Nor were the academics silent on this debate. While some, such as Stephen Ellis, tried to locate the debate within a Cold War perspective, one of the most virulent attacks on Slovo came from Archie Mafeje, a South African scholar who was based in exile. Mafeje's historical critique of the role of both the CPSA and SACP, informed, as it were, by the belief that Slovo was "a confirmed Stalinist until the writing of the essay under review", argued that the Party was formed by "white émigré communists [who] depended to a very large extent on the Soviet Union and had virtually no constituency inside the country". For him, the Party "succeeded in splitting the black national movement right in the middle for its own purposes. Having lost the support of white workers... it sought a constituency within the black national movement *without giving up its privileged position*, as a 'vanguard party'" (emphasis original). Thus, concluded Mafeje, "had it not been for its [SACP's] self-interested interference, a number of differences, say, between the Unity Movement and the ANC, and between the ANC and the PAC could have been resolved".[26]

# 8
# The Alliance

To be true to history, we must concede that there have been difficulties as well as triumphs along our path, as, traversing many decades, our two organizations have converged towards a shared strategy of struggle. Ours is not merely a paper alliance, created at conference tables and formalized through the signing of documents and representing only an agreement of leaders. Our alliance is a living organism that has grown out of struggle. We have built it out of our separate and common experiences.[1]

THIS IS HOW TAMBO SUMMED up the SACP-ANC history in his address on the occasion of the 60th anniversary of the Party in July 1981. The alliance has for years been a key mechanism for the interaction between the Party and the ANC. As shown throughout this book, it was through the alliance that the two organisations influenced each other, coordinated their actions in struggle, and managed their membership.

The alliance, as a model of a political front, had its roots in the March 1947 pact between the ANC and the Transvaal and Natal Indian Congresses which was signed by their respective presidents in the persons of Drs Alfred Xuma, Yusuf Dadoo and GM Naicker. Famously known as the Doctors or the Xuma-Dadoo-Naicker Pact, the joint declaration was informed by the realisation on the part of three organisations of "the urgency of co-operation between the non-European peoples and other democratic forces for the attainment of basic human rights and full citizenship for all sections of the South African peoples". Through the pact, the three organisations "resolved that a joint declaration of co-operation is imperative for the working out of a practical basis of co-operation between the

National Organisations of the non-European peoples". Having put forward their set of demands for change in the joint declaration, the three organisations were "of the opinion that for the attainment of these objects it is urgently necessary that a vigorous campaign be immediately launched and that every effort be made to compel the Union Government to implement the United Nations decisions and to treat the non-European peoples in South Africa in conformity with the principles of the United Nations Charter". Thanks to the pact, the three parties were "to meet from time to time to implement this declaration and to take active steps in proceeding with the campaign".[2] This joint commitment, with its follow-up mechanism of regular meetings among the three parties, gave birth to the Defiance Campaign of the 1950s. In the course of these mass defiance campaign activities, including the adoption of the Freedom Charter in 1955, the Congress alliance came into being as a front that brought together organisations of the oppressed in the form of the ANC, the Coloured People's Congress and the South African Indian Congress, as well as the trade union body SACTU and the Congress of Democrats (COD) of white activists.

With the shift to exile in the early 1960s, the Congress alliance collapsed. The *Report on Organisation* presented by the CC to the Augmented Meeting of 1970 would state:

> A unity in action between all the oppressed groups is fundamental to the effective advance of our liberation struggle. Previously this unity was expressed in the Congress Alliance. In the post-Rivonia situation a number of changes occurred in the relationships between the groups which formally constituted the liberation front. The Congress Alliance in the form in which it was moulded in the '50s ceased to exist. Between Rivonia and 1966 the only two organisations which continued to operate collectively but... for all practical purposes independently, were the ANC and the Party [SACP]... For all practical purposes there was no functioning SACTU organisation inside the country. Neither the [Coloured People's Congress] nor the SAIC existed either within or outside the country...[3]

As to relations between the ANC and the Party, the same report explained:

> This [the formation of MK] was not the first occasion when the Party and the ANC co-operated intimately in the prosecution of our revolutionary tasks; it had its precedents in the impressive mass struggles of the '50s. Although for historical reasons no formal relationship was ever created between the Party and the ANC, it is no exaggeration to claim that in the pre-Rivonia period they were the two most powerful pillars of the liberation front. There is no constitutional formula or framework within which this close relationship would fit. It did not even express itself in a joint meeting and certainly not in any sort of formal agreement; yet it was uniquely close and was understood by most.[4]

It was indeed the relationship between the ANC and the SACP, and later SACTU, that came to constitute the alliance in exile. The story of the alliance in exile began with the London Memo of 1966 which was addressed to the ANC leadership on 'Problems of the Congress Movement'. The essence of the argument in the Memo was that "a nation at war requires a Council of War" built around organisations that comprised the Congress alliance. The authors of the Memo admitted that:

> ...the machinery of the Congress Alliance as it existed in the past is clearly inadequate for the tasks which face our movement today. We are faced with the sort of problems which many revolutionary people have faced at a certain stage in their history. The preparations for revolutionary struggle including armed struggle and guerrilla warfare call for new forms of organisation [and] new forms of alliance... We feel therefore that attention should be directed to the creation of new forms of alliance or revolutionary front organisation suitable to our struggle and in accordance with South African conditions.[5]

The Memo then called for an inclusive but ANC-led 'top-level meeting' to take forward this discussion.

The ANC subsequently established a Sub-Committee to examine the London Memo and make recommendations. This Sub-Committee met in August 1966, with Kotane, Marks and Nokwe present, and agreed with the idea of a top-level meeting. The committee made the following observations:

> We also agree [with the London Memo] that from time to time and as circumstances change the Alliance, its machinery, its form might have to be changed in order to make it function more effectively in new conditions. Indeed the history of the alliance demonstrates that from time to time it had adapted itself to changing conditions with the view to making it more effective.
>
> Its foundations were made in [the] Xuma-Dadoo-Naicker pact in 1946 [sic]. This established cooperation between the ANC and what is now the SAIC. These organisations with the support of the Franchise Action Council jointly launched the Defiance Campaign... Subsequent to the formation of the COD it too joined the Alliance and so did SACTU.
>
> The next historic stage was for the preparation for the Congress of the People and the establishment of the National Action Council. The Freedom Charter was the embodiment of the common aspirations and objectives of the members of the Congress Alliance...
>
> The machinery which was agreed upon to give effect to this historic pledge [in the Freedom Charter] was [the] joint Executive Committee meetings and in between them the National Consultative Council. These were the organs through which each organisation could make proposals of policy and action to the others, which were free to accept, modify or reject the proposals made. It was never disputed that because of the situation in South Africa the African National Congress was the leader of the Alliance.[6]

The Sub-Committee then went on to explain two "problems which have faced the cooperation and joint action of the liberation force of the Congress Alliance" in exile. The first problem was the abortive attempt to establish the United Front comprised of the ANC, SAIC, PAC, SWAPO and SWANU (South West African National Union). With the failure of the United Front, according to the Sub-Committee, "the problem then arose: what form of machinery must be established" in exile? The Sub-Committee continued:

> Should there exist an alliance externally as exists internally? The question was debated and discussed and it was decided that the situation internally and externally differ; internally the Congress Alliance and its constituent organisations exist because of objective reasons and they had definite functions. The conditions externally differ and require that the image of the African National Congress as the leading organ of the liberation movement should be projected. This was no fiction which was being created but was a fact which had been implicitly accepted at home and required projection abroad.

The second problem raised by the Sub-Committee was that when the ANC turned to armed struggle, it presented its idea to its alliance partners but the SAIC and the Coloured People's Congress never accepted the idea. It was then the view of the Sub-Committee that this fact made the idea of a Council of War comprised of constituent organisations of the alliance impossible. However, the Sub-Committee emphasised that members of the SAIC and Coloured People's Congress were free to (and did) join the armed struggle in their individual capacity.

A point to note here is that in its detailed, nine-page analysis of the history of and challenges facing the Congress alliance, the Sub-Committee – comprised of leading figures of the Party – made no reference at all to the SACP. This was a confirmation that the Party was not part of the Congress alliance. This may have been so due to the fact that the Party was banned and underground during the heyday of the Congress alliance in the 1950s.

Interventions such as the recommendations of the Sub-Committee resulted in the ANC convening a consultative meeting of the Congress alliance in November 1966 in Dar es Salaam. The meeting, in its resolution, "reaffirmed that the ANC is the leader of the National Liberation struggle in South Africa". In this resolution, the meeting also "agreed that at the moment conditions do not exist for the formation of an FLN-type of organisation for the direction of the struggle in South Africa". The FLN – the National Liberation Front of Algeria – was formed in 1954 out of the merger of a number of groups that were fighting for the independence of Algeria. The inclusion of the reference to the FLN was clearly intended to dismiss the idea of forming a new organisation in exile to replace the ANC. However, a Consultative Congress Committee (CCC) was established as a sub-committee of the ANC for coordination, consultation and cooperation with various forces of the liberation movement. The CCC would eventually be replaced with the Revolutionary Council at the ANC Morogoro Conference of 1969.

But the Party was left out of the CCC. At its plenary session of 1967 the CC, in one of its resolutions, commended the ANC for having convened the consultative meeting, and noted that:

> We understand that a machinery has been set up by the ANC to draw in the various elements of the liberation movement and coordinate their work. We welcome and approve of this decision. However, as an independent organisation... we feel that our Party too should be included in the proposals for greater cooperation of the liberation movement. We are prepared to take part in such detailed discussions as may be mutually agreed upon on all questions of common concern...[7]

The exclusion of the Party from the CCC would be rectified later. In the CC's 'Notes for Guidance in Discussion' which was developed for Party structures in preparation for the ANC's Morogoro Conference, the SACP was clear in its mind that: "We are not now faced with the question of whether or not the Congress Alliance should be recreated in its old form. This is historically and practically out of the question".[8]

The Revolutionary Council established at the Morogoro Conference replaced the CCC. What followed, as discussed in Chapter Two, was the first SACP-ANC formal meeting in exile to tackle contentious issues affecting the relations between the two organisations.

Slovo's verbal report to the CC plenary session of 1972, cited in Chapter Three, indicated without doubt that SACP-ANC relations at the beginning of the 1970s were not free of the difficulties of the 1960s. Slovo's report was not an exaggeration of tensions that existed between the ANC and the Party during that period. Some key ANC figures even monitored what was published in the *African Communist*. For example, Alfred Nzo, then secretary general of the ANC, wrote a long letter in March 1972 to Marks and Kotane (while the two were hospitalised in Moscow) to update them on developments within the ANC. The letter included a paragraph on Johnny Makhathini as follows:

> Our office in Algeria is coming out more boldly and openly as one of the centres of this reactionary intrigue [the 'dissidents']. Not so long ago Johnny Makatini [sic] circulated to all the offices of the ANC including the office of the Acting President a letter in which he was complaining of the publication in the African Communist of a letter written to the editor of the AC by one of the Algerian comrades in exile. The letter which he claims was anti-Algerian appeared in the last issue of the AC. Of course, it is known that Johnny had long given himself the task of scrutinising and adversely commenting on some of the articles that appear in the AC. This in the past was done secretly and communicated to certain quarters. What is new now is that he has publicly circulated his views and this may mean an all-out open campaign to isolate the Party from the African National Congress.[9]

Similarly, one senior Party member wrote to Slovo in November 1974 from Dar es Salaam about a certain senior ANC comrade:

> ...the old chap seems to be having too many ideas in his head...

he wants to bring back... Makiwanes... and all the dissident groups. In a word, he wants to bring back all the anti-Party groups. His main worry as I can see is our FAMILY [the Party]. This is reflected in the remarks he made when they came back from the trip with the 'headman'... that the AC projected his Vice President as a chief ideologist... As he was saying that, I was searching for the AC in question. I opened the chapter which has your interview and showed him that there's no such a thing in the AC. He kept quiet, but his face registered disapproval of my explanation.[10]

The history of the alliance went through five phases from its inception in the 1940s to the unbanning in 1990: the Xuma-Dadoo-Naicker Pact period of the 1940s; the Congress alliance of the 1950s; the United Front-Consultative Congress Committee-Revolutionary Council phase of the early exile period in the 1960s; the strengthening of ANC-SACP relations in the late 1970s and early 1980s; and the advent of the Tripartite Alliance in the mid-1980s. But during the 30 years or so of the exile experience this alliance did not exist for 20 of those years (that is, in the 1960s and most of the 1970s). As shown in the previous chapters, relations between the ANC and the SACP only became organisationally more structured in the early 1980s, culminating in the Tripartite Alliance comprised of the ANC, SACP and SACTU.

What hampered the development of a well-structured relationship between the ANC and the SACP in the 1960s and 1970s? Undoubtedly the preference on the part of some key figures in both the ANC and the Party for relations between the two organisations to continue to operate as they did in the pre-Rivonia period – that is, through personal contact and unity in the terrain of struggle, rather than through a structured coordination mechanism – played a role. So too did differences in the understanding of the 'vanguard' and 'leading' role of the Party in a revolutionary struggle that is led by a nationalist movement, the ANC, as well as the decision taken by the Party leadership in exile (probably influenced by the underground years of the 1950s) to opt for a style of work in which Party members were required to conceal their membership and the existence of Party structures from ANC members. Finally, the decision taken by the Party leadership in exile requiring all Party members wherever and irrespective of their area of operation, including in the ANC and its MK, to be primarily accountable to the Party and not to structures in which they were operating also played a part.

A related challenge with which the alliance had to constantly deal was the ongoing contradiction between the demands of ANC leadership and the aspirations of other constituent organisations of the alliance. The organisations that form this ANC-led alliance are not there as an act of self-liquidation but to pursue their own interests which they believe can best be achieved through membership of a group. What helped the alliance to survive was the ANC's ability to assert itself and lead and the other member organisations were able to simultaneously assert their independence and accept that same ANC leadership. Had the ANC failed to assert itself and lead, it would have probably been dissolved into an FLN-type organisation or something like FRELIMO.

The Party tried to take decisive policy steps to overcome challenges entailed in its relations with the ANC. Notable here, as discussed earlier, were the 'Notes for Discussion' of the 1960s; the resolution of the 1970 augmented meeting on 'The Party as a Leading Force and Relations with the ANC'; the 1980 CC Discussion Document on the 'The Role of the Party and its Place in the National Liberation Movement'; the CC resolution of September 1981 on 'Party Work in Fraternal Organisations'; and cadre policy as articulated in the 1984 Constitution. Debates about the form, content and future of the alliance were always there, especially at critical turning points of the struggle. These debates, instead of weakening the alliance, in fact helped strengthen it to advance the cause of the struggle. With the ANC becoming the ruling party with the end of apartheid in April 1994, intra-alliance relations would get a new spin.

# 9
# Building a 'Mass' Party

ON ITS RETURN TO THE COUNTRY, the Party was offered a home at the offices of COSATU on Rissik Street, in Johannesburg's city centre. It was from these offices that the likes of Slovo and Hani performed their Party work, with Geraldine Fraser-Moleketi as their secretary. A few years later, Fraser-Moleketi would become a full cabinet minister and chairperson of the Party. The establishment of a legal SACP introduced new factors and players as new members flooded the ranks of the Party. The leadership from exile, the underground, and MDM had to be made into a collective. Party districts of the legal SACP were to be established in the months following the unbanning in all key centres – in Johannesburg, the East Rand, the West Rand, Port Elizabeth, Cape Town, East London, Durban and Bloemfontein.

Yet the underground machinery of both the SACP and the ANC did not automatically fold with the unbanning. On the contrary, the underground was encouraged and strengthened, especially since the leadership and membership of the liberation movement had doubts about the sincerity and commitment of the regime. When the future of the underground was discussed at the ANC's NEC meeting of 15 February, there was consensus that it should be maintained. For example, Slovo argued that the "new ANC... will not affect u/g [the underground]. They will be separate and only coordinated at top level". Mbeki maintained that "as we go into uncertain ground, we shall need our own security organs... Even after suspending hostilities, we have to keep our units".[1]

Kasrils was one of the leaders charged with servicing the underground in the immediate post-unbanning period. As he explained: "The lifting of the ban on the ANC and SACP had not meant that our underground networks had been dissolved, and these required supervision. Our contacts were reliable and extensive and

I was able to move around the country. I seldom slept in one place for more than a week at a time. Accommodation ranged from homes in affluent suburbs, to township lodgings and rural homesteads".[2] For their part, SACP units on the ground inside the country had to interrogate the new situation brought about by the unbanning. According to one underground operative:

> After the February 2nd unbanning of the ANC and our Party, all the units in our regional underground network immediately discussed the new situation… At first there were two schools of thought. Some comrades were jubilant. After 40 years the regime, which had hoped to bury us once and for all, was forced to admit that the communist movement is unshakably rooted in the soil of our country. In their jubilation these comrades were arguing that we should now immediately surface our underground. But a second school of thought had different ideas. "Nothing has really changed", they said. "The apartheid regime is still in power. The SADF has not yet suffered a decisive internal 'Cuito Cuanavale'. We must proceed in our usual way".[3]

The Tongaat meeting had brainstormed ideas around either Orlando Stadium (in Soweto) or Soccer City (nearby Soweto) as a venue for the launch of the Party. Billy Nair had his own doubts about whether Soccer City could be filled for a Party rally. He told the meeting that: "I am worried we should not be overconfident about filling the FNB [Soccer City]. In fact the last rally was not the first time that the stadium was not filled. Even when comrade Walter [Sisulu] was released. I prefer the Eastern Cape or elsewhere. I don't know about relying on the Southern Transvaal. There appears to be something radically wrong there".[4]

Preparations for the launch rally went full steam ahead in the months following the Tongaat conference, with Maharaj and Kasrils amongst the key organisers. A make-shift extended PB met in Troyeville, Johannesburg in June to consolidate preparations for the rally. The group that had expressed reservations at the PB meeting in

Lusaka about making their Party membership public did not attend, sending a clear signal of their intention to leave the Party; and when they eventually did so, they would be joined by about half of the entire CC elected at the 7th Congress in 1989.[5] As to the rally, doubts were still being expressed whether Soccer City would be filled, but Maharaj was confident that it would be done. When it came to agreeing on the list for the interim leadership which would be announced at the rally, Maharaj raised his objection to the inclusion of the name of Harry Gwala because of a negative view he had of the role that Gwala played in the violence in KwaZulu-Natal. When Maharaj did not get the support of the meeting, he tendered his verbal resignation from the Party on the spot.[6]

Subsequent to this PB meeting, a press conference was convened by Slovo to announce the launch rally. The event was used by the Party to address some of the public's concerns about the role of the Party, by emphasising in the press statement that the Party "will underline our commitment to achieving a multi-party democracy in a united, non-racial South Africa", because "we believe political pluralism is valid for now, for the transition period, and for a socialist future". The media statement also reaffirmed "the leading role of the ANC in the immediate struggle for national liberation", and that "the SACP fully supports the present ANC-led negotiation initiative within the framework of the Harare Declaration".[7] By emphasising commitment to a multi-party system and political pluralism, the Party wanted to assure South Africans that it was not going to follow the example of communist parties in the former socialist countries. The reference to the Party's support for the negotiations was directed at advocates of the Red Plot who portrayed the Party as a threat to the negotiations. The affirmation of the leading role of the ANC was intended for some nationalists within the liberation movement who still harboured fears about the Party's takeover of the ANC.

Towards the launch, several preparatory events were organised, including rallies in different parts of the country, such as one that took place in the Transkei with 70 000 people in attendance. Eventually, the public launch of the legal SACP took place on its 69th anniversary, 29th July 1990, and was attended by some 45 000 people. The venue,

Soccer City, would host the opening and closing matches of the FIFA World Cup 20 years later. In his address, Slovo took a swipe at what he referred to as "a three-fold lie" being spread by the government about the Party and himself, in the wake of the discovery of the Tongaat documents and the arrest of some Vula operatives including Maharaj. The 'lies' were that Slovo was at the Tongaat meeting; that the SACP would not be bound by the ceasefire agreed between the ANC and the government; and that Vula was an SACP operation.[8] As for Kasrils, he was still on the run, and could enter the stadium only through the back door. Nor was the group that had doubts about making their Party membership public present at the rally. This was the beginning of their parting of the way with the Party.

The introduction at the rally of a 22-person Interim Leadership Group (ILG), drawn from the exile, Robben Island and MDM leadership, did not mean, at least constitutionally, that the CC had ceased to function. The two bodies would exist side by side until the election of another CC at the 8th Congress 17 months later. Whether the CC was actually fully functional is difficult to establish, especially as a significant number of its members who were elected at the 7th Congress in 1989 had joined the Mbeki-Zuma-Pahad exodus from the Party on their return to the country from exile, and that Maharaj had resigned over the inclusion of Gwala in the ILG. If how the Troyeville extended PB meeting was put together is anything to go by, then the CC existed as a collective more in theory than practice. Notwithstanding this, after the launch rally, Slovo continued to discharge his responsibilities as the general secretary, opening Party meetings, and speaking on behalf of the CC.

The launch of the Party was followed by a series of activities which accompanied the establishment of Party districts and branches in different parts of the country, and these included a rally in Port Elizabeth in November 1990 which attracted 140 000 people. Thus the Party's membership soared at a time when communist parties across the globe were undergoing a period of serious decline. At the national workshop of February 1991, which was attended by 50 participants from the Party's six regions, an event described by Slovo as "the most important event of the Party since its launch",

1991 was declared "The Year of building a Legal Party", and a target set for growing the Party membership to 30 000 by the time of the 8th Congress in December of that year.[9] Regions were required to set their own interim membership targets, hence about a month later after the workshop a circular was sent out by headquarters that "we require the membership target from each region set for 1 May 1991. Furthermore, we will thereafter require targets for each significant date as set out in the Programme of Action arising from the National Workshop".[10] This Programme of Action was built around, among other things, the membership recruitment campaign, mass mobilisation activities relating to May Day and the Party's 70th anniversary celebrations, as well as socio-economic issues like 'jobs for all', the living wage, the bread price and rent crisis. As a result, the months leading to the 8th Congress witnessed the launch of districts and branches across the country, the celebration of the 70th anniversary of the Party in the regions, and the holding of regional congresses for the election of regional leadership.

One challenge facing the ILG and the CC was how to translate the popularity of the Party into organisational strength on the ground. This popularity, as Slovo argued at the ILG meeting at the end of May 1991, was due to two factors: "a general groundswell of a socialist perspective… [and that] we were seen as the guardians of that socialist [sic]"; and, "a perception, assisted by enemy exaggeration, [that] the Party is the militant hard core of the Alliance".[11] Nevertheless, an organisational machinery was established at the headquarters and provinces. Hani was appointed assistant general secretary by the ILG to deputise Slovo whose attention was absorbed in ANC work. An organising sub-committee was established comprised of Hani as the convener, Kasrils and Gwede Mantashe, who was then the national organiser for the National Union of Mineworkers. Mantashe was being considered for the position of the Party's national organiser but it was felt by the ILG that he would have "to be reinforced due to not having worked nationally".[12] A few years into post-apartheid South Africa, Mantashe rose to the position of the chairperson of the Party to succeed Geraldine Fraser-Moleketi, and was later elected secretary general of the ANC.

Party cadres in the ILG, the CC, and across the regions, were all overstretched due to demands on their time from the ANC and other fraternal organisations. Some of these cadres were overstretched to the detriment of Party work as they had to prioritise the ANC. One such Party cadre was Jeremy Cronin who described his situation in August 1991: "The particular [Party] branch that I'm a member of is not yet fully launched... The major organisational task that we've been battling with has been to build a strong ANC. We see that as the prime task of communists as well as non-communists here in South Africa and that's been a very complicated, difficult task".[13] Regions were experimenting with the position of full-timers, especially in the organising department, but this was constrained by limited financial resources. By the time of the ILG meeting of the end of May 1991, Transvaal, whose definition included the Free State, was leading with 3 200 members, followed by the Border region in the East London area, with 2 104 members. In total, the Eastern Cape which in Party terms was comprised of the Border, 'Eastern Cape' – which referred to the area around Port Elizabeth – and Transkei had 3 350 members. KwaZulu-Natal, which was made up of the Natal Midlands and Southern Natal regions, boasted 891 members. The Western Cape had only 450 members.[14]

Regional structures varied in strength from province to province. By the end of May 1991, at the time when the annual expenses of the Party averaged R1 000 000, each of the regions was allocated between R10 000 and R15 000 by headquarters annually. Regions raised their own funds mainly from membership subscription and the sale of Party publications. The Eastern Cape indicated in its report to the ILG dated 21 July 1991, that it had deposited R2 075 in the bank account of head office between 7 June and 25 June 1991. Western Cape had a total income of R9 000 around the same period, R8 000 of which was absorbed in office expenses, with R1 000 paid to headquarters for literature.[15] Vehicles were provided for regions but with the understanding that "in event of an accident, individual to pay for repairs if it is the fault of the driver". Traffic fine "tickets to be paid by the driver not by [the] office", while head office took charge of insurance.[16]

Notwithstanding these efforts, the Southern Natal region reported in July 1991 about the state of branches in the region that "15 area groups have been established in areas around Durban. Areas like Stanger, Port Shepstone, and Empangeni are proving to be difficult due to the lack of transport". During the first six months of 1991, the Eastern Cape region created its own finance, working and political committees, and established an interim district committee in Uitenhage, disbanding the one in Port Elizabeth, and setting in motion the process for the creation of others for Grahamstown and the surrounding areas, the Midlands around Cradock, and Tsitsikamma in the Graaff Reinet area. Branch after branch was mushrooming across the region. By contrast, the Western Cape was not progressing as impressively as the Eastern Cape. The region reported in July 1991 "the lack of significant progress, particularly in the rural areas".[17]

Problems varied from region to region. They ranged from "losing support among Indians and Coloureds" in KwaZulu-Natal and the Western Cape; the "need to reflect our social composition at leadership level" in the Western Cape; violence in KwaZulu-Natal; "poor organisation of branch meetings" in the Eastern Cape; and the fact that the 'Transvaal' covered a very large area, stretching beyond to the Free State and the Northern Cape.[18] Nonetheless, between January and November 1991 the number jumped from 5 000 to 21 000 members, but this was still below the 30 000 target set for 1991. Thanks to this astronomical growth in membership, 414 delegates representing 300 branches based in eight regions across the country were to attend the 8th Congress that was to take place in December 1991.[19]

Trying to generate money from the propaganda organs of the Party, the *African Communist* and *Umsebenzi*, had its own difficulties. For instance, it was reported to the ILG of end May that "8 000 [copies] given to COSATU, [but] not a single copy sold". For their part, regions were required "to state what no [number] of *Umsebenzi*s they can sell", and a call made for the "need for an accurate honest assessment". In this regard, the Southern Natal region reported to the ILG of 21 July 1991 that: "Sale of party publications is still very low. We have not as yet established an effective distribution network. We have asked comrades to write articles for AC [*African Communist*] and *Umsebenzi* but have not received any contribution".[20]

As to the alliance, the ILG of end May 1991 observed that the mechanism was "working more effectively than ever before", and that "this year the Alliance as a structure has made the most significant impact on the policy of the movement as a whole".[21] However, the same could not be said for the regions. For instance, the Southern Natal region observed in July 1991 that "the Alliance in this region has not met in the last few months. Nobody takes responsibility for convening Alliance meetings".[22] In the Western Cape, around the same period, "progress has been registered in building the Alliance at an executive level. However this does not include reaching consensus on key tactical and strategic questions facing the Alliance in the region." Indeed, the ILG had observed at its May meeting a "worrying aspect of growing tensions between members of the ANC Regional Executive Committee (REC) and members of the Party" in the Western Cape, and a decision was taken "to look into and emphasise the role of the Alliance" in that region. In the Transkei region, it was reported around the same period about the alliance that "no meeting has been held up to now. Settings for it had been disrupted time and again by various issues…" In the Eastern Cape region, it was reported, "activities of the Alliance are very minimal".[23]

Greater attention was given to the organisation of women into Party structures, and regions were required to report on this aspect of their work. As a consequence, in the Eastern Cape, between two and four women were elected to leadership structures across the region to substantial positions of organiser, secretary, and political commissar. A popular front of 22 women's organisations, including the Party, was created in the Western Cape. In Phiri, a township in Soweto in the Transvaal region, women were the core of the Party membership.[24]

The fact that the Party, as it prepared for the Congress, was moving away from the exile organisational model to a 'mass party', did not enjoy unanimous support across Party structures. Gwala, considered a hardliner by some in the Party and the man that Maharaj was prepared to trade his membership of the Party for the inclusion of his name in the ILG, referred to the new type of Party as an "amorphous mass".[25] Nor was the Party moving forward as a cohesive force following the quiet resignation of many of its CC members. This led to the PB members who were at the Lusaka meeting breaking into two groups: those who remained in the Party, such as Slovo, Hani and Kasrils, and the three – Mbeki, Zuma and Pahad – who were at neither the Troyeville PB meeting nor the rally, and would eventually leave the Party. Moreover, the departure from the Party of this group was not a painless affair. Differences between the two groups persisted throughout the 1990–94 transition, affecting the negotiations and the alignment of forces within the ANC. To be sure, differences between the two groups were not only over whether to go public or not about one's Party membership; there were other related factors. On the one hand, the bond of friendship between Mbeki and Zuma was very strong. According to Zuma's biographer Jeremy Gordin, "Zuma and Mbeki were almost joined at the hip; they operated as a team…"[26] On the other hand, Mbeki and Hani were perceived as competitors for succession to the throne of the ANC. Zuma touched on this matter in his interview of August 1993: "When we were still abroad [exile] those two names always emerged from the press. It was nothing new really and the press has always said Thabo is the successor, there is a competition between Thabo and Chris".[27] Another issue that caused the schism between the two groups was over the concept of the Party. As shown elsewhere, Mbeki was known to be a proponent of the 'Party of Kotane' concept, that is, a Party that worked quietly under the leadership of the ANC. Slovo, by contrast, argued for a very active and independent Party and this, indeed, was a thorny issue in exile as Oliver Tambo never concealed his preference for the Party of Kotane.[28]

Six months before the 8th Congress, the ANC held its National Conference in July 1991 in Durban, the first in the country in over three decades, where Mandela was elected president and Cyril Ramaphosa secretary general. The conference became a playing ground for the realignment of groupings in the liberation movement. On the one hand were the groupings which had their roots in the SACP between those around Slovo and Hani and those associated with Mbeki and Zuma. The other area of realignment was between the exile group and the non-exiles from the UDF, trade unions and other MDM formations. The election of Ramaphosa as secretary general at the expense of exile stalwart Alfred Nzo became possible thanks to the strong backing and support he received from the Slovo-Hani group. Ramaphosa's election was a defeat for the Mbeki group, and Zuma could only settle for the position of deputy to Ramaphosa. According to Ramaphosa's biographer Anthony Butler, "The decisive factor in overcoming Ramaphosa's reluctance to stand [for ANC secretary general position] was that leaders of the SACP had asked him to do so... SACP support came close to the guarantee of success he required".[29] Zuma's biographer also pondered this matter: "Ramaphosa? Where had he come from? Why wasn't Zuma the SG?", and pointed the finger at Slovo: "there was... agreement that Alfred Nzo, the incumbent SG, needed to be replaced by someone younger and more dynamic. Zuma said he would stand against Nzo. Zuma was effectively Mbeki's 'deputy'... So Slovo and the fellows looked around for someone they preferred to oppose Zuma... They came up with Ramaphosa..."[30]

If there is anything this conference is still remembered for it is the tension between Mbeki and Hani over the position of deputy president of the ANC. What caused the tension was that when Hani got to know of Mbeki's intention to run for the position, he then made himself available, vowing not "to serve under Thabo".[31] To settle the dust, the two were persuaded to step aside in favour of a veteran in the form of Walter Sisulu.[32] The conference was not the last battle ground between the Slovo-Hani and Mbeki-Zuma groups for influence in the ANC.

The 8th Congress, the first in the country since that of 1962 which had adopted the *Road to South African Freedom*, met under challenging circumstances. Firstly, at the international level, the collapse of the socialist bloc was a recent memory, and this created a crisis over the future and understanding of socialism. The Congress had to ponder this question, and define what socialism meant for post-apartheid South Africa. Secondly, while the Party membership had increased astronomically from about 2 000 around the time of the unbanning to some 25 000, over 90% of participants at the Congress were new members. This would have implications for the depth and quality of Party membership during the post-apartheid transition. And as a significant number of CC members elected at the 7th Congress had now left the Party, it meant that the CC elected at the 8th Congress would reflect the changing character of the Party and its membership. Finally, the Congress took place as the country was bracing itself for the first sitting of the multi-party negotiation forum so, inevitably, the Congress had to reflect on this matter.[33]

At the 8th Congress Slovo returned to his previous position as chairperson, and Hani was elected the general secretary. Other CC members elected included Charles Nqakula as deputy general secretary, as well as additional members, such as Jeremy Cronin, Kasrils, Chris Dlamini, Sydney Mufamadi, John Gomomo, Billy Nair, John Nkadimeng, Blade Nzimande, Essop Pahad, Fraser-Moleketi, Raymond Suttner, Sam Shilowa, Govan Mbeki, Thenjiwe Mtintso, and Jenny Schreiner.[34] Dlamini, Gomomo and Shilowa were among the important voices in the COSATU leadership at the time.

The Congress reviewed *Path to Power* and adopted a new programme – *Manifesto of the South African Communist Party: Building Workers' Power for Democratic Change* – an outcome of a very heated debate on the meaning of communism due to the collapse of the former socialist bloc. Even though Slovo was unsuccessful in his attempt to argue for 'democratic socialism' at the Congress, the *Manifesto* shifted from the optimism that characterised both the 1962 programme and *Path to Power*, by acknowledging the international conditions unfavourable for the struggle for socialism. This was achieved not without some difficulty, as was acknowledged four years later: "it is no secret (we made no secret of it) that there were many inner-Party tensions, differences and uncertainties – the rejection, by the 1991 Congress, of the main slogan of the Congress 'Forward to Democratic Socialism' was just one indicator".[35] While the concept of negotiation was developed further, including the notion of the 'strategic initiative' that the liberation movement had to maintain during the negotiations, the *Manifesto* failed to propose, in detail, an alternative form of socialism in its critique of 'distorted socialism'.

Admittedly, there was continuity in thinking in the *Manifesto* on the negotiations with what was put forward in both the *Road to South African Freedom* and the *Path to Power*. The programme also tried to begin to tackle issues related to governance, such as the need for a 'growth strategy'.

As to the issue of membership, with branches and districts replacing exile-days units and regions as organs of the Party, the new constitution, an amendment of the one adopted at the 6<sup>th</sup> Congress in 1984, revised the recruitment policy and did away with the probation system, thus converting the SACP into a 'mass' Party.[36]

The election of Hani to the position of general secretary at the Congress was a big catch for the Party which needed a person of Hani's calibre and popularity to carry the Party through the political transition in the country.[37] According to Cronin: "The public face increasingly of the SACP after his election as General Secretary at the end of 1991 was Chris Hani and he, I think more than any other alliance leader, moved tirelessly through mass meeting after mass meeting, small village meetings, activists' meeting and so forth week after week, more of that, more mobilisational work than anyone and it clearly redounded hugely to the credit of the SACP in the first place but to the movement more broadly". For Cronin, Hani "had a unique combination of solid credentials, the revolutionary track record and a credibility which few have".[38]

To his critics who thought his decision to accept the Party position was going to cost him politically, especially in the ANC's succession race, Hani's response was that this step in his life "has got something to do with my own history and the history of my participation in the struggle. I came into the movement from the ranks." He continued that: "...I have always enjoyed being involved physically in building the movement in organisation. It is true that I have been re-elected into the National Executive Committee of the ANC, probably receiving the highest votes, which was an indication of the people's confidence in me as part of the ANC leadership". He had observed that: "Strangely many people have said that I am one of the heir apparent. I have never considered myself as an heir apparent. I thought that when the Communist Party needed somebody, I should assist for the simple reason that, I see the Communist Party, despite what has happened in other parts of the world, as a key vehicle in empowering the ordinary working people in South Africa, especially the black workers..."[39]

Despite this explanation, his decision did not enjoy the support of many cadres on the ground. James Ngculu recounted how this decision was received in the ranks of Umkhonto we Sizwe (MK):

> ...it became clear that we were going to lose Chris Hani as Chief of Staff of MK. It was obvious that he was keen to take over the post of General Secretary of the SACP. At the Venda conference [of MK] delegates had expressed their opposition to the redeployment of Chris to the SACP, and people strenuously pleaded with Chris not to leave MK. Others even felt that if push came to shove, he should hold both posts. However this was an untenable suggestion, though it was a clear indication of the desire to retain Chris as army Chief of Staff. Those of us who knew Chris and had intimate discussion with him realised that it was no longer helpful to plead with him not to take the post because he had made up his mind after a lot of soul-searching. Thus, MK lost Chris. However, for many months thereafter his office at SACP headquarters received visits from thousands of MK members. Chris was unable to turn people away.[40]

For Zuma, speaking in August 1993, Hani took his decision well aware of its implications: "He made his own decision. People should have known. He was asked not to go, the ANC wanted him to stay. The army, MK, wanted him to stay. He made his decision and went to lead the Party. So why to think that he was still interested in the succession..."[41] Zuma was of the view that when Hani accepted the Party's general secretary position, he ruled himself out of the succession race in the ANC because, to borrow his biographer's formulation, he could not serve 'two masters'.

The 8th Congress formalised Party regions into ten, namely: Eastern Cape, Border, Eastern Transvaal, Natal Midlands, Orange Free State, PWV (Pretoria, Johannesburg, and the Vaal), Southern

Natal, Transkei, Western Cape, and Western Transvaal. The leadership that had emerged out of regional congresses and the 8th Congress was drawn from the exile and UDF/MDM streams of the liberation movement. Regional leaders, such as Smuts Ngonyama, January Masilela, Ben Martins, Jabu Moleketi, Loretta Jacobs, Mpho Scott, Nomvula Mokonyana, Dumisani Makhanya, Gwede Mantashe, Trevor Oosterwyk, Fred Carneson, and Lizo Nkonki, and those elected to the CC, such as Thenjiwe Mtintso, Ronnie Kasrils, Essop Pahad, Jenny Schreiner, Charles Nqakula and Kay Moonsamy, were all set for a mixed future in post-apartheid South Africa. Others were to pass away under tragic circumstances, while others were to occupy senior positions in the high echelons of the democratic government.[42] Indeed, some of these leaders were to leave the Party voluntarily and involuntarily for another role in post-apartheid South Africa. One such leader is Smuts Ngonyama who is now a member of the Congress of the People (COPE), a political party that broke away from the ANC. And Dumisane Makhanya and Jabu Moleketi, as shown later, would be among the most vocal critics of the Party.

The challenge after the 8th Congress was to consolidate the organisational and membership growth the Party had experienced in the two years since the unbanning. To that end, a party-building workshop was held in early February 1992 at the University of Fort Hare in the Eastern Cape to take stock of the organisational state of the Party.[43] While the Party's financial policies were to be strengthened and formalised, the organisational situation on the ground varied from region to region. It was noted at the party-building workshop that: "There was a common trend permeating Party building in all the regions, where recruitment was not methodical and branches were unable to sustain their membership". In areas such as the PWV, district structures presided over very weak branches. Some regions were affected by political violence, while others, such as the Border, were constrained by the repressive Bantustan machinery of the Ciskei regime. The Western Transvaal region where the core membership was drawn from the working class in the main was weakened by retrenchments that were taking place on the mines in the area.[44] It was felt that the Party, in its recruitment, must target primarily the working class, linking with trade union structures in the process. The intelligentsia was another target group, and so were women, who continued to receive dedicated attention thanks to the influence of CC members such as Thenjiwe Mtintso.

Financial resources remained a constraint across regions, some having no petty cash at all, nor an office to operate from, nor fund-raising activities or a financial structure. Accordingly, the party-building workshop recommended a joining fee of R2 and a monthly subscription of R1. Other fund-raising activities considered included jumble sales, concerts, film shows, cake sales, Christmas and New Year parties, and bazaars.[45]

On the ideological front, political education continued to occupy an important place in the Party, a political education school even being considered as well as night schools. The position of a full-time political education coordinator was in the pipeline. In the PWV region, for instance, political education activities centred around 'campaigns', cadre development, and topical issues, such as negotiations and the anticipated elections for a democratic government. The Natal Midlands, for its part, established its own Moses Mabhida Party School which, among other things, ran workshops for its members on economic issues and to impart critical skills in administration, organising, and propaganda work. The Eastern Cape set up a regional commissariat comprised of branch representatives that developed a three-year political education programme.[46]

The vanguard role of the Party was not to be abandoned but, if anything, escalated. The party-building workshop generated ideas in this area, including that "the Party should intervene decisively in the theoretical and ideological struggles as the leading force for socialism in our motherland". The Party was urged to "establish commissions and committees to deal with topical matters like the economy, land, [and] social welfare". Furthermore, "the Party should… establish strongholds in the various regions to provide political leadership to all other structures there, including those within the Tripartite Alliance".[47]

'Campaigns', which referred to mass mobilisation activities, became an important feature of Party work, targeting socio-economic issues such as hunger, health and housing; general issues related to the negotiations, like the call for the Constituent Assembly and the Interim Government; and those touching on international matters like the campaign for the lifting of the United States-imposed embargo on Cuba. Accordingly, at the party-building workshop "regions were asked to draw up programmes... to galvanise support around the Hunger Campaign... to culminate on Budget Day... with massive national demonstrations".[48] The Border region reported to the CC meeting of 25 January 1992 on Campaigns that: "We celebrated the Great October Socialist Revolution by holding district workshops as well as by holding... an indoor rally at Gompo Hall, East London... the Party also participated in the campaign leading up to the 30th anniversary of MK".[49]

Negotiations were the central preoccupation of the Party during this period.

# 10
# Negotiations

ONE OF HANI'S FIRST ACTS as general secretary was to speak on behalf of the Party on 20 December 1991 at the inaugural plenary session of the Convention for a Democratic South Africa (CODESA), a multi-party forum for negotiating the road to and content of post-apartheid South Africa. The CODESA process comprised plenary sessions and four Working Groups, and ran until May 1992 when the parties – mainly the ANC and the government – deadlocked over constitutional issues.

At the inaugural session of CODESA, or CODESA I, Hani acknowledged that "the SACP, in alliance with the ANC and COSATU has grasped the first opportunity that has arisen as a result of our struggles to secure a negotiated settlement of the apartheid conflict", and that "the CODESA process is a victory for our people! We believe that it is our responsibility as a vanguard organization of the working class, together with our allies, to pursue this process with the utmost vigour." He also made it "clear that we are not mesmerized by the whole process. We want it to succeed and get on track and remain on track. But that is not our only preoccupation. We are in this process because we want it to lead to a democratic result. We are in this process because there are a majority of South Africans who do not have a say in the rules governing their own lives. We are in this process because there are millions of South Africans who need a new government that will listen to their needs." The SACP, according to Hani, "want this process to succeed because without a new constitution there can be no peace. Peace must be based on a secure foundation, on a lasting constitution enjoying overwhelming support of the majority of our people. Such a new constitution must also provide the framework within which this society can be transformed from a paradise for a small minority and misery for most others, to one where all enjoy peace and social justice." For the SACP, continued Hani, "these are our broad goals, but how do we proceed from here? We believe, with the ANC, that it is essential that this meeting emerges with decisions that are enforceable, that we are all bound by these decisions."[1]

From this perspective, and with this agenda in mind, the Party would participate actively in the negotiations process. The Party's position during the 1990–94 transition, especially with regard to negotiations, created a heated debate both within the organisation and outside. The *African Communist*, in the editorial of its 3rd quarter issue of 1990, tried to tackle the problem of negotiations and compromise: "To enter into discussions with the government does not in itself constitute a compromise, but compromise of one sort or another may eventually be forced upon us by circumstances. The test will be whether that compromise opens the way to the ultimate achievement of our objectives, and whether the alternative to compromise would constitute a setback for the revolutionary cause".[2]

The Party was active in the 'talks about talks' during the transition to the negotiations and the multi-party talks themselves. The 'talks about talks' took the form of two meetings between the ANC and the government of May 1990 and August of that year, which resulted in the *Groote Schuur Minute* and the *Pretoria Minute*. These meetings laid the ground for CODESA I which began on 20 December 1991 and CODESA II of May 1992, the *Record of Understanding* concluded between the ANC and the government in September 1992, as well as the gathering of the Multi-Party Negotiating Forum which began its proceedings on 1 April 1993. This four-year negotiation process had to survive not only the assassination of Hani in April 1993, but also the 'rolling mass action' and political violence which took thousands of human lives all over the country.

Notwithstanding the meetings that Mandela held with representatives of the apartheid state while he was in prison, the first formal contact between the ANC and the government which took place in Cape Town on 4 May 1990 and gave birth to the historic *Groote Schuur Minute*, was preceded by a series of informal, preparatory engagements between an ANC team, led by Mbeki, and the government's intelligence service agents. Mbeki worked in the main with Aziz Pahad and Zuma – and all were still members of the CC and the PB, even though they were acting under the directives of ANC president Oliver Tambo. For the Groote Schuur and Pretoria meetings, and the gatherings of CODESA and the Multi-party Negotiating Forum, Slovo and, to a lesser extent, Kasrils, were other Party members who were at the helm of the ANC's negotiations structures.

Maharaj, another important player, was deployed as the co-head of the joint secretariat of CODESA. But, like Mbeki, Aziz Pahad and Zuma, he had formally left the Party by the time of CODESA and the subsequent negotiations. However, and this also applied to Mbeki, Pahad and Zuma, he had not left the Party because of a fundamental disagreement over ideology or critical organisational issues. He left because of the issue he had with Gwala and his personal problems with Slovo.[3] In theory, if the differences over Gwala and the positioning of the legal Party had been amicably resolved, perhaps all four would have continued as Party members, maybe even still be serving on the CC and the PB.[4] Unfortunately, this did not happen. In fact, the divisions between the Slovo and the Mbeki groups spilt over into the negotiations and the ANC.

The two groups jostled for influence and control over the ANC's negotiation structure, the Negotiation Commission. Mbeki had led the process from its inception in the late 1980s when very few in the ANC and the SACP leadership believed in negotiations. However, after the 1991 conference of the ANC, with Ramaphosa elected secretary general, Mbeki was removed in what observers described as a 'palace coup' or 'putsch', by Ramaphosa while he, Mandela and Zuma were out of the country.[5] Ramaphosa's ascendency, with the support of the Slovo group, meant that the role as chief negotiator was taken away from Mbeki. The seriousness of the tension between the two groups was no small matter as is evidenced by what Sydney Mufamadi told Mbeki's biographer, Mark Gevisser, about what happened at the ANC's 1991 national conference when Mbeki was given a standing ovation by delegates in response to his intervention during the debate on sanctions. Gevisser recounted: "Mufamadi was seated next to Slovo and Kasrils. 'What do you think?' he asked them. They were convinced. Given their militant profiles, however, they drew the line at applause. 'They were still afraid to associate themselves with this moderate – they did not stand up".[6]

Of course, there were issues of strategy and tactics, and the approach to the negotiations, over which Mbeki and Slovo differed. Gevisser explained: "Mbeki's primary detractors were fellow-exiles: mistrust of him had developed in exile, particularly among the senior leadership of the SACP. And now, the way he led a faction out of the SACP in July 1990 was further proof, to them, that he was not to be trusted, ideologically or politically". As to Slovo, continued Gevisser: "That internal leaders such as Ramaphosa found themselves instinctively closer to the Slovo/Hani group than to Mbeki had less to do with ideology than with style. Anxious, themselves, about the fate of their exhilarating, edgy experiment in popular democracy that had arisen out of the 1980s, they saw in Mbeki's exclusiveness the embodiment of the hierarchical and authoritarian ANC in exile. In contrast, Slovo and Hani's new, above-ground SACP became a vehicle for mass-based militancy".[7]

Nor was Ramaphosa hostile to the Party. If anything, he had tried to join the Party by being recruited through Maharaj, but his application was turned down on security grounds, and his biographer put the blame squarely on Zuma, who is accused of having instigated the conspiracy to deny Ramaphosa the prestige and privileges of Party membership.[8]

There is even a dispute between the biographers of Ramaphosa and Mbeki about the comparative role and contribution of the two men to the negotiations process. Gevisser blamed the deadlock at CODESA II on Ramaphosa's style of negotiation. He suggested that: "Ramaphosa played his intensely dangerous game of brinkmanship, forcing a break-down by making a final offer that he knew his opponents would refuse". And rightly so: "Mbeki was horrified", wrote Gevisser, because "he would have found a way of framing an offer with language vague enough to take the process to another level".[9] By contrast, Ramaphosa's biographer, Anthony Butler, taking from Tim Cohen, divided the period of the negotiations into "before Cyril and after Cyril". After going to some length to acknowledge the contributions of Mbeki, Zuma, Slovo and the others, as well as the comparative strength of each of these individuals, Butler summed up his reading of the ANC negotiation team: "The most complex and contested parts of the formal processes were inevitably led by Ramaphosa. His negotiating skills were of a higher order than those of his colleagues, and he retained the ability to manage the mood and the agenda of the discussion at will."[10]

Perhaps the complexities on the ground were less individualised than is suggested by the two biographers. No doubt: the two men played their role, and decisively so. But critical was the role of others such as Maharaj who anchored the administrative machinery of the negotiations at CODESA and post-CODESA multi-party talks; Zuma who criss-crossed the country, especially KwaZulu-Natal, quelling the fires of violence; and many cadres who ran up and down the corridors of the negotiations, drafting documents, researching ideas, and working in ANC and SACP branches. The success of the negotiations could not have been due to the brilliance of a single individual. In fact, Kasrils had a point when he joked with some members of the government's negotiating team at the beginning of CODESA that "the government and Vula are running the ball" because, as he explained, "Mac Maharaj was the co-head of the overall administration. Janet Love worked at his side. Pravin Gordhan was a co-chair of the Management Committee. Mo Shaik headed the Indian Congress delegation in our commission".[11] What he omitted, of course for obvious reasons, is that the same individuals were all involved with the Tongaat meeting of the SACP.

There were, however, moments where the contribution of an individual led to a decisive breakthrough, and Mbeki and Slovo came out on top in this regard. Mbeki led the thinking on negotiations, including the strategy, when the process began. Some of his ideas, like the two-stage transitional arrangement in the form of the Transitional Executive Council and a Government of National Unity, made the leap to post-apartheid South Africa possible.[12] But it is Slovo's contribution that is most often singled out because he is credited with having convinced the ANC to offer to suspend unilaterally the armed struggle as part of the *Pretoria Minute*. His 'sunset clause' proposals gave the negotiations process the needed momentum.

From the beginning of the talks, the government was uncomfortable with the involvement of Slovo who, to them, symbolised the 'communist plot' that they feared and loathed. At the Mbeki meeting with the government's national intelligence in preparation for the Groote Schuur gathering, one of the issues discussed, among other thorny matters the two parties had to clear off the road, was the participation of Slovo. Niel Barnard, leading the government side, thought that would not be a problem. But when he consulted De Klerk by phone that evening, the apartheid president raved about how he was not going to sit around the table with communists, and only gave in after persuasion from Barnard.[13] As shown already, the issue came up again towards the *Pretoria Minute* following the discovery of the Tongaat documents by the apartheid security forces. All in all, the Party's participation in the talks was something the government would have wished to avoid, but only conceded because they needed the ANC as a partner in the negotiations. Eugene Louw, then a minister in the apartheid government, spoke for his side on this matter in 1991 is his response to the question: "Do you think that the ANC is more or less controlled at the leadership level by the SACP?" His reply was that:

> Yes, there is a very strong element of communism involved there. They play a very important role… I think the SACP would like to bring about an uprising among the black people whom they could convert to their ideology. They probably find that the easiest way for them to get people together is to spread the gospel of communism, that is my summary of it… For you to gain control over SA it is necessary for all to get together and nationalise everything and take over the western civilisation and replace it by the communist ideology.[14]

Slovo was not the only target of the onslaught from the government. In August 1990, at the height of the Vula frenzy, the government, as part of its anti-communist onslaught, withdrew the temporary indemnity that it had granted Kasrils, Maharaj and Hani to enable them to participate in the 'talks about talks'. Similarly, in October 1992, Kobie Coetsee, De Klerk's justice minister, said that "the ANC would be well advised to sever its links with the Communist Party, and especially one Mr Hani".[15]

This aside, Slovo's role during the negotiations was indeed more than simply being key to the engineering of Ramaphosa to the position of chief negotiator. Just before the beginning of the NEC meeting to prepare for the Pretoria meeting of August 1990, Slovo approached Mandela with the proposal that the ANC should offer to unilaterally suspend the armed struggle so as to give the apartheid side something to sell to their constituency and some confidence in the process. Mandela was initially unconvinced, but later relented upon further reflection on the proposal. The idea was presented to the NEC by Slovo and adopted.[16] That is how the ANC came to suspend the armed struggle. Apparently, Mbeki had floated the idea several years before Slovo but it never became the ANC official position.[17] Either way, the suspension of the armed struggle created controversy in the ranks of the liberation movement but nonetheless demonstrated to the government the commitment of the ANC to the negotiations. Arguably, it made a huge contribution, giving movement to 'talks about talks'.

The second idea attributed to Slovo is about the sunset clause proposal that helped unlock the negotiations. Even here, Mandela gives Slovo credit for the idea even though Mbeki had made a similar proposal earlier and the same Slovo had led the charge against it.[18] With Slovo now converted, he packaged the idea into the article 'Negotiations: What Room for Compromise?', wherein he proposed a set of compromises, including sunset clauses, amnesty, and power-sharing provisions, which could be put forward by ANC negotiators, for unblocking and advancing the negotiations.[19] According to Slovo there were "certain retreats from previously held positions which would create the possibility of a major positive breakthrough in the negotiating process without *permanently* hampering real democratic advance" (emphasis original).[20] The response from within the Party was divided between those who supported Slovo, such as Jeremy Cronin and Raymond Suttner, and those who argued against him, such as Jordan and Gwala. The response of the latter group concentrated on three areas, namely: the relationship between strategy and tactic, and that Slovo had elevated negotiations to strategy; the lack of consultation in the development of the compromises in question; and the role of struggle and the masses themselves during the course of the negotiations.[21] As for the academic Left, the overwhelming view was that the SACP had shifted to the right – that the SACP had abandoned 'insurrection' and revolutionary change of society in favour of reforms.[22] Whatever the verdict on Slovo's proposal, it helped unlock the process.

Slovo explained how his proposal got to be accepted by the NEC of the ANC:

> Well I published the paper in the *African Communist* and it was given wide publicity in the daily press. That triggered off quite a heated discussion throughout the ranks and the ideas contained in the paper were then presented to the National Working Committee of the ANC which had before it, not my paper, but a draft which covered quite a few of the points I dealt with in my paper. That was debated, I think at two meetings. It was then, on the basis of the debate, redrafted, adopted by the National Working Committee and then placed before a full meeting of the National Executive which then adopted the amended draft. So that was the process.[23]

He tried to downplay the involvement of the Party in pushing his sunset clause proposal through ANC structures. When he was asked the question: "The SACP and COSATU, have they as organisations formally endorsed the strategic perspective?", his response was "I'm not sure", and that:

> I know there's been a conference or a Central Committee meeting of the Party but I would say by and large it is accepted. For example, there was a regional conference of the PWV region of the Party which broadly speaking accepted the main content of the strategic perspective. So the issue is still being

discussed in a way. It is policy, it's policy adopted by the NEC of the ANC. It's still up for discussion at grassroots level and regions are continuing to debate it and to discuss it. Until it is changed it remains policy. But by and large the impression I have both within the ANC at the regional level and within the allied organisations, maybe they don't agree, I wouldn't claim that everyone agrees with every sentence, but the broad thrust of the document I believe is accepted.[24]

However, Cronin was not that modest in acknowledging the role played by the Party in getting the ANC to adopt Slovo's proposal. He told Padraig O'Malley in August 1993 that Slovo's proposal was "pushed by the Party, by Joe [Slovo] and the Party caucus".[25]

The other SACP personality worth singling out in this context is Gwala who, together with Winnie Mandela, Peter Mokaba, Bantu Holomisa and Hani, constituted what some considered the 'hawks' in the ANC. As shown in the author's chapter on the SACP in the 1980s, Gwala was in no way a stranger to controversy.[26] With the violence in KwaZulu-Natal and the intransigence of the Inkatha Freedom Party leader, Gasha Buthelezi, the outcomes of the negotiations were never a certainty. Buthelezi remained a serious threat and an obstacle to the transition to the post-apartheid order right up to the last days leading to the founding elections. And as Maharaj's case demonstrated, Gwala was considered in some ANC and SACP circles part of the KwaZulu-Natal problem.

Nor was Gwala convinced of a negotiated settlement to the South African question, let alone Slovo's sunset clause. As he put it in response to the question about Slovo's sunset proposal: "I would be happier if before negotiations resume [after the collapse of CODESA] if we, as the NEC, called a special consultative conference of the organisation and get a mandate from the people themselves, the constituencies. I will not be happy to go with a thing which is not receiving the majority support like this one which has been rejected by some regions among them Southern Natal, all the regions of Natal have not gone along with this Strategic Perspective and I believe the other regions have criticised this very strenuously".[27] His controversial role was to earn him a six month suspension by the Party, his membership reinstated in the months before his death in June 1995. "There had been serious allegations of sectarian behaviour in the Midlands region, and we had failed to secure comrade Gwala's co-operation in trying to get to the bottom of the allegations", the Party leadership explained the basis for the suspension.[28]

Charles Nqakula, Hani's successor as the Party general secretary, described Gwala as "Man of Steel" in his tribute to him: "I like to believe that the SACP... made a very important contribution to the negotiated transition in our country. If we did make such a contribution, it was only because we had comrades of the calibre of Joe Slovo and Harry Gwala who, as communists and loyal ANC members, were prepared to go toe-to-toe against each other in public debate. Neither of them settled into backroom manoeuvres against the other".[29]

Frustrated and with little to show out of the negotiations, and following the killing of 46 people in Boipatong by the Inkatha Freedom Party members in June 1992, the ANC decided on 'rolling mass action' in the form of protest marches, strikes, stay-aways and boycotts, not only as a show of force, but also to put pressure on the apartheid government. The Boipatong incident led the ANC to walk out of the negotiations, resulting in the collapse of CODESA.[30] Between the collapse of CODESA in June 1992 and the Bisho massacre of September the same year, temperatures ran high in the streets across the country. This of course was exacerbated by the ANC accusing the government of complicity in the political violence.

Even though there was an alliance machinery for coordination and exchange of views on the 'rolling mass action', there were nonetheless divergent views on strategy and tactics. Hani gave a sense of the intensity of debates in the alliance in his interview with O'Malley on 15 July 1992: "You must remember that we are an Alliance, the ANC, the Party and COSATU and that we are discussing with a number of groups and formations in this country who are expressing their own concerns, the churches, the big business and other organisations. We would like to pull into mass action as many of these organisations and formations as possible, so that we really deal a blow to this stubborn, unyielding and provocative government." He told O'Malley that: "we are going to be having meetings, I think today or tomorrow, we are going to be having meetings of the Secretaries of the Tripartite Alliance, that is myself, Jay [Naidoo] and Cyril [Ramaphosa]. We will look into all this and again. What I would say, because as the weeks go by we must come up with a more coherent approach, but I am not worried about everything being put forward, that is general brainstorming, we have not begun to mix together, or to weave together common tactics and common strategies. The Alliance Campaigns Committee is meeting and is also discussing these problems."[31]

It was in this context that some leading figures of the Party publicly advocated the need to deploy mass action against the apartheid government. Hani was one such leader, even being perceived to be opposed to the negotiations. When he was asked in August 1991, in the period leading to CODESA, whether the resuscitation of the armed struggle was an option in the event the negotiations failed, he placed his hope in the role the international community could play: "I think the international community wants a settlement in South Africa. It's desperate for a settlement. And they know that it would not be in the interests of the international community if negotiations fail. I don't know what leverage the international community has on De Klerk and his government but for us, first of all, I'm referring to the ANC, the PAC, COSATU, and AZAPO [Azanian People's Organisation], would have to sit down and say, how do we pressurise the international community to exert very, very strong pressure on this government to proceed with negotiations with seriousness".[32] However, with the collapse of CODESA and at the height of the 'rolling mass action', his attitude towards the negotiations had hardened. His view in July 1992 was that: "We look back at our own failures and weaknesses in the past, we talked to De Klerk against the background of a lull and I think we saw illusions that everything would be solved at CODESA, the people must just wait and should be passive spectators, and I think that was one of the weaknesses of our negotiations strategy. We also allowed this government to play with us, to put us on a merry-go-around. We had no responses to violence, we had no responses to provocations, so that the government was doing nothing about the violence." When asked about his impression of De Klerk, his reaction was that "...to hell with him, specifically because De Klerk has never accepted a full democracy as universally accepted..." He was clear in his mind that "we are not going to return to negotiations simply to refute what happened after CODESA II, and De Klerk wants us to return to that situation".[33]

Cronin attempted to defend Hani:

> I think that what increasingly he was doing, initially his irritations were directed against negotiations in general and although he supported the decision to suspend the armed struggle he didn't do it very enthusiastically and mass audiences could associate with his lack of deep enthusiasm for it. But I think increasingly he did come to understand that we were on a negotiating terrain. He couldn't run away from that and that the problem was not that we were negotiating or that we had suspended the armed struggle but that a correct balance needed to be found between negotiating, preparing for government, and maintaining the traditions of mass democratic struggle. Increasingly his interventions became of that kind so that he became an irritation for lots of forces but above all the other side because he was not easily demonised as a Peter Mokaba or as a Harry Gwala. Chris could have gone that way, he could have become demagogic in his interventions but by and large he wasn't.[34]

Slovo would try to distinguish Hani from the Gwala-Mokaba group:

> In the case of Hani I think he was not just misunderstood but misrepresented. I think Hani was a very profound supporter of the negotiating process, he's always been so since we started the process and remained so to the end of his days. I think he regarded his own specific role with his charisma and his capacity for getting responses from people on the ground, to devote his energies on the campaign trail but not in conflict, I don't believe ever, with the negotiating process. So whether

he from time to time made the kind of noises that have been described as war talk, we've all done that in the heat of the moment after massacres and so on and so forth, but I think that doesn't describe what Hani was about. He didn't belong to that grouping. There is a small grouping like that which has been reluctant to fall in with the importance of the negotiating process. It's a question of degree really rather than basic substance.[35]

The reaction to Cronin's article on what was called the 'Leipzig option' was another case in point. In the article, published in 1992 when the negotiations were delivering little results and the pressure was on, Cronin took issue with three perspectives on mass action, namely: the 'don't rock the boat' approach to mass action which "sees the path to democratisation as depending primarily upon negotiated pacts between elites" and that the "greatest threat to democratisation comes from 'radicals' to the right and left"; the 'turning on the tap' perspective which saw mass action "as a weapon 'to bring the other side to its senses', 'to produce a change of heart'"; and the 'Leipzig way' which was a "perspective of a mass uprising that builds dual power, that over-throws an incumbent regime and replaces it with the emergent organs of popular power. It is a perspective in which the people transfer power to themselves in an insurrectionary moment".[36] The 'Leipzig way' was a model of insurrection that had played a part in the collapse of socialist regimes in Eastern Europe. Contrary to what was generally believed in the popular media, Cronin was not convinced of the practicality of the 'Leipzig way' perspective. His preference, at the time of the writing of his article, was for an approach that was aimed, as he put it, at achieving "both a significant negotiations breakthrough and maintain mass momentum"; that is: "this means achieving a difficult balance between effective mobilisation to achieve at least partial breaks, while not raising unrealistic (and therefore ultimately demobilising) expectations about what any particular breakthrough might deliver".[37] Cronin would revise some of his ideas on this subject,[38] but when he was asked in July 1992, "You talked about the boat people who would be like the Thabos [Mbeki]?", his reply was "I wouldn't identify names, but yes".[39]

For its part, the government saw 'mass action' in negative terms, as proof of the SACP's determination to scuttle the negotiations. This was clear in De Klerk's reply to Mandela after the collapse of CODESA:

> ...the use of this kind of mass mobilisation to make and impose demands in the negotiation process is just as unacceptable as the use of violence for this purpose. Our information indicates that the SACP and COSATU have played a dominant role in redirecting the ANC from negotiations to the politics of demands and confrontation which are inherent in mass mobilisation.
>
> Insurrectionist thinking is currently flourishing within the ANC and is being propagated by a cabal with close links to the SACP and COSATU. These elements undermine the attempts of many ANC realists to negotiate in good faith and also induce within the ANC the spirit of radicalism and militancy of the insurrectionist school, which was evident at the SACP's 8th congress in 1991.
>
> The ANC/SACP have been trying to create the impression that they and the South African Government are the only adversaries... The ANC's rhetoric has been radicalised and is now virtually indistinguishable from that of the SACP...[40]

To be sure, some elements in the regime's security establishment fed their leadership at the top with fabricated information aimed at reinforcing the myth of an impending 'Leipzig option' as part of the Red Plot scare. How they manipulated the Tongaat documents was one case in point but certainly not the last attempt. Again, at CODESA, in the deliberations of Working Group 1 which was charged with tackling the question of political violence and intimidation, Hernus Kriel, the justice minister, replied to criticisms levelled by delegates against his government with what he thought was a 'top secret', high quality intelligence, pulled out from one of his files: "On December 4, 1991 at a meeting of the South African Communist Party in a

Hillbrow hotel, Walter Sisulu said that 'for every township resident killed we must respond by killing 10 policemen'. Chris Hani said that 'if MK is not integrated into the SADF we must begin killing SADF soldiers'. And Jay Naidoo said that 'when we get to power the first thing we must do is ban Inkatha'."[41] As it turned out, and to his embarrassment, the information was a fabrication. The event in question was not even a formal gathering, but a cocktail party hosted by the Party for its international guests who were in the country to attend the 8th Congress. Moreover, neither Walter Sisulu nor Jay Naidoo was in attendance. The support for the negotiations that the Party expressed in its statements was not for public posturing; it was genuine and sincere as reflected in the circular Hani sent out to regions in February 1992 in his capacity as the general secretary: "As you are aware, the SACP is committed to the negotiations process and supports the present talks at CODESA."[42]

It was with the massacre in Bisho, Ciskei, in September 1992, that the 'rolling mass action' approach was on the headlines more than ever before. This is what was posted on one website in 2006 about this Bisho incident:

> In 1992, 60 000 members of the ANC were led into a direct confrontation with 500 black troops of one such homeland – Ciskei. The Ciskei Government had warned them not to cross the border. But Ronnie Kasrils, a senior member of the South African Communist Party... played a key role in leading this sea of people straight into a confrontation with the Ciskeian army. 2½ minutes of automatic gunfire by the black soldiers left 28 dead and hundreds injured. So the modus operandi was the same as at Sharpeville [in 1961], and as always, the whites were blamed for the massacre... the Ciskeian army was merely defending their position and they were not the ones attacking. This is an example of how communists and revolutionaries DELIBERATELY led people to their deaths for the sake of publicity and for fighting their war in the Western media where they would then make exaggerated claims and then take the incident out of context [emphasis original]. This

is how terrorists and communists use civilians, their deaths and suffering for propaganda purposes.

At the end of this [video] you will see a slightly smiling Ronnie Kasrils, who was the mastermind behind this slaughter. They milked it for every ounce of political gain in the world political arena.[43]

This view was not isolated at all, and was even shared quietly by some within the ANC who accused SACP leaders, notably Kasrils, of 'adventurism' and 'recklessness'. In fact, Cronin attributed the Bisho incident to proponents of the 'Leipzig option': "I think that possibly the dominant current amongst the direct participants in the Bisho thing was a kind of Leipzig option notion, not well thought through, but this idea of falling dominoes. Gqozo would go, we would take Bisho. But within the broader movement there was no consensus on any of that and so there were different versions and in the aftermath of all of that of course a lot of reassessment and, to put it politely, maybe a reinterpretation of what motivations were knocking around".[44]

The Party's CC had to respond to the barrage of criticism levelled against its members. The CC statement on 'Bisho and the anti-communist campaign', while pointing out that the "SACP reaffirms its commitment to a negotiated settlement" and that "the SACP views the future with confidence", challenged the interpretation of the Bisho incident that was making rounds in the media, and defended the role played by its members, emphasising that they participated in the march as part of the alliance leadership: "We... reject with contempt the attempt to attribute to Communists, and in particular to white Communists, decisions that were at all times collective and tri-partite in character. Those making these insinuations reveal their own innate bigotry and racism".[45] According to Charles Nqakula, the Party's general secretary after Hani, "the SACP was not the prime mover of this thing [the Bisho march]. It was discussed by the entire Alliance who said what, when and where, I would never be able to tell you, I can't quote chapter and verse of how this idea evolved. And as you saw on that day, it was the leadership of the Alliance that participated, that is why you saw a Cyril Ramaphosa from the ANC, a Chris Hani from the SACP, and John Gomomo from COSATU towards an Alliance project." In fact, he elaborated, "this kind of programme was discussed by the entire Alliance, both at the regional as well as the national level. We have a national coordinating committee, campaigns coordinating committee of the alliance, and this programme was submitted to that committee. The committee agreed and it was taken to the regions and the regions agreed. And from the Ciskei we would have gone, as you correctly say, to KwaZulu and then to Bophuthatswana as part and parcel of that programme. But it was mass action to open up for free political activity."[46]

However, a subsequent investigation of the massacre by the Goldstone Commission apportioned part of the blame to Kasrils for what was regarded as an irresponsible act on his part to have led marchers to break the razor wire, provoking the Ciskei military to open fire. The incident had a sobering effect on the leaders nonetheless, with Mandela and De Klerk signing a *Record of Understanding* a few days later in September. Ramaphosa who, according to his biographer, "almost lost his life there" and "whose mother was desperate with shock and fear" because of the Bisho incident, acknowledged that: "Bisho brought some measure of realism to bear on our mass action campaign." Similarly, Raymond Suttner, then a CC member, concurred that because of Bisho "any idea of removing the 'regime' evaporated under gunfire".[47] When the parties reconvened, post-CODESA, for another round of multi-party negotiations, the ANC was now armed with Slovo's sunset clause proposal.

The assassination of Hani in April 1993 at his home in Boksburg, tragic as it was, added another impetus to the process. Gwala described in November 1993 how he received the news of Hani's death:

> Chris Hani was an exceptional character and his popularity was next to Nelson Mandela, if not on a par with him among the youth. His assassination set the country ablaze. No-one could believe it. Many people, including leaders who had seen many of these killings broke down in tears. I remember we were in Cape Town attending a funeral when the news was broken. Tony Yengeni who broke the news just collapsed and

everyone was hysterical about what had happened because in the dark moments of our struggle Chris would always be a beacon of light and would give encouragement to everyone. His name was a household word. Everyone mentioned his name with admiration.[48]

For Tokyo Sexwale:

I think in many terms the consequences of his death could have been worse. It could have been worse had we not had a very strong leadership. The whole Alliance stood... to try to say to people hold, hold, we understand the hero (is gone), one of the best sons of this country is dead, and has been slain, but we should be circumspect in our reaction. It could have been worse in that sense, because this country could have broken up into pieces had Chris not operated within a very strong collective. Had he just been a man unto himself, a leader who fought other leaders, but because he was a leader amongst other leaders the collective was able to hold the country together.[49]

What Sexwale was referring to here was how Hani's death was leveraged by the ANC leadership, resulting in the parties agreeing on an election date. This was the central thrust of Mandela's message in his televised address to the nation after the assassination, headlined on his written text 'Nothing Will Stop Us!': "Chris Hani championed the cause of peace, trudging to every corner of South Africa calling for a spirit of tolerance among all our people. We are a nation in mourning. Our pain and anger is real. Yet we must not permit ourselves to be provoked by those who seek to deny us the very freedom Chris Hani gave his life for."[50] This was so because many believed that the assassination was the work of the 'third force' to derail the negotiations, and lead the country into a civil war.

The assassination also led to an increase in popular support for the Party and general interest in its work. Nqakula, who took over from Hani, cited a contemporary survey conducted by Markinor that suggested that the support for the Party had increased from 15%

before Hani's assassination to 22% after, and that Slovo was now the second most popular person in the black community. "...[I]n terms of our own structures and organisation on the ground", observed Nqakula, "a lot of people have shown a lot of interest in the Party and they've been joining the Party. And what is even more interesting to us, is the amount of support and solidarity we have received from white people. There have been many who have made inquiries in terms of joining the Party, particularly Afrikaners, because comrade Chris had begun to speak with white people, and in particular, Afrikaners..."; and that "what has happened is that not just people inside South Africa have now become so sympathetic to our cause, but people abroad as well".[51] Cronin made the same observation that "we've had another major influx of recruits into the party since the death of about 10 000 so we've gone from 40 000 to nearly 50 000".[52]

In another setting, an incident such as Hani's assassination would have led to a civil war; in South Africa's case, it brought the political parties and their leaders to their senses. Hani's death bequeathed to the country the election date of 27 April 1994. His assassins are still in jail, but within the Party there is a conviction that his murderers were not "acting alone".[53]

The Party's organisational machinery established after the unbanning was not a bystander during the negotiations. With the beginning of multi-party negotiations, the Party deployed some of its leading personnel in the CODESA Working Groups; regions, for their part, were urged to establish a 'negotiations forum' to feed negotiations issues to the branches and source their input, organise workshops and related activities, and advise on technical matters. Two models were adopted by the regions. Some, like the Eastern Cape, established a stand-alone forum comprised of representatives of the Regional Executive Committee, branches, and cadres with the necessary technical expertise. Others, like the Western Cape and the PWV, gave the responsibility to the REC. As it was explained in the case of the PWV region: They "moved from the position that the first task of the negotiations forum would be to ensure participation at all levels of the process of our entire membership. They felt the REC was best posted to be the structure to deal with coordination on the matter and, therefore, would be the most appropriate negotiation forum."[54] It cannot be ruled out, however, that the preference for the REC was informed by a concern to avoid establishing a structure that would compete with the REC, especially that the negotiations were the central and dominant focus of the liberation movement. Those who served on the negotiations forum stood the chance of attracting the limelight; and as negotiations were likely to result in elections and the installation of a new political dispensation, they stood a better chance of getting good positions in the new government.

At national level, the CC and the PB were kept abreast of developments at CODESA, including progress in the Working Groups. This information was, from time to time, conveyed to the regions, including through the use of *Umsebenzi* and the *African Communist*. Party positions were developed on each of the issues on the negotiating table. One such issue was on traditional leadership, and the position that was taken on the matter was informed by a paper developed by Blade Nzimande who was to become the general secretary of the Party in 1998.[55] The position that the Party delegation took to CODESA's Working Group 2 on constitutional issues was that while the SACP "accept that provision must be made for a role for traditional leaders... such a role must however be guided by functions relating to their traditional jurisdiction", and that "there shall be no special representation of traditional leaders in the central legislative".[56] So important was this issue to the Party that Hani sent out a circular to regions on it, even attaching a copy of Nzimande's paper.[57] When it came to the future of the homelands, a subject of discussion in Working Group 4, Party structures in those parts of the country were urged to "collect data on the areas that the Party can use to challenge the puppets in those areas who push certain untenable positions at CODESA".[58] Furthermore, SACP, ANC and Transvaal and Indian Congress delegates to this Working Group agreed to meet on a weekly basis to coordinate their positions, and also engage other members of the Patriotic Front.[59] All in all, the Party had an approach and position on each of the issues that was on the negotiation table, from the Constituent Assembly to the Interim Government. But the Party's positions were in line with those taken by the ANC as there was coordination through the alliance mechanism.

But this was not a one-way equation with the Party toeing the ANC line. How Hani dealt with intra-alliance complexities during exchanges on post-apartheid constitutional arrangements in the period leading to the collapse of CODESA shows this:

> I want to take you back to CODESA talks. The 75% on the Bill of Rights was widely and comprehensively discussed by the entire line. There was a feeling that the Bill of Rights is an important document because it guarantees the human rights of individuals, prevents a situation where individuals become victims of a powerful state without protection from the courts and other mechanisms. So the Alliance felt on the Bill of Rights, there was no problem about accepting 75%. But we went to CODESA II with an agreement that we were going to press for a two thirds majority in terms of the adoption of the constitution. But as you remember there was a deadlock, the government was refusing to budge. The government was insisting that on everything, the Bill of Rights and the constitution, it should be 75%.
>
> The ANC's Constitutional Commission was meeting the other side quite a few times before CODESA II in order to break the deadlock, so that would be possible to put before CODESA II an agreement coming from the Working Group II. The government was stubborn.
>
> Then a sort of hurried up meeting was called of the Patriotic Forces in CODESA, of which I was a part as the SACP. The Party stood up very vigorously and opposed any form of concession. We said two thirds is a universally accepted standard in terms of adopting the constitution. We argued that after all that a two thirds majority is a later concession and it is going to be very difficult to get two thirds as shown by the Namibian example. It would demand a lot of work on our part in terms of mobilising the people, in terms of assuring that when elections take place for a Constituent Assembly, we actually have about 70% supporting our position and the position of our allies...

Then some of our people in the ANC as well as some components of the Patriotic Front said that let us offer 70% in order to facilitate movement forward. We were defeated when a vote was taken, so our position was defeated. But after that we went to the ANC later and we said that we are of the view that there should have been a meeting of the Tripartite Alliance before the meeting of the Patriotic Front because the Tripartite is part of the struggle in this country, and therefore it is important before you open up and not for us not to trust each other amongst ourselves. But you see, the government was foolish and it rejected that 70% and for us as the parties right now to get to the original position of 66%. We got a lot of flak from the ground from our members, both ANC and the party and COSATU, and the people were very, very critical of that concession.[60]

When he was asked the question "So, would it be fair to say that in future discussions, the SACP will not accept a 75% threshold on veto threshold for a Bill of Rights?", his response was that: "We will discuss it with our colleagues in the ANC and COSATU; we will come forward very strongly…"[61]

In fact, the Party did not get everything it wanted to see out of the negotiations. For instance, when Nqakula was asked in August 1993 about the degree of his satisfaction with the Interim Constitution which the parties had just agreed on, his response was that: "…on a scale, therefore, of 1–10, we in the Party cannot claim to be satisfied to a 50% kind of position. To us, and of course we accept that Interim Constitution, it is an Interim Constitution as far as we are concerned and the constitution makers subsequently are not going to be bound by that constitution. They may throw it out in its entirety, but it is not the kind of satisfactory measure that would have satisfied our interest in the Party. And on a scale of 1–10, therefore, I would say our registration would only be four."[62] At one CC meeting in 1993 where a presentation by Slovo on the state of negotiations was discussed, the "Central Committee congratulated the SACP negotiating team for the very significant (and widely acknowledged) role that it played in the process".

While Essop Pahad pointed out to the meeting that "the driving role of the ongoing ANC/government bilaterals (in which cde [comrade] JS [Slovo] played a leading role) was certainly an important and positive factor", for his part, Brian Bunting noted that "we have scored a major negotiations victory and the SACP has played an important role. My concern is that in the past three years the Party's independent voice on key issues like the Reserve Bank, foreign investment and nationalisation has not always been sufficiently clear or loud."[63] Even with the final Constitution which was adopted in 1996, the Party did not get everything it wanted. Nqakula spoke about this fact in October 1996 in relation to the Party's preference for a constituency-based electoral system: "The view of the SACP was constituency basis but the view of the majority of the Alliance was party lists and that is what has gone into the Constitution. But we have it on good authority that this is going to change, but for the elections it shall not have changed."[64]

# 11
# Elections and Freedom

THE ELECTIONS OF APRIL 1994 were an historic breakthrough, and many Party members were elected to sit on the benches of the post-apartheid parliament, while others, like Slovo and Kasrils, became cabinet ministers in the new, ANC-led government. For COSATU, which had deployed 20 of its leaders to the ANC's elections list, two of its members were given cabinet positions and another two were given responsibilities as chairs of parliament's portfolio committee. This period was not just the beginning of a new era for the country; SACP-ANC and intra-alliance relations were also opening another chapter. The SACP now had to deal with the ANC not just as an ally, but also as the ruling party.

The Party had to adapt both organisationally and ideologically to these changed conditions. Regions that were formalised at the 8th Congress were to give way to nine provinces that were established by the Constitution of the new South Africa. But the process was not instantaneous; for example, the provincial structures of the Free State and the North West were inaugurated in April 1996, and, in the case of the former, it was the product of the merger of the Bloemfontein and Welkom districts.[1]

Hardly a year into his portfolio as the minister of housing, Slovo died of cancer in January 1995. In paying tribute to him at the burial ceremony, Mandela spoke of Slovo as "a leader, a patriot, a father, a fighter, a negotiator, an internationalist, a theoretician and an organizer".[2] Just before Slovo's death, Jack Simons was one amongst several Party stalwarts to pass away. And others would follow: Harry Gwala, Govan Mbeki, Billy Nair, Sonia and Brian Bunting, Raymond Mhlaba, Ray Alexander Simons and Fred Carneson. As one after another of this generation of loyal party members passed on after decades of uninterrupted service to the liberation struggle, the way was opened for a new generation to take over the leadership of the Party.

It took the Party about four years to adapt to the post-apartheid period and develop its own independent profile. Initially, after the 1994 breakthrough, the Party saw itself as some sort of a watchdog; as Nqakula put it in 1995: "We are like some kind of check on the ANC". For Nqakula, "the SACP plays the role where we (advise) the ANC when they are going to be troubled, when there are problems with respect to some of the positions in the process of governance wittingly or unwittingly institute or illustrate movement away from those very important policy positions of the ANC". The Party's role, according to Nqakula, was "to ensure that the ANC in the first instance does not go astray in terms of the policies".[3] Cronin recounted an incident in July 1994 which served as a dress rehearsal for the years ahead: "After the elections there was some attention around the Party particularly in the July period when there was a round of workers' strikes and the ANC or some leading figures in the ANC, including the President, came out criticising COSATU workers, portraying them as an elite... The Party intervened, a few days went by, but we intervened quite firmly on that issue disagreeing politely with the President but disagreeing. That led to a fairly high profile moment of tension between the SACP and ANC which we succeeded in resolving."[4]

The performance and future of the Party after April 1994 is still being debated. Three views on the role of the Party in post-apartheid South Africa are worth singling out in this regard. Within the ANC, the Party came to be seen by some as an irritation because of the public stance it took on a number of issues concerning the transformation of the country, resulting in public spats conveying a picture of an alliance at the brink of collapse. For example, Dumisane Makhanya, described by some as "the ruling party's rottweiler" and by others as a member of the 'authoritarian clique' around Mbeki, dismissed Cronin as "not only white, middle-class and educated, but a Catholic to boot", and that the 'African revolution' did not need "a white messiah to succeed".[5] Makhanya, once a Party member himself, died in October 2004, but his attack on the 'white messiah' would not be the last.

For the Left, the SACP was thought to have little influence except for giving legitimacy to the ANC's 'neo-liberal' policies. For example, one academic critic of the Party, David Thomas, argued that "the SACP has consistently prioritised the maintenance of the ANC-dominated Tripartite Alliance above all else. This has meant that the Party's efforts to contest political space in the post-apartheid era have been tempered and moderated by its unwavering commitment to the ANC."[6] Similarly, former party member Dale McKinley, taking from other Left critics by characterising April 1994 as the 'historic compromise', suggested that "from a peculiarly romanticised attachment to classic guerrilla warfare, to a rhetorically heavy notion of insurrectionary people's power, to social and political contracts with capital, the strategic thrust of the ANC's struggle for national liberation, consummated in the post-1994 period, has consistently underestimated and seriously undermined the potential and actual struggle of the people themselves." And that: "The SACP and COSATU, as well as the working-class sections of the ANC, accepted, albeit cautiously, the 'historic compromise' that had emerged from negotiations".[7] Rumours even circulated within Left circles, as reported by Ferial Haffajee, that "the South African Communist Party is going into business. Soon it will start one or more companies either on its own or with partners".[8] McKinley would be expelled from the Party in August 2000 for, as it was explained, "publicly and consistently attacking the leadership of the ANC, and to a lesser extent the leadership of COSATU and the SACP", including "publicly and consistently promoting positions that undermine the SACP".[9]

Naturally, the Party, for its part, viewed its role in post-apartheid South Africa in a more positive light. Nqakula defended the role of the Party in more concrete terms in October 1995:

> In fact our people understand, let's take education for instance and the new education system that is in place now in the country. Most of what has happened in terms of that transformation is credited to Blade Nzimande who is a Party person, he is the Deputy Chairperson of the Party. He has played a tremendous role in terms of transformation of

education. He has been involved in that sector for a number of years and people credit him for the advance that has been made in the area of education. You will remember when Joe Slovo was alive that people credited him with a lot of intelligent thinking around the question of housing and they saw that contribution as a contribution that essentially came from socialist thinking and there are a number of comrades who are occupying quite senior positions in the government of national unity who are communists. As I say, their role there is construed by our people as a very important role and, as I say, they have delivered in a number of areas. The Chairperson of the Constitutional Joint Committee is Pravin Gordhan and that person is a fantastic thinker. Many of the arrangements that relate to the present elections, for instance, were authored by him, he is quite incisive in his thinking. I could name a number of those people and he is also a Central Committee member. So no-one can accuse the Party of having been involved in a dispensation that is not delivering. The Party's role is clearly defined and people can see what communists have been able to do during this conjunction.[10]

Over the years, the Party developed an analysis and concept of its role in the new dispensation. The 11th Congress which met in July 2002 adopted a political programme which advanced the following position.

> In the present political reality, the leadership role of the ANC [in the Alliance] includes the fact that it is as the ANC that we contest elections, and it is under an ANC direct mandate that thousands of SACP members (along with other ANC comrades) participate in national and provincial cabinets and legislatures, and in local councils.
>
> The role of the SACP is, essentially, to be a Party of strategic influence and activism, to play a vanguard role in consistently representing the immediate and long-term interests of the working class and the poor, within the context of a multi-

class liberation movement and NDR [National Democratic Revolution]. The Party seeks to play this consistent class role by, amongst other things, propagating socialist values, a socialist perspective, and programmes of action that are capable of building momentum towards, capacity for, and elements of socialism.[11]

The 9th Congress convened twelve months into the new political dispensation, in April 1995, attended by some 600 delegates representing 70 000 members, adopted the programme *Strategic Perspectives* to replace the *Manifesto*, with the slogan: "Socialism is the Future: Build it Now!" The slogan was timely and in line with the notion of the NDR which the Party had advanced since the days of its 1962 programme. In that programme, the phase of national liberation (the NDR), led by the ANC, serving as a stepping-stone towards socialism was set out. Now that a new, national democratic order had been ushered in, now that the Colonialism of a Special Type has been defeated with the end of apartheid in 1994, it was time to work for the advance towards socialism.

When Mandela spoke at the 9th Congress on behalf of the ANC, he made the observation that: "Looking at delegates gathered in this hall, one is struck by your youthfulness – except of course for us on the podium. This is perhaps the best answer to those who have expressed doubt in the future of the Party."[12] This 'youthfulness' was a reflection of the wave of new members who had swelled the ranks of the Party after the unbanning. This was both a strength and a weakness; it helped grow and sustain the Party as communist parties in other parts of the world were in serious decline, but it also brought forward new members whose experience with the Party was just a few years old. As Hani, Slovo and others of the earlier generation passed on, the face of the Party increasingly became that of cadres who had joined the organisation after the unbanning. This was in stark contrast to the ANC where the mantle of leadership remained in the hands of members who had been in the organisation for decades. Over the years, the likes of Essop Pahad, Fraser-Moleketi, Mufamadi and Kasrils dropped out from the leadership of the Party and disappeared into new roles in society. This new reality, inevitably, came to affect how the alliance functioned under the new conditions, including Party-ANC relations. Indeed, it would be observed about the 9th Congress that "inside the Party there has been uneven, but tangible consolidation of a leadership collective – despite the very heavy loss of both our former General Secretary, comrade Chris Hani, and our former Chairperson, comrade Joe Slovo".[13]

In *Strategic Perspectives*, the Party distinguished itself from two tendencies, namely: what it called the 'far left', with its 'wholly utopian' notion of socialism, which stated that "no significant advances can be made until socialism is achieved", and "tendencies that are characterized by economism and narrow reformism". The latter, argued *Strategic Perspectives*, "while occasionally invoking 'socialism', are so immersed in the immediate here and now that the goals of broader structural transformation, of revolutionary socialist change, are forgotten".[14] Moving from the premise that "the present phase of our NDR is one in which the key tasks are to advance, deepen and defend the April 1994 democratic breakthrough", the Party outlined its understanding and vision of socialism in some detail in *Strategic Perspectives*. The approach was to build socialism now, progressively, through struggles and advances in key areas. In this regard, for the Party, the most important achievement of the 9th Congress was "the consolidation of our Party's internal strategic unity".[15] Indeed, in 2002, the Party would observe that "the strategic slogan first advanced in 1995 – 'Socialism is the future, build it now!' has, over the past seven years, acquired greater substance and meaning. It has enabled us to engage actively and confidently on the terrain of the NDR *as socialists*" (emphasis original).[16]

At the centre of the approach articulated in the *Strategic Perspectives* was the Reconstruction and Development Programme (RDP), a socio-economic and governance transformation plan, which was initiated from within COSATU, and developed by the alliance in the months leading to the elections as a blueprint for post-apartheid South Africa.[17] The RDP was meant to serve as an electoral pact connecting the ANC to its more radical alliance partners, the SACP and COSATU. Cronin spoke about the evolution of this programme in August 1993: "Within COSATU, within the Party, within Civics increasingly, with a whole range of formations, we're drafting, we're already going into our fourth draft of the suggested reconstruction programme so it's beginning to happen and hopefully by November COSATU and SANCA [South African National Civic Association] will probably jointly convene a mass democratic movement type conference which will look at reconstruction and then in December the ANC will convene a sort of ANC but very broad conference looking also at reconstruction and at the election manifesto that the ANC will go into the elections with".[18] Cronin saw the RDP as a victory for the Party and, in October 1994, celebrated the fact that "the ANC went into elections not just on a token blank cheque but upon a programme and quite an elaborated programme [that is, the RDP]".[19] In fact, he thought that the RDP "has the possibility of being a socialist oriented document".[20] For the Party, as argued in *Strategic Perspectives*, "... the RDP is essentially a programme of internal redistribution... and restructuring", and that it had a "...people-centred and people-driven character". This approach was to entail engaging in struggles for the "decommodification of the basic needs", as well as "transforming" and "rolling back" the market.[21]

The enthusiasm that prevailed within the Party over the RDP was not misplaced, nor was it limited to the Party in the liberation movement. Three months after the 9th Congress, in July 1995, the alliance met at the executive level to take stock of developments following the April elections. While "the overwhelming consensus of the Tripartite Alliance executives meeting of 20th July 1995 was that the principal challenge in our present situation is to ensure effective, ANC-led, political coordination of our overall transformation process", it was however emphasised that "in many ways the battle-lines of our struggle have shifted on to the terrain of the RDP" and that in this regard the "challenges are safeguarding the fundamental vision of the RDP, that is, its developmental growth-path; and ensuring effective implementation of the RDP". There was also consensus that "the unity of the Alliance needs to be deepened, based on a common strategic programme (essentially the RDP), and a mutual respect for the specific roles, constituencies and autonomy of the three partners". It was acknowledged that "our own fragmentation, which leads to weak implementation, opens the space for our strategic opponents" who will stop at nothing to find ways to undermine the RDP: "Since the April 1994 election, no major forces in our country, or externally, have dared to openly attack the RDP. Instead, they seek to undermine it by posing as its most consistent and reliable proponents. They wish to introduce a fundamentally different 'RDP', in which 'growth' is delinked from developmental objectives..."[22] This consensus on the RDP was short-lived; within a year, the battle lines on macro-economic policy were drawn in the alliance between the ANC on the one side, and the Party and COSATU on the other.

Mandela opened his speech to the 9th Congress with the following words: "It is not given to a leader of one political organisation in a country to sing praises to the virtues of another. But that is what I intend to do today". This, arguably, was to be for the last time, at least by the time of the writing of this book, that a president of the ANC would make such a flattering statement to a gathering of the Party's congress. When Mandela and his successor, Mbeki, addressed the 10th and subsequent Party congresses, the environment was acrimonious and tense. At the centre of the tension was the replacement of the RDP by Mandela's government in 1996 with a new macro-economic policy framework, *Growth, Employment and Redistribution* (GEAR), which the Party dismissed as 'neo-liberal'.[23]

One big gripe the Party had was with how GEAR had been introduced without any proper discussion or consultation. Cronin told O'Malley in his interview of October 1996 that: "As the Deputy General Secretary of the Party I was consulted in the last weeks before it was unveiled but as an ANC NEC member I was never consulted before it was unveiled, so they were more nervous about the SACP and COSATU because it was along with COSATU that we were being told, given glimpses, and then finally in the days just before it was unveiled we got a pretty full version of what was coming. The problem was the ANC wasn't there, there were a couple of ministers from the ANC but not the ANC as a political structure driving it. So that's our first package of concerns, process".[24] Nqakula tried to be more composed when he was interviewed by O'Malley on the same subject, and tried to "set the record straight around the tabling of the macro-economic strategy, that before it was tabled and government's intention was that it needed to be tabled quite soon, no less a person than the President, Nelson Mandela, invited some comrades from the alliance to a meeting. The Party was represented as was COSATU together with representatives of the ANC. The intervention that President Mandela made in that meeting, and this was before the tabling of this document to parliament, was that it could not be the last word on the economic debate in this country".[25] While the two Party leaders differed in their tone and approach to this sensitive issue, they nonetheless were of the same view when it came to the role that the ministry of finance played in suppressing the debate on GEAR and declaring the policy to be non-negotiable. By September 1998, even though he did not share Cronin's assessment that "you can already smell authoritarianism tendencies in the air", Nqakula's attitude towards GEAR was hardening. "If anyone says we are part of government then we must be seen to be part of government. Therefore we must participate in the formulation of government policies", was how he expressed his growing frustration.[26]

Over the years, with the GEAR in place since 1996, the SACP came to develop a concept called the '1996 class project' to characterise what was emerging in the country. This concept had two dimensions to it: it was, on the one hand, about the impact of the '1996 class project' on the state, and, on the other, how this 'class project' affected the configuration of the ANC and the alliance in general. At its National Policy Conference of September 2008, the Party defined this concept:

> Over several years the SACP has developed an analysis of the post-1994 South African transition. We have argued that, notwithstanding important advances, monopoly capital in our country has succeeded in asserting a relative hegemony over the broad direction of our post-apartheid state and society. This hegemony was secured, in part, thanks to a leadership collective around cde [comrade] Mbeki. It was a leadership collective that attempted to drive a neo-liberal restructuring

programme that required the marginalisation of the SACP and COSATU, the demobilisation of the ANC, the suppression of popular struggle, and the forging of a close alliance between monopoly capital, senior state leadership and an emerging BEE [black economic empowerment] faction of capital closely linked to our movement.[27]

How this class project affected the ANC was articulated in one CC-approved Discussion Document: "It is also worth noting that the 1996 class project simultaneously sought to reshape the ANC as a modern political party, whilst simultaneously appealing to past traditions of the pre-1990 alliance ostensibly to 'imprison' the SACP and the left to 'outmoded' alliance traditions and methods as an attempt to 'liquidate' it. This was argued in terms of 'this is no longer the SACP of Kotane' whilst rapidly dismantling the ANC of Oliver Tambo and Nelson Mandela, largely using the new terrain of ascendancy to state power…"[28]

The two sides, the SACP and ANC, did not take their differences lightly, and indeed attempts were made to find an accommodation that could settle the storm. One effort in this regard, after some discussion by the ANC's NEC and NWC (National Working Committee) on how to deal with attacks from the Party and COSATU, was Mbeki's attendance of the CC meeting of November 1996 where he presented his paper entitled 'The State and Social Transformation', wherein, using Marxist-Leninist tools of analysis of the South African post-apartheid transition, he tried to defend the logic that drove his government in the direction of GEAR. The CC was not convinced of his argument, especially the emphasis placed in the paper on the need to tackle the huge government deficit inherited from the apartheid era. The CC felt that the government's approach to the reality described in Mbeki's paper should not be state-centric and defeatist; it should leverage the collective, mass strength of the workers and the poor to take on the apartheid-era legacy and challenge the forces of global capital. At the end of this exchange, the two sides returned to their respective corners in the ring; the fight was not over as yet.[29]

The 10th Congress opened in July 1998. It was convened in the months leading up to the elections of 1999, and was a turning point in building an independent profile of the Party in the new South Africa. One of the decisions taken by Congress was "to continue to build and strengthen the SACP as an autonomous formation within the context of the ANC-led alliance".[30] The Congress adopted a programme for "building socialism where we live and work" which, as Nzimande explained as the newly elected general secretary, rested on three pillars: first, was "building organs of people's power through the strengthening of community-based initiatives in the area of development, dealing with crime, school governing bodies, and collective efforts towards the general upliftment of the mass of the people in areas where they live"; second, "building effective participation by workers in decision-making processes in their work-places"; and finally, "making every effort to rebuild popular and mass structures in the educational arena, in order to mobilise students, teachers and parents in the enormous effort of educational transformation". And that "all this is to be underpinned by specific campaigns in various provinces, including the intensification of political education and general cadre development".[31] In essence, this programme, as was explained in the Congress Declaration, "focuses upon the need to build People's Power, and to do so in the context of mass mobilisation that works hand in hand with progressive governance structures".[32] In 2002, the 11th Congress would acknowledge this turning point: "Since the Party's 1998 Congress, the SACP, in its own right, has more confidently led a series of campaigns and struggles – particularly around co-operatives and for the transformation and diversification of the financial sector. The 11th Congress provided an important forum in which to assess these struggles".[33] These campaigns, especially the one targeting the financial institutions, kept the Party in the public space, and projected the image of an organisation which was not just concerned about GEAR.

The 10th Congress was an attempt to address the difficult yet persistent question inherent in the Party's two-stage approach to socialism. The Congress opted for a double-edged approach: to engage, on the one hand, the ANC in its capacity as a liberation movement by using the alliance mechanism and, on the other, to engage the ANC in its other capacity as a governing party from a civil society platform that is available to non-state and non-alliance actors. The success of this approach would depend, on the one hand, on ANC responses and, on the other, on the extent to which the Party could resolve a much bigger ideological question, the one which confronts all communist parties, which is: What is the significance and substance of socialism in the post-Cold War era? At the organisational level, the Party had opted for tools of engagement in the form of campaigns and struggles around cooperatives and the financial sector.

At the 10th Congress, the CC's political report pointed out that "macro-economic policy has been one of the major areas in which, in the collective view of the SACP, there have been serious strategic shortcomings..." The Party's concerns, as explained in the CC's political report, were in four areas. Besides the concern with "the process by which it was formulated", the Party's other problem with "GEAR relates to its content, or rather its guiding assumptions. Fundamentally it conceives of macro-economic policy as being directed at stabilising the economy. We believe, however, that macro-economic policy should be aligned much more actively with our transformational goals". The third issue "is that it is far too rigid. For instance its budget deficit reduction targets are entirely arbitrary"; and fourthly, "we are convinced that, in regard to reducing the budget deficit, GEAR has failed to explore all the practical alternatives".[34] Two years on, after the 10th Congress, Nzimande was still calling for engagement with government: "Because of our disagreements around government's macroeconomic policy (GEAR), people shy away from talking about problems facing our economy. GEAR is not going to be an intro point of the debate we are calling for".[35]

Mandela, when he addressed the 10th Congress, launched what was probably the ANC's first major offensive against the Party. Mbeki, following Mandela to the podium, took issue with what he thought were 'charges of treachery' that the Party was levelling against the ANC with regard to GEAR, and felt that "none of us should go around carrying the notion in our heads that we have a special responsibility to be a revolutionary watchdog over the ANC".[36] Accordingly, at its first meeting after the 10th Congress, the newly elected CC deliberated on the lashing delegates received from Mandela and Mbeki and "it was agreed that these two interventions were relatively unprecedented and unfortunate in their tone and character". While the CC committed itself to implementing Congress's directive that the Party should seek a meeting with the ANC to discuss the criticism levelled by the two ANC leaders, the CC emphasised that "the SACP is an independent organisation within the Alliance, and it is an organisation that will continue fearlessly to raise its perspectives and concerns. We have raised publicly SACP concerns with certain government policies because these are public concerns, and not because we are trying to score points".[37]

In this context, with Nzimande elected general secretary at the 10th Congress and Mbeki assuming the country's presidency to succeed Mandela after the 1999 elections, the scene was now set for the escalation of the tension between the Party/COSATU and the ANC over GEAR and the internal workings of the alliance. Nzimande and his COSATU counterpart, Zwelinzima Vavi, led the charge, targeting Mbeki as the brain behind and the face of the 1996 class project.

This battle for hegemony over the direction of the country was not limited to the leadership level, between certain individuals at the helm of both the SACP and the ANC. Structures of the two organisations on the ground were involved, and so was the 50th national conference of the ANC which took place in Mafikeng in December 1997. Leading up to the conference, the media was predicting doom and the imminent collapse of the Alliance. They reported daggers drawn and a fight brewing between what were perceived as divisions between the leadership and the grassroots on the one hand and, on the other, the Left and the moderates. The various outcomes of the conference were celebrated by the Party: "At the end of the five days of Conference, the cynics and opportunists were left shaking their heads. They had, once again, badly miscalculated on the maturity, depth of experience and unity of the ANC and its Alliance".[38] As the conference was preceded by intensive debates in the ANC and the entire Alliance over thorny issues, this helped avert a crisis at the event. "A case in point", explained the Party, "is government's macro-economic framework policy, GEAR. Contrary to many press reports, the 50th ANC Conference did not rubber-stamp GEAR. The positions elaborated in the Alliance Summit were re-affirmed and developed... The ANC agrees that GEAR, like any other policy is 'not written in stone', and has to be assessed in an ongoing way. The Mafikeng Conference also reaffirmed the centrality of RDP objectives to all other policies, including macro-economic frameworks."[39] But this victory for the Left was just symbolic at best as it did not deter the government from implementing its GEAR policy.

The ANC-SACP divisions over macro-economic policy were felt throughout the liberation movement, with Mbeki being accused by Nzimande of wanting to "provoke the allies to walk out of the alliance".[40] Within the Party, those who were seen as 'Mbeki's people' – Essop Pahad, Fraser-Moleketi, Mufamadi and Nqakula – were phased out by not being elected to the CC at subsequent congresses. Nqakula, Hani's successor as general secretary, was replaced by Nzimande before being phased out in subsequent years after a short stint as chairperson. Pahad, once the Party's spokesperson during the negotiations, was shown the door from the CC. Fraser-Moleketi, once the administrative anchor at the Party headquarters after the unbanning, even succeeding Nqakula as the chairperson of the organisation, was eventually moved out of the CC. In this way, the position of the 'youthfulness' of the Party that Mandela had observed at the 9th Congress was consolidated.

The workings of the Alliance were also affected by squabbles over GEAR and the 1998 turning point in the Party. The Alliance functioned relatively well in the immediate months of the post-April 1994 transition, with the secretariats of the three organisations meeting on a weekly basis, culminating in the summit at the executive level in July 1995 the purpose of which was to assess the performance of the ANC-led government since the first democratic elections. The mood at the summit was characterised by optimism built around the RDP and the consensus on the need for an effective ANC-led centre. The ANC's leadership was not questioned. Instead, it was felt that ANC structures, notably the National Working Committee and the office of the secretary general, should be strengthened in order to enable them to effectively lead government and the entire

Alliance. There was consensus that the NWC should "function as a key political centre that is able to drive the RDP", and that its work should be reoriented "away from week-to-week crisis management, towards strategic oversight of RDP implementation". One concern which was raised, and which would pose a challenge later, was the emerging tendency on the part of cabinet ministers to run ahead of the ANC without proper consultation: "One of the major weaknesses in our movement these past 18 months has been a tendency for ANC ministers to move ahead with major transformation programmes without having run these effectively through ANC, and Alliance constitutional structures".[41]

If the alliance summit of July 1995 was held in the spirit of optimism, this was less so for that of September 1997. In his opening address to the latter summit Mandela spoke about "unresolved matters facing the Alliance" and said that "frankness is what is required at this summit... frankness is what the alliance requires among ourselves to thrash issues out and resolve them".[42] He proposed a formula whereby the Alliance partners would accept that while there would be areas of convergence among them, "there are issues where it may be very difficult for us to agree and I think we should be realistic enough to appreciate that this is going to be the position".[43] This is the formula of 'agreeing to disagree' in order to contain differences and keep the Alliance together. The summit was indeed an opportunity for the three organisations to refine their understanding of the NDR and their respective roles within it. The problems over GEAR were attributed to what was referred to as a 'stageist' understanding of the NDR, where the SACP and COSATU regarded it as a stage towards socialism, while some in the ANC thought the post-1994 era had ushered in a transition towards a fully-fledged capitalist dispensation. While "the strategic task of the ANC and its alliance is the consolidation of a united, non-racial, non-sexist and democratic South Africa", it was argued in the report of the summit, on the other hand "the ANC's two key alliance partners, the SACP and COSATU, have both adopted socialist programmes" and that "their commitment to socialism, and this is stated clearly in the official policy statements of both formations, is not in opposition to the NDR or the ANC". If there was any consensus that emerged from this summit, it was that the days of the RDP were over.

The alliance would meet again at summit level in October 1998, its deliberations informed by the Discussion Paper on 'The State and Social Transformation' which tackled the question of the role of the state in post-apartheid South Africa.[44] But it would take over three years before another summit-level meeting could take place. The Alliance joint secretariat explained in its report to the summit of April 2002:

> During 1999 an Alliance Summit was planned but not held, and a ten-a-side meeting was instead held towards the end of the year. In the year 2000 no Summit or ten-a-side was held among the Alliance partners. While 2001 commenced with a series of positive bilateral discussions, particularly between the ANC and COSATU, the end of the year, as we all know, was perhaps the lowest point in Alliance relations since the democratic breakthrough. Aside from secretariat meetings, there has been a growing void in official political interactions between us as alliance partners. This, amongst other factors, contributed towards a breakdown of trust and the emergence of public misunderstandings and even attacks, providing fertile ground for the media and others to intensify divisions.[45]

At the heart of the problems affecting the workings of the alliance was the difficulty experienced in implementing Mandela's formula of agreeing to disagree in order to keep the mechanism together. Consensus had evaporated on the basics of the alliance; there was no longer a common understanding of the character of the alliance, how to manage the challenges that arise out of intra-alliance relations, modalities for strengthening the coordinating structures of the alliance, the role of the Alliance in policy development and implementation. The warning made at the summit of July 1995 had not been heeded of cabinet ministers running ahead of the ANC and its alliance in policy development and implementation. A view prevailed that alliance structures, especially the ANC, were being used as a 'rubber stamp' for what had been decided in government corridors.[46]

As the relations between the ANC and the Party became more and more strained, those between the Party and COSATU went in the opposite direction. In fact, at their bilateral meeting of February 1998 the latter two organisations even agreed to establish "SACP work-place units" which "may be based on an industrial location, cutting across several work-places and COSATU affiliates". This agreement was necessitated by the fact that "both the Party and COSATU acknowledge the need to build a communist party political presence at the work-place itself. But how, in doing this, do we avoid creating parallel structures, SACP structures that second-guess, or even undermine the democratic trade union structures? While these things have to be worked out in specific circumstances, the bilateral agreed that there would need to be a clear understanding that the role of the SACP structure would not be a trade union role but rather an ideological and political education role".[47] For its part, COSATU took numerous decisions at its policy forums, aimed at strengthening its relations with the SACP. One consequence of this was the increase in the alienation of the ANC within the alliance with the SACP and COSATU beginning to question the ANC's centrality and leadership in the tripartite mechanism.

International relations are an important component of the work of a communist party, and the SACP is no exception. As shown elsewhere, during the exile years, this component in the life of the SACP was dominated by relations with the states and ruling parties of the socialist bloc and parts of southern Africa.[48] After the unbanning, with the socialist countries now in the shredder of history, these relations were reoriented towards like-minded political parties as well as the social and anti-globalisation movements. Besides Slovo's visit to Moscow in April 1991 and that of Hani in 1992 when he was in transit to China and North Korea, there does not seem to have been any systematic contact between the Party and the former Soviet Union and its Communist Party of the Soviet Union in the 1990s. In April 1992 Slovo admitted that during the heyday of SACP-USSR relations "we didn't meet the very top very often, but we met people at the middle levels", and when he was asked the question, "Do you keep in touch with any of these people through all the turmoil of the last couple of years?" his response was that: "Oh the odd friend has written a letter but one can't say that there's any kind of structured contact with any of them now."[49]

During the period under review, the Party's international work would entail relations with states such as Cuba and China on the one hand, and on the other, solidarity work in support of struggles for self-determination in places such as Palestine and the Western Sahara, as well as the promotion of democracy and peace in parts of Africa. In his defence of the record of the Party in the aftermath of the 10th Congress, Nzimande, as the newly elected general secretary wrote: "Our Party enjoys international prestige, and this is due in no small measure to the attempts we have made to maintain fraternal relations with many left-wing and socialist forces throughout the world. We are also an active component of international attempts in fostering a renewal of socialism and socialist forces world-wide".[50]

# Conclusion

THE PARTY, AS AN ORGANISATION, underwent a number of changes during the exile period, some of which were revisited after the unbanning in 1990. To begin with, the leadership structure of the Party was unstable throughout the exile period for a number of reasons. Leading figures in the Party before the exile period, apart from Kotane and Marks, included Rusty Bernstein and Michael Harmel. In exile, however, Bernstein's prominence at the leadership level dropped, and Harmel, whose role continued to be central, especially within the Secretariat, was transferred to Prague to represent the Party on the board of the *World Marxist Review*, and died in June 1974. With the hospitalisation of both Kotane and Marks in 1970, and the death of Marks in August 1972, the leadership of the Party had to rely mainly on Slovo and Dadoo. While Kotane only died in May 1978, he was not in a position to effectively execute his responsibilities as the general secretary between 1970 and his death.

Mabhida, in taking over the general secretaryship in 1979, moved the Party to new heights particularly in terms of its relations with the ANC, but the Party was soon to be deprived of his services after the 6th Congress in 1984. He spent the next two years in and out of hospital and died in March 1986. His position was only filled by Slovo at the 7th Congress three years later. Effectively, the Party was without a general secretary between 1970 and 1978 and then between 1984 and 1986. The business of running and leading the Party during these periods was in the hands of those who were central in the secretariat. In the 1980s this role fell to the Politburo.

Of all these exile Party leaders, with the exception of Bernstein, only Slovo survived until the unbanning in 1990. Slovo played a critical role in building the external mission, by steering the setting up of the Secretariat in London, playing a leading role in attempts to resuscitate the underground inside the country, and occupying a key role in Party-ANC relations. However, Slovo only became chairperson following the death of Dadoo and the general secretary at the 7th Congress, contenting himself during most of the exile period with confining his leadership role to serving the Party in the Secretariat and the PB. All in all, Slovo's role during the exile period remains a complex area that will require detailed research, especially on how he managed to gain prominence from 1963, overshadowing Party leaders who were more senior than him, such as Bernstein, Harmel, even Kotane and Marks.

The exile period also produced a new leadership for the Party, especially from the 1970s, notably Mac Maharaj, Chris Hani, Josiah Jele and John Nkadimeng, and with the co-option of the youth in the 1980s, January 'Ché' Masilela.

The substance of the membership of the Party also underwent both quantitative and qualitative changes during the exile period. As the membership increased, first in the mid-1970s and again in the 1980s, more and more youth joined the Party. With the unbanning in 1990, the Party experienced a dramatic growth in membership, this time the ranks of the organisation being swelled by people many of whom had little or no exile experience.

As to relations with the ANC, it was not one-way traffic, with the ANC being nothing but a pawn of the Party. There is no doubt that the Party, especially with its September 1981 resolution on working in 'fraternal' organisations, was serious and systematic about its determination to influence the direction of the ANC, as exemplified, for example, by the Lusaka Regional Committee circular to its units of 23 April 1986:

> The ANC Department of Political Education is to start its work soon. Units must ensure that all members take active part in the work of this organ – attend the discussions, make effective Party input into the whole programme and assist whenever necessary. We consider this work very essential in that it is one important forum for Party ideological work within the liberation movement, for our education and establishing

which among NLM cadres have the potential to become Party members.[1]

The reason why the Party wanted to influence the direction of the ANC was not because of a conspiratorial, Soviet agenda as some have suggested, but because, unlike its counterparts in other parts of Africa, the SACP was informed by a conviction that its socialist ideal could be achieved through the attainment of the national democratic order. The Party was also convinced that its Marxist ideology was superior, and that its Leninist organisational principles and practices promoted high political standards and instilled in its cadres a special form of discipline.

Thus the relationship between the ANC and SACP was more dynamic than some have argued. The ANC, for its part, thanks largely to the leadership of Tambo, was conscious in its effort to ensure that it was not controlled by the Party – that it remained independent as a nationalist movement. At the same time, however, the two organisations did influence each other in a number of areas, especially in matters pertaining to ideology, strategy and tactics, and organisational practice. This contradictory, mutual pull in the relationship between the two organisations contributed to the ups and downs that the relationship experienced during the exile period. A careful and patient reading of the ANC archives should help in drawing a picture of how this dynamic relationship evolved and developed in exile. Indeed, Tambo pointed out in his July 1981 address on the occasion of the 60th anniversary of the SACP that: "It is often claimed by our detractors that the ANC's association with the SACP means that the ANC is being influenced by the SACP. That is not our experience. Our experience is that the two influence each other. The ANC is quite capable of influencing, and is liable to be influenced by others. There has been the evolution of strategy which reflects this two-way process".[2]

The question to ask is whether there was continuity or discontinuity between the SACP of the period 1953–63 and that of the exile years. At the leadership level, the emergence of Slovo as a central figure was a factor. Ideologically, the Colonialism of a Special Type thesis was developed further, especially with regard to elements pertaining to the relationship between the Party and the ANC. So was the theory of armed struggle, as the Party shifted from the detonator and the rural-based guerrilla warfare theory to a 'people's war'. Organisationally, districts gave way to regions, and working underground was mastered in exile, including what the Lusaka Region termed a "conspiratorial characteristic in our style of work". Finally, in terms of membership, the Party in exile had to do with members located in artificial environments, such as army camps, and even those who were in places such as London considered themselves to be refugees. For that matter, the primary purpose of Party work was directed towards 'home'.

Following the unbanning of the ANC and SACP, a more important challenge faced the Party at the ideological level. At one level, how was the struggle for socialism to be executed during the 1990–94 transition, and, at another level, what and how should socialism be constructed in the 21$^{st}$ century, in the light of the collapse of the Soviet Union and other former socialist countries? These questions were to persist after the first democratic elections in April 1994, and stand at the heart of the substance of the role of the Party in the post-1994 transition, and in the relationship between the Party and the ANC as both a liberation movement and a governing party. The Party, like its communist counterparts in some post-colonial African countries, is faced with the difficulty of having to survive as a socialist force within an alliance that is led by a nationalist movement.

## The SACP Today

The year 1998 was a significant turning point in the life of the SACP, but it was just the beginning of the process of fundamental transformation of the Party, including its relations with its historical ally, the ANC. At the time of writing, Jacob Zuma is the president of the country following a bruising succession battle with his long-time friend, ally in the ANC, and comrade in arms, Thabo Mbeki. Mbeki was recalled by the ANC before the end of his second term as president of the country after losing to Zuma in the presidential electoral contest at the National Conference in December 2007. Some of his supporters – products of the UDF, Terror Lekota and Sam Shilowa – left the ANC in anger to form their own party, COPE, only to spend years at each other's throats over the leadership of their breakaway creation.

Nzimande is still the SACP's general secretary and Gwede Mantashe now the secretary general of the ANC. But the chemistry between the two organisations is not as it was. For instance, in 2001, Jabu Moleketi, once a leader of the SACP after the unbanning, argued that the Party was "stuck in a time warp". Mantashe, in his capacity as the chairperson of the Party responded: "When the Party was unbanned in 1990, some of the graduates of the Lenin school left the SACP with the prediction that it would wither away. Moleketi's attack mirrors the disappointment of some of these graduates that the Party has actually not withered away but has grown and that the global challenge to neo-liberalism is growing".[3]

If there is an SACP-ANC exchange to be remembered, it is certainly the one of 2006 following the release of the CC discussion document entitled 'Class, National and Gender Struggle in South Africa: The Historical Relationship between the ANC and the SACP'. The document was the product of the work of a CC commission which was established to implement the directive of the Special National Congress of April 2005 which instructed the CC to examine the Party's relationship to the state, including the question of whether the time had not come for the Party to contest elections on its own. The document, which used the '1996 class project' model of analysis of the race, class and gender contradictions in post-apartheid South Africa, was not well received by the ANC, resulting in a meeting between the ANC National Working Committee and the Party leadership in June 2006. In its response, the ANC argued, among other things, that "both in content and style, the Discussion Document reflects many distortions of historical facts. It refers, literally, to rumours… It also resorts to subjective interpretations of the debates that took place when the SACP re-established itself as a legal organisation in 1990… In its subjectivism, the document stylistically tends cogently to explain the difficulties the SACP faced during many moments in its history and the choices it decided to make. Yet, when it comes to interpreting actions of the ANC leadership, conspiracy theories are brought into play".[4] Subsequent to the NWC-SACP meeting, the SACP responded to the ANC's critique: "There are many issues, including... some criticisms in the NWC document with which we agree, or around which we are prepared to concede that better formulations would be more appropriate. However, the core critique contained in the NWC argument is based on a radical misunderstanding of the fundamental strategic argument of the CC paper. This misunderstanding is not innocent. It is a symptom of an economistic reformism (we use these words advisedly and without any intention of mere labelling) that has tended to dominate some of the strategic thinking within our movement".[5]

Recently, a young man who was not there during the days of Slovo and Hani spoke for some in the ANC, a group referred to as nationalists in the media, when he lambasted what he called 'yellow communists': "The yellow communists are driven by greed. They sing anti-corruption songs. They are the most corrupt. There is everything wrong with the communists trying to take over the ANC".[6] Echoing the words of Dumisani Makhanya many years earlier, he dismissed Cronin as a 'white messiah' in his public exchange with him over the question of the nationalisation of the mines. This young man is Julius Malema, the former president of the ANC Youth League. After he was booed out of an SACP special conference, one of his supporters, the Northern Cape provincial secretary of the Youth League, reacted: "We will not keep quiet in the spirit of protecting the tripartite alliance whilst some hooligans and fakes who masquerade as leaders mobilise stupid delegates to insult our ANC NEC and ANCYL members". The provincial secretary appealed: "We humbly wish to warn these rented hooligans and dogs and their masters that we will defend the ANCYL leadership and ANC NEC with our lives, even if it means kicking this unbecoming behavior out of them we will do that". One branch secretary of the Youth League in Mpumalanga was similarly enraged: "The ANCYL in Mpumalanga has always asserted that the SACP at its branch level is led by renegades who have lost seats in the ANC BECs [branch executive committees]... We have never heard anything communist in the branches and districts of the SACP except demands for deployment on Alliance basis and attacks to [sic] the ANCYL president".[7]

The consensus on the ANC's leadership of the alliance is on shakier ground than ever before, with the SACP and COSATU calling for the 'reconfiguration' of the tripartite mechanism. Accordingly, the 12th Congress of the Party, held in 2007, resolved that:

> The Alliance requires major reconfiguration if the NDR is to be advanced, deepened and defended, and if we are to achieve the SACP's medium term vision objectives of building the working class hegemony in all sites of power, including the state. That this reconfiguration of the Alliance must include the following elements: (a) the Alliance must establish itself as a strategic political centre; [and] (b) this political centre must develop a common capacity to drive strategy, broad policy, campaigns, deployment and accountability. At the same time, this reconfiguration of the Alliance must respect the independent role and strategic tasks of each of the Alliance partners.[8]

The Party's provincial secretary for KwaZulu-Natal motivated for this view in one of the SACP's discussion documents:

> ...the SACP proposes that the Alliance should be reconfigured and become the strategic political centre to drive policy, campaigns, deployment and accountability. This means having an Alliance Deployment Committee and the Alliance mechanisms to develop and implement policy instead of the ANC. To put it more directly, the SACP is deeply concerned that the National Democratic Revolution will not be deepened and defended unless the centrality of its leadership lies with the Alliance, rather than with the ANC. This is notwithstanding the fact that the ANC has led this revolution even during difficult moments of our struggle.[9]

Similarly, at its special provincial council of September 2008, the

Western Cape SACP took a resolution 'On the SACP and State Power', the content of which reinforced the notion of the 'reconfigured' alliance. The provincial council felt strongly that:

> As the Party we should conclude an agreement with the ANC within the Alliance prior to the elections... that the 2009 elections be fought on the basis of a 70–30% allocation of seats between the ANC, SACP & COSATU... SACP candidates must be accountable to the SACP – with the party having the right within a broad Alliance strategy to direct them as well as to recall them... In respect of the next local government elections, the September 2008 SACP National Policy Conference must debate the need for the SACP to contest the next local government elections in its own right.

This position was informed by the experience in the province which was articulated in the resolution: "Our recent experience in the Western Cape in the midst of a ground breaking provincial Alliance Declaration taught us that the mere request for consultation on the deployment of our cadres into government will not necessarily yield the outcomes expected but create further tensions particularly where there are no shared perspectives and understanding on the Alliance as the strategic political centre." Hence the view of the provincial council was that: "For the SACP a reconfigured Alliance as the strategic political centre must be premised on an understanding that the Alliance as a whole will jointly develop policies, jointly manage the implementation of policy, jointly deploy cadres into government and state machinery, jointly exercise accountability of deployed cadres and collectively manage the execution of the election manifesto."[10]

Blade Nzimande, apart from being general secretary of the Party, is the minister of higher education and training and his deputy, Jeremy Cronin, deputy minister of transport. But this has not pleased the SACP's other ally in the Alliance, COSATU, which has called on Nzimande to resign from his cabinet position to return to his post at the Party headquarters. COSATU's general secretary, Zwelinzima Vavi, told the SACP's Young Communist League, formed in December 2003, that: "The absence of full-time officials, in particular at national and provincial levels in the SACP, will hamper the left's ability to carry through its programme of radical transformation of our society and for socialism" and that "this is an honest view [that is] informed by our love of the SACP not by any newly found hatred or disdain of the SACP".[11] KwaZulu-Natal's secretary of the National Union of Mineworkers of South Africa, one of COSATU's affiliates, in defending the call made by his federation, attributed the decline in the Party's profile to the deployment of its office-bearers to government positions: "We have seen, during both the auto and public-sector strikes, the SACP being a tourist in the midst of class struggle for equitable distribution of income. It's pathetic for the vanguard to behave like Christians waiting for the revelation [to] pronounce its class role".[12] But the Party is unmoved; instead, a Special National Congress was convened in December 2009 to allow, as stated in one of the resolutions, for "SACP secretaries to be full-time or part-time as the political terrain, balance of forces, strategic considerations, and organizational challenges, among other issues, dictate", and effect necessary amendments to the SACP's constitution which had hitherto made the general secretary position full-time.[13] Speaking on behalf of the CC on the matter, Nzimande pointed out that: "The SACP has never conceived of itself as a non-governmental organisation. In the current reality of South Africa, the SACP, together with its Alliance partners, is committed to building popular and working-class power both outside of and within the state".[14]

Even though the financial situation of the Party has stabilised, however, challenges are far from over. A discussion document on the 'Role and Character of the SACP', which was prepared for the 11th Congress, which was held in July 2002, attributed this improvement to the debit order system which requires Party members in state institutions to contribute a percentage of their monthly salary to the organisation: "Over the last several years, the SACP has made major strides, particularly through our Debit Order campaign, in building a basis for effective financial sustainability". But, as the paper put it: "This remains one of the most challenging questions facing the SACP. Financial sustainability is essential for the implementation of our strategic objectives and programmes, and for improving our capacity for tactical flexibility. We need to use the next four years to attain financial sustainability, improving, in particular, the capacity of Party structures at all levels to raise funds. The more the Party is reliant on our own mass-base, the more we are able to fulfill our strategic watch-word: 'WITH AND FOR… THE WORKERS AND THE POOR'" (emphasis original).[15]

So much has changed since the Party was banned, went underground, then into exile, and finally, was unbanned. This change has not just been organisational, ideological or at the level of strategy and tactics; it has also been about people – both leadership and the general membership. As the country has changed over the 90-odd years since 1921 when the CPSA was formed, the Party has also changed; its influence on the country has been as immense as the country's influence on it.

# Acknowledgements

THIS BOOK IS A REVISED VERSION of the *South African Communist Party in Exile* which was published by the Africa Institute of South Africa (AISA). Chapters Four to Eleven are a revision of relevant sections of the *South African Communist Party in Exile* as well as the two chapters the author contributed to the South African Democracy Education Trust (SADET) project on the history of the liberation struggle in South Africa. The photographs in the picture section come from the Unsorted SACP Archives and from the Essop Pahad Papers. As such, they have not been catalogued, referenced or dated and it has therefore not always been possible to identify everyone in each photograph.

# Notes

**Introduction**

1 Resolution on 'The South African Question' adopted by the Executive Committee of the Communist International following the Sixth Comintern congress, South African Communist Party Documents, 1928, http://www.marxists.org/history/international/comintern/sections/sacp/1928/comintern.htm.

2 The role of the Party in the formation of MK remains in dispute. See, for example, Nelson Mandela's account in his *Long Walk to Freedom: The Autobiography of Nelson Mandela*, Randburg: Macdonald Purnell, 1994, pp. 262–271; and Joe Slovo's in *Slovo: The Unfinished Autobiography*, Johannesburg: Ravan Press, 1995, pp. 145–150.

3 See, in particular, S Johns, 'Generation of Histories of the Communist Party of South Africa', Paper presented at the International Historical Conference, Moscow, 25–26 June 1997; S Johns, *Raising the Red Flag: The International Socialist League and the Communist Party of South Africa, 1914–1932*, Bellville: Mayibuye Books, 1995. For the Party's own publications, see A Lerumo, *Fifty Fighting Years: The South African Communist Party, 1921–1971*, London: Inkululeko Publications, 1971; SACP, *South African Communists Speak: Documents from the History of the South African Communist Party, 1915–1980*, London: Inkululeko Publications, 1981; B Bunting, *Moses Kotane: South African Revolutionary*, London: Inkululeko Publications, 1975.

4 See, for example, G Ludi and B Grobbelaar, *The Amazing Mr Fischer*, Cape Town: Nasionale Boekhandel, 1966; N Mitchison, *A Life for Africa: The Story of Bram Fischer*, London: Merlin Press, 1973; DE Albright, (ed), *Communism in Africa*, Bloomington: Indiana University Press, 1980; J Depelchin, 'Anti-Communism and the Attempts to Re-Write the Histories of National Liberation in Southern Africa', *UFAHAMU*, vol. 16, no. 1, 1987/88; P Duignan and LH Gann, *Communism in Sub-Saharan Africa: A Reappraisal*, Washington DC: Hoover Institute, 1994; DR Kempton, 'New Thinking and Soviet Policy towards South Africa', *Journal of Modern African Studies*, vol. 28, no. 4, 1990; HP Pike, *A History of Communism in South Africa*, Germiston: Christian Mission International of South Africa, 1985; TG Karis, 'South African Liberation: The Communist Factor', *Foreign Affairs*, vol. 65, no. 2, 1986; WJ Booyse, 'The Revolutionary Program of the South African Communist Party', *International Freedom Review*, vol. 2, no. 1, 1988; M Ottaway, 'Liberation Movements and Transition to Democracy: The Case of the ANC', *Journal of Modern African Studies*, vol. 29, no. 1, 1991; A Prior, 'South African Exile Politics: A Case of the African National Congress and the South African Communist Party', *Journal of Contemporary African Studies*, vol. 3, nos 1/2, 1983/84; T Lodge, *Black Politics in South Africa since 1945*, New York: Longman, 1983.

5 See, for example, V Shubin, *ANC: A View from Moscow*, Bellville: Mayibuye Books, 1999; S Ellis and T Sechaba, *Comrades against Apartheid: The ANC and*

*the Communist Party in Exile*, London: James Currey, 1992; C Bundy, (ed), *The History of the South African Communist Party*, Cape Town: University of Cape Town Summer School Lecture Series, 1991; I Liebenberg *et al*, (eds), *The Long March: The Story of the Struggle for Liberation in South Africa*, Pretoria: Haum, 1994; P Laurence, 'South African Communist Party Strategy since February 1990', *South African Review*, vol. 6, 1992; T Lodge, 'Post-Modern Bolsheviks: SA Communists in Transition', *South Africa International*, April 1992; D Kotze, 'Morogoro: Out of the Whirlwind', *Politikon*, vol. 16, no. 1, 1989. For the Party's own account of its history, see *The Red Flag in South Africa: A Popular History of the South African Communist Party, 1921–1990*; R Kasrils, *Armed and Dangerous: My Undercover Struggle against Apartheid*, London: Heinemann, 1993; LR Bernstein, *Memory against forgetting: Memoirs from a life in South African politics, 1938–1964*, London: Viking, 1999; Slovo 1995.

6 The author has contributed to this project the chapters on the SACP in 1980s and 1990s.
7 Shubin 1999.
8 D Ottaway and M Ottaway, *Afrocommunism*, New York: Africana Publishing Company, 1981.
9 J Ruedy, *Modern Algeria: The Origins and Development of a Nation*, Bloomington: Indiana University Press, 1992, p. 139.
10 For a discussion of communist parties in Africa, see J Markakis and M Waller, (eds), *Military Marxist Regimes in Africa*, London: Frank Cass, 1986; A Hughes, (ed) *Marxism's Retreat from Africa*, London: Frank Cass, 1992; B Turok, *Africa: What Can be Done?*, London: Zed Press, 1987; Ottaway and Ottaway 1981.
11 Oliver Tambo, 'Our Alliance is a Living Organism that has Grown out of Struggle', (Address on the Occasion of the 60th Anniversary of the SACP, London, 30 July, 1981), *Sechaba*, September Issue, 1981, p. 4.

## Chapter 1

1 Cited in Ludi and Grobbelaar 1966, p. 53.
2 For an account of Fischer's life, see *Ibid* and Mitchison 1973. However, Ludi's account should be read with caution because it was meant to incriminate Fischer.
3 Unsorted SACP Archives, CEC, 'Minutes and Recommendations' of the CC meeting of May 1965. These archives are at the SACP headquarters.
4 *Ibid*.
5 *Ibid*.
6 *Ibid*.
7 *Ibid*., CEC letter to 'Noel', 25 June 1965.
8 *Ibid*., CEC, 'Report Handed to JB for Hull Comrades', 1966.
9 *Ibid*.
10 *Ibid*., CEC, 'Aide Memoire', undated, but written during 1966.
11 *Ibid*., CEC, 'Outline of Talks to Groups', undated, but c.1966.
12 *Ibid*.
13 *Ibid*.
14 *Ibid*.
15 *Ibid*.
16 Unsorted SACP Archives, 'Minutes of the recommendations and decisions of the full Central Committee meeting held on the 13th and 14th January, 1967'.
17 *Ibid*., 'Proposed draft [letter to ANC acting president] prepared by Secretariat', undated.

18 *Ibid.*, 'Notes of full Central Committee meeting held on the 23rd, February 1968'.
19 *Ibid.*, 'Minutes of the London Committee Meeting, 10 August 1976'.
20 *Ibid.*, Kotane to Dadoo, 7 June 1967.
21 *Ibid.*, Secretariat to Kotane, undated.

**Chapter 2**
1 Unsorted SACP Archives, CC, 'Report on Organisation to the 1970 Augmented Meeting'.
2 *Ibid.*, CC, 'The Results of the Consultative Conference of the ANC and the Tasks of the Party', 1969.
3 *Ibid.*, Tambo to Slovo, c.1970.
4 Ellis and Sechaba, 1992, for example.
5 For a detailed discussion of the dissidents, see L Callinicos, 'Oliver Tambo and the Politics of Class, Race and Ethnicity in the African National Congress of South Africa', *African Sociological Review*, vol. 3, no. 1, 1999; Shubin 1999, pp. 84–93; Lodge 1983, pp. 300–305.
6 Cited in Lodge 1983, p. 303.
7 Unsorted SACP Archives, 'Current Trends within the Organisation (ANC): Report by a Group of Comrades', March 1972.
8 *Ibid.*, CC, 'Notes for Guidance in Discussion', undated.
9 SACP, *Road to South African Freedom*, pp. 41, 46.
10 Unsorted SACP Archives, Marks to Secretariat, 6 December 1971.
11 *Ibid.*, 'Notes on the Discussion between a Delegation from the CC of the SACP and the NEC of the ANC', undated.
12 Kasrils 1993, p. 101.
13 Unsorted SACP Archives, Secretariat to 'Patrick', J/DJ/3/5/12/69, undated.
14 See Shubin 1999.
15 Unsorted SACP Archives, SACP to CPSU, 6 September 1970.
16 *Ibid.*, 'Report of the Final Stages of the Attempted Implementation of Operation J'.
17 *Ibid.*
18 *Ibid.*
19 *Ibid.*
20 Shubin 1999, p. 105.

**Chapter 3**
1 Unsorted SACP Archives, 'Report on Organisation', undated, but probably prepared for the 1972 CC meeting.
2 *Ibid.*, 'Verbal Report to CC Plenary Meeting by JS, September 1972'.
3 *Ibid.*, CC to 'Phoenix', 2/21/3/75, undated.
4 *Ibid.*, CC to CPSU, 2 May 1972.
5 *Ibid.*, CC to CPSU, 5 February 1978.
6 *Ibid.*, 'Discussion Notes on London District', undated, but probably 1973.
7 *Inner-Party Bulletin*, December 1979, pp. 13, 15.

**Chapter 4**
1 *Inner-Party Bulletin*, November 1982, p. 1.
2 Unsorted SACP Archives, SACP to CPSU, 15 January 1984.
3 *Ibid.*, p. 2.

4 Tambo 1981, p. 4.
5 Unsorted SACP Archives, 'Minutes of the Meeting of the CC held in Moscow, 17 September 1981'.
6 *Ibid.*, CC, 'Notes for Guidance in Discussion', undated.
7 *Ibid.*, London Committee report to the PB, January 1983.
8 ANC, *Statement to the Truth and Reconciliation Commission*, August 1996, pp. 49, 51.
9 Unsorted SACP Archives, PB Minutes, 11–12 May 1981.
10 *Ibid.*, CC, 'Notes for Guidance in Discussion', undated.
11 *Inner-Party Bulletin*, December 1984, p. 1.
12 *Ibid.*, March 1985, p. 9.
13 Unsorted SACP Archives, CC, 'Directive of the Central Committee of the SACP to all members, units and other structures on security measures to be taken', September 1985.
14 See WB Simons and S Whites, (eds), *The Party Statutes of the Communist World*, The Hague: Martinus Nijhoff Publishers, 1984.
15 *Inner-Party Bulletin*, December 1984.
16 *Ibid.*, January 1986.
17 SACP, 1984 Constitution.
18 Unsorted SACP Archives, PB Minutes, 11–12 May 1981.
19 University of Cape Town Archives, SC BC1081, 'The Simons Papers'.
20 *Ibid.*
21 *Umsebenzi*, vol. 4, no. 1, 1st Quarter 1988, p. 17.
22 *Ibid.*
23 Mayibuye (University of Western Cape) Archives, MC02-3, ANC Papers, 'Memorandum to the CC on the need for an inner-party bulletin', undated.
24 Unsorted SACP Archives, PB Minutes, 3 September 1981.
25 *Ibid.*, LC Report to the Secretariat, 9 May 1972.
26 *Inner-Party Bulletin*, September 1985, p. 2.
27 According to Tom Lodge: "In 1989 at its seventh congress in Havana, the SACP was believed to have 5000 members, a total which represented a doubling of its size in 1984". See Lodge 1992, p. 172.
28 PB Report to 7th Congress, June 1989.
29 *Inner-Party Bulletin*, June 1989, p. 4.
30 See issues of *Umsebenzi*, especially from 1987.
31 *Umsebenzi*, vol. 4, no. 1, 1st Quarter, 1988, p. 17.
32 PB report on 'Internal' work to the 7th Congress, undated.
33 *Ibid.*
34 *Ibid.*
35 *Umsebenzi*, vol. 3, no. 4, 4th Quarter, 1987, p. 17.
36 *Ibid.*, vol. 4, no. 1, 1st Quarter, 1988, p. 17.
37 *Ibid.*, vol. 3, no. 4, 4th Quarter, 1987, p. 17.
38 *Ibid.*, vol. 4, no. 3, 3rd Quarter, 1988, p. 17.
39 *Ibid.*, vol. 5, no. 1, 1st Quarter, 1988, p. 13.
40 *Ibid.*, vol. 4, no. 3, 3rd Quarter, 1988, p. 5.
41 *Inner-Party Bulletin*, September 1985.
42 PB Minutes, 20 December 1984.
43 *Inner-Party Bulletin*, June 1989, p. 18.
44 Unsorted SACP Archives, 'Report of the Industrial Sub-Committee', undated.
45 *Umsebenzi*, vol. 4, no. 4, 4th Quarter, 1988, p. 13.
46 *Ibid.*, vol. 5, nos 3&4, 4th Quarter, 1989, p. 18.

47 *Ibid.*, vol. 5, no. 2, 2nd Quarter, 1989, p. 21.
48 'Decisions of the Special PB Meeting held to consider Preparations for the Coming Harvest [7th Congress]', 18 March 1989.

**Chapter 5**
1 Cited in Raymond Suttner, 'The Character and Formation of Intellectuals within the ANC-led South African Liberation Movement', in Thandika Mkandawire, (ed.), *African Intellectuals: Rethinking Politics, Language, Gender and Development*, (Dakar: CODESRIA, 2005), p. 127.
2 Cited in *Ibid.*, p. 132.
3 *Ibid.*, p. 134.
4 Cited in Marion Sparg et al, (eds.), *Comrade Jack: The Political Lectures and Diary of Jack Simons, Novo Catengue* Johannesburg: STE Publishers, 2001, p. 8.
5 *Ibid.*, p. 24.
6 *Ibid.*, p. 25.
7 *Ibid.*
8 *Ibid.*, p. 11.
9 *Ibid.*, p. 12.
10 Kasrils 1993, p. 120.
11 UWC–Robben Island Mayibuye Archives, Records of the ANC Lusaka and London (1960-1991), 'Report on Ideological and Political Work (Kwabe Conference)', Box MCH01-47.
12 Ray Alexander Simons, *All my Life and all my Strength*, Johannesburg: STE Publishers, 2004, p. 327.
13 Thomas G. Karis and Gail M. Gerhart, (eds.), *From Protest to Challenge: A Documentary History of African Politics in South Africa, 1882–1990, Volume 5: Nadir and Resurgence, 1964–1979* Pretoria: UNISA Press, 1997), pp. 387–392.
14 Cited in 'Twenty Years of Sechaba [sic] Journal of the ANC', *Sechaba*, May 1987, p. 28.
15 See, for example, the following issues of *Sechaba*: August 1979; August 1981; and September 1986.
16 Cited in Padraig O'Malley, *Shades of Difference: Mac Maharaj and the Struggle for South Africa*, New York: Viking, 2007, p. 164.
17 Interview with General Andrew Masondo, SADET Oral History Project.
18 *Ibid.*
19 Ahmed Kathrada, *Memoirs*, Cape Town: Zebra Press, 2004, p. 288.
20 The High Organ was the leadership core on the Island, and its composition was essentially comprised of Nelson Mandela, Govan Mbeki, Walter Sisulu, and Raymond Mhlaba. Of the four, the latter and Mbeki were known SACP leaders.
21 *Ibid.*
22 Cited in Fran Lisa Buntman, *Robben Island and Prisoner Resistance to Apartheid*, New York: Cambridge University Press, 2003, p. 101.
23 Cited in *Ibid.*, p. 93.
24 On these divisions, see, for example, 'Memorandum on ANC "Discord" Smuggled out of Robben Island, 1975', in Karis and Gerhart 1997, pp. 406–411.
25 Interview with Wilton Mkwayi, SADET Oral History Project.
26 I am grateful to Gail Gerhart for sharing this document with me as well as her correspondence on the document with Ahmed Kathrada. The document was entitled 'Marxism and Inqindi'. See also, Kathrada 2004, pp. 293–95.
27 *Ibid.*

## Chapter 6

1. Essop Pahad Papers (unsorted), 'Agreement between the Socialist Unity Party of Germany (SED) and the South African Communist Party (SACP) on cooperation in 1980 and 1981'. The Papers are kept at the offices of SADET in Pretoria.
2. Unsorted SACP Archives, CPSU letter to Moses Kotane, undated.
3. UWC-Robben Island Mayibuye Archives, Yusuf Dadoo Papers, SACP letter to the Central Committee of the Bulgarian Communist Party, 3 February 1983, Box 1.5.9.
4. Dadoo Papers, Moses Mabhida to Dadoo, 2 March 1983, Box 1.5.11.
5. *Ibid.*, Essop Pahad to Dadoo, 10 March 1983, Box 1.4.5.
6. For correspondence pertaining to these aspects of the Party's relations with fraternal parties, see Dadoo Papers, Box 1.
7. *Ibid.*, SACP to Communist Party of Israel, 6 July 1976, Box 1.3.8.
8. *Ibid.*, Communist Party of Israel to SACP, 21 July 1976, Box 1.3.5.
9. See Essop Pahad Papers for the unpublished manuscript of *Dr YM Dadoo, A People's Leader: A Political Biography*.
10. *Ibid.*, Communist Party of Jamaica to SACP, 28 September 1982, Box 1.5.5.
11. *Ibid.* Iraqi Communist Party to SACP, undated, Box 1.3.19.
12. Records of the ANC, 'International Meeting of Communist and Workers' Parties: June 69: Report of the SACP Delegation', Box MCH02-1.
13. Records of the ANC, 'Report on the Work of the Delegation of the SACP to the International Conference of Communist and Workers' Parties, Moscow/1969', Box MCH02-1.
14. Essop Pahad Papers, 'Proposals on Restructuring *World Marxist Review*'.
15. Pahad, *Dr YM Dadoo*, p. 217.
16. Pahad, *Dr YM Dadoo*, p. 219.
17. *Inner-Party Bulletin*, March 1983, p. 2.
18. Unsorted SACP Archives, 'Our Visit to China'.
19. I had suggested in my *South African Communist Party in Exile* that this process began in 1979. See p. 55.
20. Essop Pahad Papers, 'Proposed Conference of Communist Parties of Africa', undated, but probably prepared for the SACP as background for the Summit of 25 May 1978.
21. Essop Pahad Papers, 'Meeting of African Marxist-Leninist Leaders', 16 June 1969.
22. *Ibid.*, 'Proposed Conference of Communist Parties'.
23. This secretariat was sometimes referred to as the Editorial Commission or the Liaison Committee.
24. For the correspondence pertaining to the work of this secretariat, see Essop Pahad Papers.
25. See, for example, Essop Pahad Papers, Liaison Committee to the CPSU, 27 June 1978; and Editorial Commission to the CPSU, 26 April 1978.
26. Essop Pahad Papers, Liaison Committee to the Portuguese Communist Party, 1 August 1978.
27. *Ibid.*, 'A Confidential Report', undated.
28. *Ibid.*, Untitled and undated one-page summary of the decisions of the meeting of 16 April 1981.
29. *Ibid.*, Untitled and undated two-page report of the meeting of the 16 April 1981.
30. The national question, in classic Marxist thought, refers to issues of race (in relation to class), liberation, colonialism and nation building.
31. According to a Sudanese friend with intimate knowledge of the Sudanese CP.
32. For this correspondence, see Essop Pahad Papers.

33 For the Maputo Manifesto and the Protocol, see Essop Pahad Papers.
34 Essop Pahad Papers, Vieira to the SACP, 10 September 1981.
35 Unsorted SACP Archives, 'Opening address by Comrade Joe Slovo to the African Conference'.
36 *Ibid.*, Pahad to Slovo, 22 December 1987.
37 *Ibid.*, 'African Seminar', undated.
38 *Ibid.*, Pahad to Slovo, 22 December 1987.
39 Unsorted Archives, Mzala's 'Report of the Implementation Sub-Committee of the International Preparatory Committee for the GDR Seminar after the Visit to Berlin on 10.3.88'.
40 The newspaper article can be found in the Unsorted Archives.
41 Unsorted SACP Archives, Taeb to the Central Committee, 14 April 1988.
42 Essop Pahad Papers, 'African Seminar'.
43 *Ibid.*, Slovo to the Congolese Party of Labour, 6 November 1989.

## Chapter 7
1 On Operation Vula, see Shubin 1999, pp. 332–339.
2 *Umsebenzi*, vol. 5, no. 2, 2nd Quarter, 1989, p. 5.
3 See my 'South Africa Communist Party in the 1980s'.
4 Unsorted SACP Archives, 'Decision of the Extended Meeting of the Political Bureau', 17 February 1990.
5 Jeremy Gordin, *Zuma: A Biography*, Johannesburg: Jonathan Ball Publishers, 2008, p. 56.
6 Mark Gevisser discusses this issue at length. See his *The Dream Deferred: Thabo Mbeki*, Johannesburg: Jonathan Ball Publishers, 2007, pp. 471–473.
7 'Editorial Notes', *African Communist*, 2nd Quarter Johannesburg: Jonathan Ball Publishers, 1990, 12; 'De Klerk's Open Agenda', *Umsebenzi*, vol. 6, no. 2, 1990.
8 'Minutes of the NEC of 15 February 1990', O'Malley Archives.
9 University of Fort Hare, OR Tambo Papers, C445-6, 'SACP/COSATU jointly prepared notes for internal distribution within the broad liberation movement', 31 March 1990.
10 Jay Naidoo, *Fighting for Justice: A Lifetime of Political and Social Activism*, Johannesburg: Picador Africa, 2010, p. 171.
11 *Ibid.*
12 *Ibid.*
13 For the history of the alliance, see my 'Notes on the History of the Alliance', *Umrabulo*, no. 33, 2nd Quarter, 2010.
14 'SACP Sessions', O'Malley Archives.
15 SACP Consultative Conference, Tongaat, 19–20 May 1990, *History in the Making: Documents Reflecting a Changing South Africa*, vol. 1, no. 2, November 1990.
16 'SACP Sessions', O'Malley Archives.
17 O'Malley 2007, p. 359.
18 'USA Cable 1', O'Malley Archives.
19 *Ibid.*
20 For the review of the media coverage of the 'Red Plot', see Kasrils, 1999, pp. 252–255.
21 Nelson Mandela, *Long Walk to Freedom: The Autobiography of Nelson Mandela*, London: Abacus, 1994.
22 J Slovo, 'Has Socialism Failed?', *African Communist*, no. 121, 2nd Quarter, 1990.

23 See, for example, J Slovo, 'The Nature of Socialism: Socialist Aspirations and Socialist Realities', *African Communist*, no. 124, 1st Quarter, 1991.
24 ZP Jordan, 'The Crisis of Conscience in the SACP', *Transformation*, vol. 11, 1990, p. 88.
25 See, for example, P Maqhawe, 'A Reply to Harry Gwala: We Owe a Duty to the Future', *African Communist*, no. 124, 1st Quarter, 1991; B Nzimande and M Skhosana, 'Debating Socialism: Civil Society and Democracy', *African Communist*, no. 128, 1st Quarter, 1992; S Roji, 'Disregarding the Lessons of History: A Response to Harry Gwala', *African Communist*, no. 128, 1st Quarter, 1992.
26 A Mafeje, 'The Bathos of Tendentious Historiography: A Review of Joe Slovo's "Has Socialism Failed?"' *Southern African Political Economy Monthly*, August 1990.

## Chapter 8
1 Oliver Tambo 1981, p. 4.
2 See the 'Joint Declaration of Natal Indian Congress, Transvaal Indian Congress, and the African National Congress'.
3 Unsorted SACP Archives, Central Committee, 'Report on Organisation', 1970.
4 *Ibid.*
5 *Ibid.*, 'London Memo on Problems of the Congress Movement', 1966.
6 *Ibid.*, Report of the Sub-Committee, August 1966.
7 *Ibid.*, Central Committee, 'The Results of the Consultative Conference of the ANC and the Tasks of the Party', 1969.
8 *Ibid.*, 'Notes for Guidance in Discussion', undated.
9 *Ibid.*, Nzo to Kotane and Marks, March 1972.
10 This letter is in the Unsorted SACP Archives.

## Chapter 9
1 'Minutes of NEC of 15 February 1990', O'Malley Archives.
2 Kasrils 1999, p. 251.
3 *Umsebenzi*, vol. 6, no. 2, 1990, p. 18.
4 'SACP Session', O'Malley Archives.
5 'Editorial Notes: Consolidating our Strategic Unity – the SACP's 9th Congress', *African Communist*, no. 141, 2nd Quarter, 1995.
6 O'Malley 2007, pp. 359–360.
7 'Public Launch of the Legal SACP Press Statement', O'Malley Archives.
8 Kasrils 1999, pp. 248–250.
9 '16–17 February 1991 Party Building National Workshop', O'Malley Archives.
10 'Circular to Regions from Central Committee', 6 March 1991, O'Malley Archives.
11 Essop Pahad Papers, 'Minutes of the ILG Meeting, 25–26 May 1991'. These Papers are unsorted and temporarily housed at the SADET Trust.
12 *Ibid.*
13 Interview with Jeremy Cronin, 26 August 1991, O'Malley Archives.
14 Essop Pahad Papers, 'Minutes of the ILG Meeting, 25–26 May 1991'.
15 Essop Pahad Papers, 'Regional reports to the ILG meeting of 21 July 1991'.
16 *Ibid.*
17 *Ibid.*
18 *Ibid.*

19 'Editorial Notes', *African Communist*, 1st Quarter (1992).
20 Essop Pahad Papers, 'Regional reports to the ILG meeting of 21 July 1991'.
21 *Ibid*.
22 *Ibid*.
23 *Ibid*.
24 *Ibid*.
25 For the debate on the 'mass' Party, see *African Communist*, no. 127, 4th Quarter, 1991.
26 Gordin 2008, p. 56.
27 Interview with Jacob Zuma, 28 July 1993, O'Malley Archives.
28 See my 'South African Communist Party in the 1980s' in *The Road to Democracy in South Africa, vol. 4, part 1 and 2 1980–1990*, (UNISA Press, 2010; and Gevisser, 2007.
29 Anthony Butler, *Cyril Ramaphosa*, Johannesburg: Jacana, 2007, p. 255.
30 Gordin 2008, p. 56.
31 According to Gevisser 2007, p. 601.
32 See *Ibid*., pp. 600–601; O'Malley, 2007, p. 391; and Butler 2007, pp. 254–260.
33 'Editorial Notes: Consolidating our Strategic Unity – the SACP's 9th Congress'.
34 For a contemporary report and analysis, see Karl von Holdt, 'The South African Communist Party: Preparing for a New Era', *South African Labour Bulletin*, vol. 16, no. 3, January 1992.
35 'Editorial Notes: Consolidating our Strategic Unity – the SACP's 9th Congress'.
36 *Constitution and Rules of the South African Communist Party as Adopted at the 8th Congress*.
37 Janet Smith and Beauregard Tromp, *Hani: A Life Too Short*, Johannesburg: Jonathan Ball Publishers, 2009, p. 216. Some surveys conducted at the time put Hani second only to Mandela in popularity.
38 Interview with Jeremy Cronin, 25 August 1993, O'Malley Archives.
39 Interview with Chris Hani, 15 August 1991, O'Malley Archives.
40 James Ngculu, *The Honour to Serve: Recollections of an Umkhonto Soldier*, (Cape Town: David Philip, 2010), p. 231.
41 Interview with Jacob Zuma, 28 July 1993, O'Malley Archives.
42 Lizo Nkonki and January Masilela were to die tragically in a car accident.
43 For the report of this workshop, see Pahad Papers, 'SACP Workshop on Party Building, Held at Fort Hare University, Alice, February 1–2, 1992'.
44 See *Ibid*.
45 *Ibid*.
46 These regional reports to the CC meeting of 25 January 1992 are contained in the Essop Pahad Papers.
47 Essop Pahad Papers, 'SACP Workshop on Party Building', undated.
48 See *Ibid*.
49 This report to the CC is in the Essop Pahad Papers.

## Chapter 10

1 SACP, 'Statement of the South African Communist Party Presented by General Secretary, Chris Hani, to the Convention for a Democratic South Africa, World Trade Centre', 20 December 1991.
2 'Editorial', *African Communist*, no. 122, 3rd Quarter, 1990, p. 11.
3 For his personal problems with Slovo, see O'Malley 2007, p. 345 and pp. 356–57.
4 Mbeki continued to use Marxist-Leninist tools of analysis long after he had left the

Party. See, Gevisser 2007.
5 The two biographers agree on this interpretation. See, Gevisser 2007, pp. 603–05; and Butler 2007, p. 262.
6 Gevisser 2007, p. 602.
7 *Ibid.*, p. 596.
8 Butler 2007, p. 290.
9 Gevisser 2007, p. 609.
10 Butler 2007, p. 290.
11 Kasrils 1999, p.259.
12 Gevisser 2007, p. 609.
13 *Ibid.*
14 Interview with Eugene Louw, 20 August 1990, O'Malley Archives.
15 Cited in 'Who Killed Hani', O'Malley Archives.
16 Mandela, *Long Walk to Freedom*, pp. 701–702.
17 Gevisser 2007, p. 598.
18 Mandela, *Long Walk to Freedom*, p. 727; Gevisser 2007, pp. 611–612.
19 J Slovo, 'Negotiation: What Room for Compromise?' *African Communist*, no. 130, 3rd Quarter, 1992. The ANC developed its own, see 'Negotiations: A Strategic Perspective', *African Communist*, no. 131, 4th Quarter (1992).
20 Slovo 1990, p. 40.
21 On the debate, see *African Communist*, no. 131, 4th Quarter, 1992.
22 See, for example, S Adam, 'What's Left?: The South African Communist Party after Apartheid', *Review of African Political Economy*, no. 72, 1997; *The Limits of Capitalist Reform in South Africa*, Marxist Theory seminar paper, UWC, April/May 1993; A Callinicos, *Between Apartheid and Capitalism: Conversation with South African Socialists* London: Bookmarks, 1992; D Pillay, 'The South African Communist Party', *South African Labour Bulletin*, vol. 14, no. 6, 1990; K von Holdt, 'The South African Communist Party: Preparing for a New Era', *South African Labour Bulletin*, vol. 16, no. 3, 1992; A Habib, 'The SACP's Restructuring of Communist Theory', *Transformation*, vol. 14, 1991.
23 Interview with Joe Slovo, 5 January 1993, O'Malley Archives.
24 *Ibid.*
25 Interview with Jeremy Cronin, 25 August 1993, O'Malley Archives.
26 See my 'South African Communist Party in the 1980s'.
27 Interview with Harry Gwala, January 1993, O'Malley Archives.
28 Charles Nqakula, 'Harry Gwala – Man of Steel', O'Malley Archives.
29 *Ibid.*
30 For a contemporary report and analysis on this mass action, see, for example, a special focus on this subject in the *South African Labour Bulletin*, vol. 16, no. 7, September/October 1992.
31 Interview with Chris Hani, 15 July 1992, O'Malley Archives.
32 Interview with Chris Hani, 15 August 1991, O'Malley Archives.
33 Interview with Chris Hani, 15 July 1992, O'Malley Archives.
34 Interview with Jeremy Cronin, 25 August 1993, O'Malley Archives.
35 Interview with Joe Slovo, 30 November 1993, O'Malley Archives.
36 Jeremy Cronin, 'The Boat, the Tap and the Leipzig Way', O'Malley Archives.
37 *Ibid.*
38 Cronin told O'Malley in July 1992 that "I've changed my mind a little bit since the paper"; see Interview with Jeremy Cronin, 13 July 1992, O'Malley Archives.
39 Interview with Jeremy Cronin, 13 July 1992, O'Malley Archives.

40 'De Klerk's reply to Nelson Mandela 2 July 1992', O'Malley Archives.
41 'Eavesdroppings or... the credulous Kriel', O'Malley Archives.
42 Essop Pahad Papers, General Secretary Circular to Regions, 19 February 1992.
43 Posted on the website of the 'African Crisis' on 17 September 2006. The targets of the website are in the main the post-independence governments in Zimbabwe and South Africa.
44 Interview with Jeremy Cronin, 25 August 1993, O'Malley Archives.
45 'Bisho and the anti-Communist Campaign', O'Malley Archives.
46 Interview with Charles Nqakula, 4 August 1993, O'Malley Archives.
47 Ramaphosa and Suttner are cited in Butler, *Cyril*, p. 297.
48 Interview with Harry Gwala, 10 November 1993, O'Malley Archives.
49 Interview with Tokyo Sexwale, 5 August 1993, O'Malley Archives.
50 Mandela, 'Nothing Will Stop Us', O'Malley Archives.
51 Interview with Charles Nqakula, 3 August 1993, O'Malley Archives.
52 Interview with Jeremy Cronin, 25 August 1993, O'Malley Archives.
53 This is a matter widely reported in the media. The SACP, in its opposition to the amnesty application of those convicted of the assassination, "is calling for the investigation into Chris Hani's murder to be re-opened. There is evidence that a conspiracy was involved, and the other members are still at large." According to the Party, Hani's killers, Clive Derby-Lewis and Janusz Waluz, "are open, unashamed, racists". See, *Umsebenzi*, December 1996/January 1997.
54 Essop Pahad Papers, 'SACP Workshop on Party Building'.
55 *Ibid.*
56 *Ibid.*
57 *Ibid.*, For other contributions on this debate in the Party, see my 'Traditional Leaders and the Current Transition', *African Communist*, no. 141, 2nd Quarter, 1995.
58 Essop Pahad Papers, 'Party Building Workshop'.
59 *Ibid.*
60 Interview with Chris Hani, 15 July 1992, O'Malley Archives.
61 *Ibid.*
62 Interview with Charles Nqakula, 4 August 1993, O'Malley Archives.
63 'Central Committee Discussion of Joe Slovo's Presentation', *African Communist*, no. 135, 4th Quarter, 1993.
64 Interview with Charles Nqakula, 31 October 1996, O'Malley Archives.

## Chapter 11

1 *Umsebenzi*, June 1996.
2 'Address by President Nelson Mandela at the Funeral of Joe Slovo', 15 January 1995.
3 Interview with Charles Nqakula, 25 October 1995, O'Malley Archives.
4 Interview with Jeremy Cronin, 11 October 1995, O'Malley Archives.
5 *Times Live*, 31 October 2004.
6 David P Thomas, 'The South African Communist Party (SACP) in the Post-Apartheid Period', *Review of African Political Economy*, No. 111, 2007, p. 135.
7 Dale T McKinley, 'Debates and Opposition within the ANC and the Tripartite Alliance Since 1994', online publication, International Journal of Socialist Renewal, http://links.org.au/node/139.
8 *Mail and Guardian*, 20 June 1997.
9 SACP, 'SACP Decision on Dale McKinley', 16 August 2000; *SAPA*, 16 August

2000.
10 Interview with Charles Nqakula, 25 October 1995, O'Malley Archives.
11 This citation is from Chapter 6 on 'The Role and Character of the SACP' of the political programme adopted by the 11th Congress.
12 Mandela's address to the 9th Congress of the SACP, online resource.
13 'Editorial Notes: Consolidating our Strategic Unity – the SACP's 9th Congress'.
14 SACP, *Strategic Perspectives as adopted by the 9th Congress*, April 1995.
15 *Ibid*.
16 'The SACP's 11th Congress – With and for the Workers and the Poor', *Umsebenzi*, September 2002.
17 Naidoo 2010, p. 215.
18 Interview with Jeremy Cronin, 25 August 1993, O'Malley Archives.
19 Interview with Jeremy Cronin, 21 October 1994, O'Malley Archives.
20 *Ibid*.
21 SACP, *Strategic Perspectives*.
22 'The Need for an Effective ANC-led Political Center', *African Communist*, Issue 142, 3rd Quarter, 1995.
23 For an academic critique of intra-Alliance debates on policy issues including the RDP and GEAR, see Tom Lodge, 'Policy Process within the African National Congress and the Tripartite Alliance', *Politikon*, vol. 26, no. 1, 1999; and Eddie C Webster, 'The Politics of Economic Reform: Trade Unions and Democratisation in South Africa', *Journal of Contemporary African Studies*, vol. 16, no. 1, 1998.
24 Interview with Jeremy Cronin, 3 October 1996, O'Malley Archives.
25 Interview with Charles Nqakula, 31 October 1996, O'Malley Archives.
26 Interview with Charles Nqakula, 10 September 1998, O'Malley Archives.
27 Cited in SACP, 'Building Working Class Hegemony on the Terrain of a National Democratic Struggle', SACP Central Committee Discussion Paper, September 2009.
28 CC Discussion Document, 'Class, National and Gender Struggle in South Africa: The Historical Relationship between the ANC and the SACP', *Bua Komanisi!*, vol. 5, no. 1, May 2006.
29 'Message from the Central Committee', *Umsebenzi*, December 1996/January 1997.
30 SACP, 'Declaration of the 10th Congress'.
31 Nzimande, 'The Role of SACP in the Alliance: Our Vision of Socialism', *African Communist*, Issue 150, 1st Quarter, 1999.
32 SACP, 'Declaration of the 10th Congress'.
33 'The SACP's 11th Congress – With and for the Workers and the Poor'.
34 SACP, Central Committee Political Report to the 10th Congress, July 1998.
35 *Business Day*, 29 November 2000.
36 'Now Mbeki Savages SACP', O'Malley Archives.
37 'Take Forward the Work of 10th Congress', *Umsebenzi*, August 1998.
38 'ANC 50th National Conference – A Milestone in the NDR', *Umsebenzi*, February 1998.
39 *Ibid*.
40 IOL News, 'SACP Taunts Mbeki While Chanting Hani Song', 13 June 2007.
41 For this report of this Alliance summit, see 'The Need for an Effective ANC-Led Political Center', *African Communist*, no. 142, 3rd Quarter, 1995.
42 This citation is in the report of this summit which is on the ANC website.
43 *Ibid*.
44 For this Discussion Paper, see *Umrabulo*, no. 5, 3rd Quarter, 1998.

45 Alliance, 'Report of the Alliance Summit', 3–7 April 2002, Kempton Park.
46 See *Ibid*.
47 'Taking Socialism Forward – SACP/COSATU', *Umsebenzi*, March 1998.
48 See my 'South African Communist Party in the 1980s'.
49 Interview with Joe Slovo, 9 April 1992, O'Malley Archives.
50 Nzimande, 'The Role of the SACP in the Alliance'.

**Conclusion**
1 University of Cape Town Archives, SC BC1081, 'The Simons Papers'.
2 Tambo 1981, p. 5.
3 Gwede Mantashe, 'Moleketi's Outburst Undermines SACP', *Mail and Guardian*, 26 January 2001.
4 ANC, 'Managing National Democratic Transformation: ANC Response to SACP Discussion Document', 19 June 2006. For the SACP document, see 'Class, National and Gender Struggle in South Africa'.
5 For a critique of the NMW's response, see 'Is the ANC leading a National Democratic Revolution or Managing Capitalism?' SACP website.
6 *Times Live*, 16 December 2009.
7 *PoliticsWeb*, 14 December 2009.
8 Cited in Sihle Zikalala, 'A Perspective on the Alliance Today', unpublished, undated SACP discussion document. The pages of the document are not numbered.
9 *Ibid*.
10 For this resolution, see 'SACP Provincial Council Media Statement', 6 September 2008, SACP website.
11 *Mail and Guardian Online*, 12 October 2010.
12 *Times Live*, 30 November 2010.
13 SACP 2nd Special National Congress Resolution, 10–13 December 2009.
14 *Africa News*, 29 November 2010.
15 'Role and Character of the SACP', Discussion Document for the 11th Congress, SACP website.

# Index

**A**
Africa 11, 83
*African Communist* 22, 23, 38, 42, 43, 44, 48, 82, 85, 100, 103, 106, 113, 122, 123, 133, 139, 151
African communist movement 13
African Communist Parties 88, 89, 90, 91
African Independence Party 89
African National Congress (ANC) 7–12, 17–23, 25–29, 32–38, 41, 43, 44, 45, 47, 48, 49, 51, 52, 55, 60, 61, 68, 69, 72–80, 85, 87, 94, 97, 98–102, 104, 106–121,123, 124, 125, 127, 128, 129, 132–142, 145–149, 151–171, 173–180
African Revolution 29, 81, 156
African Socialism 11, 12
Afrikaners 150
Alexander, Ray 72 *see also* Simons, Ray Alexander
Algeria 12; 20, 86, 88, 89, 112, 113
Alliance 100, 107, 123, 141, 147, 148, 149, 152, 154, 158, 160–64, 167–170, 179, 180, 181
Alliance Campaigns Committee 142
Alliance Summit 168, 170
amnesty 138
ANC Youth League 178, 179
Anglophone parties 88
Angola 12, 41, 42, 43, 45, 48, 49, 53, 55, 69, 72, 87, 89, 90
anti-communist 63, 99, 137
Anti-Apartheid Movement 20, 44
apartheid 31, 34, 41, 48, 49, 72, 100, 104, 105, 115, 153, 137, 138, 141, 142, 159, 164
    security forces 15, 54, 102, 137
    spy 15
Arab-Middle East 91
armed struggle 8, 27, 35, 69, 109, 136, 138
assassination 148, 149, 150
AZAPO 142

**B**
banning 8, 10
Bantustan machinery 129
    system 79
Barnard, Neil 137
Basotho Congress Party 33
Benin 90
Berlin 89, 90, 91
    Wall 94
Bernstein, Lionel 'Rusty' 8, 9, 14, 22, 23, 40, 173, 174
Bill of Rights 152, 153
Bisho massacre 141, 146, 147
Black Economic Empowerment (BEE) 164
Black, Douglas 15
Bloemfontein 116, 155
Boipatong 141
Boksburg 148
Bophuthatswana 148
Border 56, 57, 121, 128, 129, 131
border controls 32
Boshielo, Flag 19
Botha, PW 87
Botha, Pik 104
Botswana 42, 48, 55, 57
boycotts 141
Bramley, Johannesburg 15
brinkmanship 135
Britain 20
Budget Day 131
Bulgaria 84
Bunting, Brian 9, 21, 22, 23, 40, 42, 44, 154, 155
    *Moses Kotane* 44
    *South African Communists Speak* 44
Bunting, Sonia 155

197

Buthelezi, Gasha 140
Butler, Anthony 125, 135

C
Cape Town 31, 34, 42, 116, 133, 148
capitalism 69, 91, 97
Carneson, Fred 129, 155
Central Committee (CC) 9, 14–24, 28, 29, 31, 34, 35, 36, 37, 39, 41, 42, 43, 45–48, 50, 51, 53, 54, 56, 58, 84, 85, 95, 96, 99, 100, 102, 108, 112, 115, 118–21, 124, 126, 129, 130, 131, 139, 147, 148, 151, 153, 158, 164, 166, 167, 168, 178, 181
Central Executive Committee (CEC) 16, 17, 18, 19, 20, 21, 22, 35, 42
Chief of Staff 73, 128
Chile 87
China 27, 87, 88, 171, 172
Cingi, Dan 71
Ciskei 129, 146, 148
Cobra 30
Coetsee, Kobie 138
Cohen, Tim 135
colonialism 9, 11, 91
Colonialism of a Special Type (CST) 9, 23, 25, 49, 159, 175
Coloured People's Congress (CPC) 8, 25, 108
communism 11, 26, 63, 70, 70, 72, 74, 98, 126, 137
communist 8, 12, 27, 45, 48, 68, 70, 75, 77, 78, 79, 98, 104, 106, 117, 118, 119, 121, 137, 141, 146, 147, 158, 159, 166, 171, 176, 178, 197
Communist and Workers' Parties of Tropical and Southern Africa 89
Communist Party 11, 28, 50, 73, 75, 77, 127, 128, 138, 171
Communist Party of China (CPC) 86, 87, 88
Communist Party of Great Britain 20
Communist Party of Israel 84
Communist Party of Lesotho 88
Communist Party of Reunion 88
Communist Party of South Africa (CPSA) *see also* South African Communist Party 7, 8, 10, 68
Communist Party of Sudan 89, 90
Communist Party of the Soviet Union (CPSU) 20, 39, 66, 83, 86, 87, 91, 171
Communist Party of Tunisia 88
comrade 45, 59, 60, 63–66, 70, 71, 73, 75, 77, 83, 102, 103, 123, 150, 154, 158
Congolese Party of Labour 90
Congress Alliance 8, 9, 21, 25, 108, 109, 111, 112, 114
Congress Movement (CM) 80, 81, 83
Congress of Democrats (COD) 8, 108, 110
Congress of South African Trade Unions (COSATU) 42, 48, 61, 65, 100, 101, 102, 116, 122, 126, 139, 142, 145, 148, 153, 155, 156, 157, 160, 161, 162, 163, 164, 167, 169, 170, 171, 179, 180, 181
Constituent Assembly 151, 152
Constitutional Joint Committee 158
constitution 49, 50, 66, 154, 155
Consultative Congress Committee (CCC) 112
Convention for a Democratic South Africa (CODESA) 132–136, 140–43, 145, 146, 148, 150, 151, 152
Cradock 122
Cronin, Jeremy 31, 34, 121, 126, 127, 138, 140, 143, 144, 147, 150, 156, 160, 161, 162, 178, 180
Cuba 12, 131, 172
Cuito Cuanavale 117
Czechoslovakia 84

D
Dadoo, Yusuf 14–17, 20, 22, 24, 25, 26, 28, 29, 37, 38, 50, 83–87, 90, 91, 106, 110, 173, 174
Dansoko, Amath 89
Dar es Salaam 14, 16, 21, 42, 48, 55, 112, 113
Davies, Rob 31
De Klerk, FW 97, 105, 137, 138, 142, 154, 148
Defiance Campaign 8, 108, 110
democracy 52, 91, 172
democratic elections 9, 98, 168
socialism 101, 105, 106, 126
dissidents 26, 27, 36
District Committee 14, 58, 66
Dlamini, Chris 99, 126
Dlamini, Stephen 77

Durban 77, 116, 122

**E**
East Africa 27, 43
East Germany 84
East London 116, 121, 131
East Rand 116
Eastern Cape 34, 43, 56, 117, 121, 122, 128, 129, 130, 150
Eastern Europe 144
Eastern Transvaal 128
Egypt 12, 89
elections 154, 155, 156, 165
Ellis, Stephen 106
Empangeni 122
Engels, Frederick 98
England 33
Ethiopia 12, 87, 89, 90
Exile 10, 11, 16, 19, 20, 23, 25, 29, 37, 49, 51–56, 69, 82, 98, 100, 103, 111, 114, 116, 119, 124, 129, 135, 171, 173, 174, 175, 176, 182

**F**
Ferreirastown 68
FIFA World Cup 119
First, Julius 17
First, Ruth 8, 14, 22, 35
Fisher, Bram 9, 14–18, 30
France 20
Francistown 31
Francophone Africa 88
Fraser-Moleketi, Geraldine 116, 120, 126, 159, 168
Fred 30
Free State 34, 57, 121, 122, 155
Freedom Charter (FC) 8, 78, 80, 81, 108, 110
FRELIMO 89, 90, 91, 115
French Communist Party 12, 86

**G**
German Communist Party 86
German Democratic Republic 41
Gevisser, Mark 134, 135
Ghana 12
Goldstone Commission 148
Gomomo, John 126, 148
Gompo Hall 131
Gorbachev, Mikhail 95
Gordhan, Pravin 136, 158

Gordin, Jeremy 99, 124
Government of National Unity 136, 158
Gqabi, Joe 79
Gqozo 147
Graaff Reinet 122
Grahamstown 122
Great October Socialist Revolution 131
Greece 32
Greek Communist Party 32
Groote Schuur 101, 134, 137
Groote Schuur Minute 133
Group of Eight 26
Growth, Employment and Redistribution (GEAR) 162–169
Guebuza 91
guerrilla warfare 35, 47, 49, 109, 157
Guinea 11, 12
Gwala, Harry 75, 76–79, 106, 118, 119, 123, 134, 139, 140, 141, 143, 148, 155

**H**
Haffajee, Ferial 157
Hani, Chris 19, 33, 34, 36, 37, 39, 42, 43, 72, 73, 99, 100, 116, 120, 124–128, 132, 133, 135, 137, 138, 140–145, 147–152, 159, 160, 168, 171, 174, 178
Hani, Gilbert 33
Hanoi 85
Harare Declaration 100, 118
Harmel, Michael 8, 9, 14, 21, 22, 23, 29, 44, 83, 86, 173, 174
*Fifty Fighting Years* 44
Havana 95
Helsinki 87
Herbert 30
High Organ 76, 78, 79
Ho Chi Minh City 85
Holden, Roberto 87
Holomisa, Banthu 140
Hull 16, 17, 18, 23, 37
human rights 107, 152

**I**
Ibrahim, Ishmael 75
ideology 11, 81, 82, 130, 134, 137, 155, 166, 175
Indian Congress 136, 151
Industrial Sub-Committee (ICS) 61

Inkatha Freedom Party 140, 141
*Inkululeko – Freedom* 37, 44
*Inner-Party Bulletin* 21, 37, 53
Interim Constitution 153
Interim Government 131, 151
Interim Leadership Group (ILG)
   119–124
International Conference of Communist
   and Workers' Parties 85, 88
Iraqi Communist Party 85
Italy 20

J
Jacobs, Loretta 129
Jele, Josiah 35, 43, 174
Johannesburg 15, 30, 31, 116, 117, 128
Jordan, Pallo 100, 105, 139

K
Kasrils, Ronnie 14, 30, 72, 104, 117,
   119, 120, 124, 126, 129, 134, 136,
   137, 146, 147, 148, 155, 159
Kathrada, Ahmed 76, 79, 99
   *Memoirs* 76
Kaunda, Kenneth 11
Keita, Modibo 11
Kerekou, Mathieu 90
Kisimayo 32
Kotane, Moses 7, 8, 9, 14, 16, 17, 20,
   21, 22, 24, 28, 29, 35, 36, 39, 44,
   62, 83, 110, 113, 124, 164, 173,
   174
Kriel, Hernus 145
Kwabe Conference 47, 48, 72
KwaZulu-Natal 102, 118, 121, 122,
   136, 140, 148, 179, 181

L
Lekota, Terror 177
Lenin 9, 38
Lenin Peace Prize 18
Lenin School 43, 53, 55, 60, 177
Lenin Vladimir 98, 106
Leninist 28, 175
Lesotho 33, 34, 39, 42, 48, 54, 72, 73
Lesotho Liberation Army 73
*Lesotho Security Act 1974* 33
Levy, Norman 15
liberation movement 11, 18, 21, 25, 29,
   34, 37, 45, 46, 40, 51, 52, 53, 69,
   74, 105, 118, 129, 138, 151, 161,
   165, 168, 174
liberation struggle 8, 10, 48, 108, 155
Liliesleaf Farm 13
London 14–17, 19, 21, 23, 25, 28, 29,
   30, 41, 42, 44, 48, 49, 55, 57, 67,
   173
London Committee 20, 24, 40, 41, 46,
   54
   Memo 109, 110
Louw, Eugene 137
Love, Janet 136
Luanda 42, 44, 89
Ludi, Gerard 15
Lusaka 36, 42, 43, 48, 52, 53, 55, 67,
   117, 124, 176
Lusaka Regional Committee 52, 174

M
Mabhida, Moses 19, 35, 42, 43, 44, 50,
   56, 84, 91, 173
Maclean, Dr May 73
macro-economic policy 166, 167, 168
Madiba 78
Mafeje, Archie 106
Mafikeng 167, 168
Maharaj, Mac 43, 75, 101, 102, 104,
   105, 117, 118, 119, 123, 134–137,
   140, 174
Makhanya, Dumisani 129, 156, 178
Makhathini, Johnny 113
Makiwane, Tennyson 26
Malema, Julius 178
Mali 11
Mandela, Nelson 13, 68, 75, 78, 79,
   104, 105, 124, 133, 134, 138, 145,
   148, 155, 159, 162, 163, 164, 166,
   167, 168, 169, 170
Mandela, Winnie 140
*Manifesto of the South African
   Communist Party: Building
   Workers' Power for Democratic
   Change* 126, 127
Mantashe, Gwede 120, 129, 177
Mao, Tse-Tung 87
Maputo 44, 89, 91
Maputo Manifesto 91
Markinor 149
Marks, JB 7, 9, 14, 17, 18, 21, 22, 28,
   29, 36, 37, 38, 110, 113, 173, 174
Martins, Ben 129
Marx, Karl 98

INDEX

Marxism  12, 13, 20, 68, 72, 73, 75, 76, 79, 105
Marxism-Leninism  7, 11, 12, 56, 63, 90, 164
Marxist  72, 75, 76, 105, 175
Marxist ideology  81, 90
Marxist- Leninist Parties  86, 88, 89
Marxist-Leninist Revolutionary Theory  72
Mascow  20, 24, 28, 35, 42, 47, 87, 90, 91, 113, 171
Maseru  34, 73
Masilela, January  69, 129, 174
Masonda, Andrew  75
mass action  133, 141, 142, 144–148
Mass Democratic Movement (MDM)  48, 57, 58, 60, 61–65, 68, 82, 102, 116, 119, 125, 129
mass mobilisation  120, 130, 145, 165
mass organisations  22
Mati, Vuyisile  71
Matsoane, Ruth  19
Matthews, Joe  9, 22 29
May Day  120
Mbeki, Govan  78, 99, 126, 155
Mbeki, Thabo  99, 100, 101, 102, 103, 119, 124, 125, 133–138, 144, 156, 162, 163, 164, 166, 167, 168, 176
McKinley, Dale  157
Mengistu, Haile-Mariam  12
Mhlaba, Raymond  155
Mhlongo, Reggie  70
Middle East  84
Midlands  122, 141
MK *see* Umkhonto we Sizwe
Mkwayi, Wilton  78
Mlangeni, Andrew  99
Mofutsanyane, Edwin  7
Mogadishu  32
Mokaba, Peter  140, 143
Mokonyana, Nomvula  129
Moleketi, Jabu  129, 177
Mompati, Ruth  19
Moonsamy, Kay  129
Morocco  12, 20, 88, 89
Morogoro Conference  23, 25, 26, 29, 37, 73, 112, 113
Moses Mabhida Party School  130
Motsoaledi, Elias  99
Mozambique  12, 41, 48, 54, 55, 57, 89, 90

MPLA  89, 90
Mpumalanga  178
Mtintso, Thenjiwe  126, 129, 130
Mtshali, Eric  35, 37
Mufamadi, Sydney  99, 126, 134, 159, 168
Multi-Party Negotiating Forum  133, 134

N
Naicker, Marimuthu Pragalathan (MP)  9, 19
Naidoo, Jay  101, 102, 142, 146
Naidoo, Phyllis  73
Naiker, Dr GM  107, 110
Nair, Billy  99, 102, 103, 117, 126
Natal  31, 34, 43, 57, 107, 121, 122, 123, 140
Natal Midlands  121, 128, 130
National Action Council  110
National Democratic Revolution (NDR)  159, 160, 169, 179
National Executive Committee (NEC)  26, 99, 100, 101, 138, 139, 140, 162, 164, 178
national liberation  12, 28, 31, 49, 72, 73, 118, 157
National Liberation Front (FLN)  112, 115
national liberation movement (NLM)  19, 46, 52, 80, 81, 85, 90, 175
struggle  21, 28, 74, 80, 112
National Policy Conference  163
National Union of Mineworkers (NUM)  120, 181
National Working Committee (NWC)  139, 164, 168, 169, 177, 178
nationalisation  154, 178
negotiations  131, 133, 134, 136–139, 141, 142, 143, 145, 146, 151, 154
Ngonyama, Smuts  129
Nigeria  20, 86, 88, 89
Nkadimeng, John  43, 102, 126, 174
Nkomati Accord  44, 54
Nkonki, Lizo  129
Nkrumah, Kwame  11, 12
Nkuku, Raymond  71
Nokwe, Duma  9, 14, 23, 29, 110
North Africa  90, 91
North Korea  171
North West  155

201

Northern Cape 122, 178
Nqakula, Charles 126, 129, 141, 147, 149, 150, 153, 156, 157, 162, 168
Ntsangane 76
Ntsiki, Naledi 77
Nyanda, Siphiwe 104
Nyerere, Julius 11
Nzimande, Blade 126, 151, 157, 165, 166, 167, 168, 172, 177, 180, 181
Nzo, Alfred 74, 113, 125
Nzula, Albert 7

O
October Revolution 38, 85, 88
Ogara, Ché 71
O'Malley, Padraig 140, 141, 142, 162, 163
Oosterwyk, Trevor 129
Operation Eagle 102
Operation J 32, 33, 34, 36, 39
Operation Vula 95, 102 see also Vula; Vula operatives
Orange Free State 128
Order of Friendship of the Peoples 84
Order of Georgi Dimitrov 84
Order of Karl Marx 84
Organisation of African Unity (OAU) 27
Ottaway, David 12
Ottaway, Marina 12

P
Pahad, Aziz 99, 100, 101, 124, 134
Pahad, Essop 84, 85, 86, 89, 101, 119, 126, 129, 154, 159, 168
Palestine 172
Pan-African Congress (PAC) 8, 21, 27, 78, 79, 80, 87, 106, 111, 142
Party of Liberation and Socialism 88
Party of the Popular Revolution (PRP) 90
*Path to Power* 95, 97, 103, 126, 127
Patrick 30
Patriotic Front 151, 153
People's Republic of Angola 87
People's Republic of China 13, 86, 87
Pepani, Christian 70, 71, 72
Phoenix 33
Politburo (PB) 42, 43, 46, 50, 51, 52, 53, 55, 57, 61, 96, 97, 101, 102, 104, 117, 118, 119, 124, 134, 151, 173, 174
political education 68, 69, 72, 74, 77, 130, 165, 174
Port Elizabeth 116, 119, 121, 122
Port Shepstone 122
Portuguese Communist Party 89
post-apartheid 9, 98, 120, 125, 126, 129, 136, 152, 155, 156, 157, 163, 164, 170
Prague 16, 17, 18, 20, 86, 89, 173
Pretoria 128, 134
Pretoria Minute 133, 136, 137
PWV (Pretoria, Johannesbug and the Vaal) 128, 129, 130, 139, 150

R
Ramaphosa, Cyril 124, 125, 134, 135, 136, 138, 142, 147, 148
Reconstruction and Development Programme (RDP) 160, 161, 162, 168, 169, 170
*Record of Understanding* 133, 148
Regional Committees 56, 58
Regional Executive Committee (REC) 123, 150, 151
Reserve Bank 154
Reunion 86
Revolutionary Council 25, 27, 37, 38
Rhodesia 25
Rivonia 13, 14, 15, 108, 109, 114
Rivonia Trial 13, 15
*Road to South African Freedom, The* 9, 47, 80, 95, 96, 125, 127
Robben Island 19, 74, 77, 78, 119
rolling mass action 141, 142
*Rooigevaar* 68
*rooigevaar* schools 10
Roux, Eddie 68
Russia 105
Rustenburg 15

S
SACP – ANC relations 8, 17, 19, 21, 22, 28, 35, 38, 44, 45, 60, 98, 109, 113, 114, 115, 155, 160, 171, 173, 174, 175, 176, 177
Salim, Ahmed 89
Savimbi, Jonas 87
Schreiner, Jenny 126, 129
Scott, Mpo 129
*Sechaba* 74, 82

# INDEX

Secretariat 23, 24, 25, 28, 31, 33, 34, 38, 40, 41, 42, 43, 53, 173, 174
security forces 15, 31, 32, 54, 137
Senegal 11, 12, 20, 88, 89
Senghor, Leopold 11
September, Reg 40
Sexwale, Tokyo 149
Shaik, Mo 136
Sharpeville 146
Shilowa, Sam 126, 177
Shope, Mark 9, 21, 22
Shubin, Vladimir 10, 11, 33
Simons, Jack 69, 70, 71, 72, 100, 155
Simons, Ray Alexander 19, 35, 43, 100, 155
Sisulu, Walter 125, 146
Slovo, Joe 8, 9, 15, 21, 22, 25, 26, 28, 29, 32, 36, 42, 43, 50, 56, 84, 91, 94, 99, 101, 104, 105, 106, 113, 116, 118, 119, 120, 124, 125, 126, 134–41, 150, 153, 154, 155
Soccer City 117, 119
socialism 9, 12, 23, 46, 49, 69, 74, 85, 91, 97, 98, 103, 126, 159, 160, 165, 169, 172, 176, 181
Socialist Party of Working People 89
Socialist Unity Party of (East) Germany (SED) 83
Socialist Vanguard Party 88
Socishe, Lawrence 33
solitary confinement 33
Somalia 32
South Africa 22, 24, 25, 28, 30, 31, 33, 34, 38, 40, 41, 42, 43, 53, 173, 174
South African Communist Party (SACP) 14, 15, 17, 20, 25, 27, 29, 33, 35, 36, 37, 49, 55, 60, 73, 74, 75, 80–83, 85–91, 94, 97–109, 111, 113, 114, 116–119, 124, 125, 127, 128, 132–137, 139, 140, 141, 145–148, 151–158, 160, 162–169, 171, 175–182
   cadre development 165
   cadre policy 50, 51, 54, 83
   cadres 24, 26, 30, 34, 45, 47, 54, 55, 62, 69, 77, 101, 121, 136, 150, 165, 175, 180
   8th Congress 120, 125, 126, 128, 129, 146
   11th Congress 158, 165, 180, 181
   50th anniversary 38
   50th national conference 167, 168

   45th anniversary
   membership 54, 55, 56, 57, 120, 121, 122, 123, 125, 126, 127, 129, 150, 174
   9th Congress 159, 160, 161, 162, 168
   probation 50, 51, 66
   propaganda 21, 22, 23, 30, 31, 37, 38, 44, 46, 49, 50, 57, 103, 122, 147
   recruitment 14, 24, 51, 55, 58, 129, 150
   7th Congress 55, 57, 60, 66, 67, 95, 97, 103, 118, 119, 173, 174
   70th anniversary 120
   6th Congress 54, 55, 56, 60, 127
   60th anniversary 12, 45, 175
   69th anniversary 118
   10th Congress 162, 164–167, 172
*South African Communists Speak* 44
South African Congress of Trade Unions (SACTU) 8, 20, 25, 34, 27, 42, 44, 60, 61, 100, 101, 102, 108, 109, 110, 114
South African Defence Force (SADF) 58, 117, 146
South African Democracy Education Trust (SADET) 10
South African Indian Congress (SAIC) 8, 14, 25, 108, 110, 111
South African National Civic Association (SANCA) 161
Southern Natal 128, 140
Southern Natal 140
Soviet 10, 175
Soviet Union 13, 17, 20, 32, 33, 98, 105, 106, 171, 176
Soweto 123
Stalin, Joseph 98, 106
Stanger 122
Stephen 30
Strachan, Jean 15
*Strategic Perspective* 140, 160, 161
*Strategy and Tactics* 25, 73
struggle 8, 9, 43, 44, 47, 49, 58, 65, 73, 81, 86, 91, 100, 107, 115, 153, 157, 161, 165, 166, 172, 179
Sudan 12, 20, 86
Sudanese Communist Party 88
sunset clause 136, 138, 139, 140, 148
*Suppression of Communist Act* 15
Suttner, Raymond 69, 126, 138, 148

203

SWANU 111
SWAPO 111
Swaziland 42, 48, 54, 55, 57

T
Tambo, Oliver 12, 14, 22, 26, 28, 29, 32, 37, 39, 43, 45, 60, 107, 124, 134, 175
Tanzania 11, 21, 27
Thomas 33, 34
Thomas, David 157
Thompson, C 15
Timol, Ahmed 31
Tloome, Dan 19, 42, 43, 95
Tongaat 102, 104, 105, 117, 119, 136, 137, 145
Toure, Sekou 11, 12
trade unions 58, 60, 61, 62, 65, 130
traditional leaders 151
transformation 156, 157, 160, 165, 181
Transkei 32, 43, 118, 121, 129
Transvaal 34, 43, 56, 57, 107, 121, 122
Treason Trial 15
Tripartite Alliance 60, 102, 114, 130, 142, 153, 157, 161, 178
Trotsky, Leon 98
Troyeville 117, 119, 124
Tsitsikama 122
Tunisia 12, 20, 89
Turok, Ben 19, 40

U
Uitenhage 122
Ujamaa 11
Umkhonto we Sizwe (MK) 8, 13, 18, 25, 27, 32, 33, 35, 37, 41, 45, 49, 58, 69, 71, 72, 73, 79, 109, 115, 116, 128, 131, 145
  30th anniversary 131
*Umsebenzi* 44, 52, 56, 57, 82, 100, 103, 106, 122, 123, 151
unbanning 176, 177, 182
underground 8, 9, 10, 14, 15, 17, 27, 31, 33, 34, 35, 44, 59, 62, 98, 102, 103, 111, 176, 182
Union of Soviet Socialist Republics (USSR) 53, 87, 94
United Democratic Front (UDF) 42, 48, 61, 102, 125, 129, 177
United Front 27, 111, 114
United Nations (UN) 108

United Nations Charter 108
University of Fort Hare 129

V
Vaal 128
Vaal uprising 48
vanguardism 28, 29
Vavi, Zwelinzima 167, 180
Venda 128
Vieira, Sergio 90, 91
Vietnam 87
Vietnam Worker's Party 85
Vorster, Premier John 84, 87
Vula 104, 105, 119, 136, 137 *see also* Operation Vula
Vula operatives 102, 105, 119

W
Wankie campaign 23, 25, 32, 38
Wankie Game Reserve 25
Waverley, Johannesburg 15
Weinberg, Eli 15
Welkom 155
West Rand 116
West, Peter 15
Western Cape 34, 43, 56, 57, 121, 122, 123, 129, 150, 180
Western Sahara 172
Western Transvaal 129
Wolpe, Harold 8
Workers Charter 101
Workers Party 89
*World Marxist Review* 84, 89, 173

X
Xuma, Dr Alfred 107, 110

Y
yellow communists 178
Yengeni, Tony 148
Young Communist League 180

Z
Zambia 21, 27, 48
Zambia-Botswana border 31
Zimbabwe 48, 54, 55, 57
Zimbabwe African Peoples Union (ZAPU) 25
Zuma, Jacob 77, 99, 100, 101, 104, 119, 124, 125, 128, 134, 135, 136, 176